Broadview Public Library District
2226 S. 16th Avenue
Broadview, IL 60155-4000

D1521184

The African-American Guide to

DIVORCE & DRAMA

ATTORNEY LESTER L. BARCLAY

The African-American Guide to

DIVORCE & DRAMA

ATTORNEY LESTER L. BARCLAY

Breaking Up Without Breaking Down

Khari Publishing, Ltd
Chicago, IL

Lester L. Barclay, Esq. is managing partner of The Barclay Law Group, PC in Chicago, IL. For over 25 years, he has practiced family law and advocated for children of divorce.

The African-American Guide to
DIVORCE & DRAMA:
Breaking Up Without Breaking Down

Lester L. Barclay

KHARI PUBLISHING, LTD
39 S. LASALLE • SUITE 900 • CHICAGO, IL 60603
Phone: 888-200-6445
Website: www.kharipublishing.com • Email: publisher@kharipublishing.com

Printed in the United States of America.

⊗ This paper meets the requirements of ANSI/NISO Z39.48-1992 (Permanence of Paper).

15 14 13   1 2 3 4 5

Cover Design: Darren Hardy, Hardy Design

ISBN: 978-1-939724-00-7 (cloth)
ISBN: 978-1-939724-01-4 (paper)

Library of Congress Control Number: 2013939249

For Sue,
my loving and dedicated wife,
and the inspirational children of our joy:
Kayin, Kia, and Kara.

Contents

Foreword

by **Judge Mablean**

I am enthusiastic about *The African-American Guide to Divorce & Drama.* Written by Lester L. Barclay—an outstanding attorney in the area of family law and advocacy for children—this groundbreaking book is both timely and necessary. Let me tell you why.

In more than thirty years of practice as a lawyer, over 25 of them handling divorce matters, and my seven seasons as the judge on the Fox Network's "Divorce Court," I have litigated and presided over hundreds of divorce cases. I know millions of my viewers watched the show every day for the entertainment provided by the accusations, the squabbling, and the humiliation by the litigants of one another. Others tuned in for my advice, to be educated on some aspects of divorce law, and for the life lessons I gave. For many viewers, it was all great fun, but to me, it was real life with real people. It was no laughing matter.

At a time when over 50 percent of all marriages end in divorce, we cannot deny the devastating impact divorce is having on our families and our communities, especially among African-Americans. I admonished all viewers to "look deep before you leap" into marriage. Most fail to do so. Many continue the same blind-sided approach to divorce. I have found that these same people who fail to look before they leap into marriage often fail to seek any advice or consider the consequences before they go to divorce court. *The African-American Guide to Divorce & Drama* helps prevent this mistake.

Stress and drama are everyday occurrences in a relationship. So when bad marriages become unbearable, naturally, people look to divorce as their way out. But, as was so aptly demonstrated on my show, divorcing couples brought their problems right into the courtroom with them. It was my job as judge to sort it out and render a decision that would allow them to part with some measure of peace. In fact, I considered my role on the show as a ministry. I genuinely cared about the couples who appeared before me and wanted to give them the best outcome possible, sometimes even against their will. In this respect, some of my harshest judgments were meted out to divorcing dads who did not want to support their children. Some fathers seem to feel that once they divorce the wife, they divorce the children, too. Nothing is farther from the truth. As stated in my book, *Judge Mablean's Life Lessons: Tools for Weekly Living*, fathers, not just mothers, have a responsibility to take care of their children, forever. If anything, once the father is no longer in the home, the responsibility is greater. He now must fight, push through all barriers, pay lawyers, inconvenience himself, change his lifestyle, put his children first over career, recreation, social life, and yes, another woman, to do whatever is necessary to fulfill his responsibility. On this point and many others, Attorney Barclay and I are in complete agreement.

Divorce is often a much more traumatic event for women, however, than it is for men. Fewer women remarry than men, and most see divorce as a failure. Yet, as I have told countless women over the years, and repeat in my book, divorce is not death. Your marriage may be over, but you still have the rest of your life ahead of you. I know from personal experience the pain and heartbreak of divorce and the courage it takes to rebuild your life as a single parent afterward. I can tell you with certainty that divorce is not easy, but as many of you already know, sometimes it is necessary. It is not death. It is a new beginning. It does not have to destroy your life or your sanity.

As Attorney Barclay so clearly discusses in *The African-American Guide to Divorce & Drama*, there are a lot of breakaway issues in a divorce. This book is so important because whether your marriage is solid or on the rocks, whether you are thinking about divorce or already separated, or even if you are already divorced, it has tools and insights that can benefit you. You will find a lot of wisdom in this book—wisdom about the law, wisdom about life. Wisdom gleaned from Attorney Barclay's 25 years of experience. I hope you will read it, use it, and share the information it contains. If ever there were a time to "look deep before you leap," it is when you decide to leave your marriage. By writing *The African-American Guide to Divorce & Drama*, Attorney Barclay has ensured that if you finally take that leap, you will land on firm footing.

Los Angeles, CA – *Spring 2013*

Mablean Deloris Ephriam, Esq.
Speaker, Author, Mediator

President/CEO/Founder
Mablean Ephriam Foundation

Acknowledgments

This book, *The African-American Guide to Divorce & Drama: Breaking Up Without Breaking Down*, is the result of a collaborative effort of many dedicated people who have my sincerest appreciation. As an attorney, though words are my stock and trade, I am nearly at a loss to find the words sufficient to thank those who helped me with this book. Yet, I must publicly thank many who gave assistance.

While all those who helped or encouraged me are too many to list in these pages, I thank and acknowledge the assistance of the following people, without whom I might never have written this book: Cynthia Battle, the Honorable William S. Boyd, Denise Brewer, Esq., Kimberly Cook, Esq., Margaret Currin, Esq., the Honorable Pamela Hill-Veal, Patrick John, Esq., Lisa McLeod, Esq., Vickie Pasley, Esq., Crystal Roberts, Esq., Deadra Woods-Stokes, Esq., Rafael L. Taylor, Esq., and Calvin Willis.

The 26 African-American focus-group divorce participants, who read and responded to these ideas in draft form, did a great service. My representatives "heard you" and incorporated many of your insightful and provocative sentiments into this important conversation. I humbly thank you.

During several very dynamic stages of development, a collaborative team gave oversight to this project. I am grateful for a good friend and writing coach, the Rev. Dr. Walter A. McCray, who has assisted me in forming and overseeing this publishing project from its inception. I especially thank consultant Mary C. Lewis of MCL Editing, Etc., for performing a crucial developmental edit of the rough manuscript in its formative stages—an invaluable service that greatly strengthened the budding concept. I am most appreciative to my editor, Dibri Beavers, who enthusiastically caught my vision and excellently used her critical and substantial skills to enhance and reshape the manuscript through the final stages of the editorial process.

Each member of the team—including several of my close legal colleagues—did far more than is here acknowledged, and the outcome of their collective contributions is far greater than the specific tasks and services they performed individually. Overall, the collaborative team helped me take what I've learned from more than 25 years of legal practice and mold it into a coherent and user-friendly guidebook that everyday people can understand.

I do not believe this project would have reached its destined end without the special encouragement and prayers of a number of close friends and professional colleagues. Though not mentioned here by name, I express my sincere appreciation for their most helpful moral support.

Lester L. Barclay
March, 2013

Testimonials for

The African-American Guide to DIVORCE & DRAMA:
Breaking Up Without Breaking Down

"The African-American Guide to DIVORCE & DRAMA is just what most attorneys who handle such cases have been waiting for to serve as a reference for clients about to go through this experience of divorce or separation. I, too, have handled divorces, and have worked very hard to help couples understand the importance of their coming to mutual agreement on everything possible before waiting for a judge to decide. When couples don't decide and put themselves and their children through adversarial processes over everything, their families come out the losers. Very often, no one gets what makes them happy–after spending a whole lot of money to get someone else to decide for them! Thank you for this great guide. If followed, it will save couples a lot of heartache, indecision and money!"

E. Faye Williams, MPA, Ph.D., D.Min., Esq.
National Chair, National Congress of Black Women, Inc.,
Commissioner, Presidential Scholars Commission
President, Natural Health Options

"This guide–The African-American Guide to DIVORCE & DRAMA–clearly illustrates how societal norms, values and culture, impact our most intimate interpersonal and familial relationships . . . More important, it reveals the social forces, the dynamics of institutional powers and various cultural influences that permeate the basic concept of 'divorce' and its emotional characteristics. An excellent pre-nuptial resource . . . But a must read for post-nuptial survival."

Dr. Joan M. Payne-Hill
Sociologist

"This 'Anthology' of The African-American Guide to DIVORCE & DRAMA is comprehensive, down to earth and quite readable. It covers the wide spectrum of human emotions generated by divorce. It should be a must read for family counselors, ministers, and of course divorce lawyers. The psychological impact of divorce can be felt through reading Mr. Barclay's timely book."

Stephen A. Parker, Ph.D. NCC
Professor Psychology, (Ret.)

Testimonials for
The African-American Guide to DIVORCE & DRAMA:
Breaking Up Without Breaking Down

"*The African-American Guide to DIVORCE & DRAMA helps us understand
the impact and effect of divorce on the family unit. It also provides much advice for
divorcing litigants who desire to resolve or minimize much of the drama accompanying
the divorce process and its aftermath. Barclay's writing style and use of numerous
real-life illustrations are spot-on. The guide evokes introspection, deliberation, and
peace-making action, especially on behalf of children of divorce. I highly recommend
the book as required reading for those contemplating divorce . . . as well as for couples
who plan to marry! Legal and other professionals will benefit greatly from Barclay's
culturally sensitive approach to drama remediation. We applaud Barclay, our
colleague, for his outstanding creative writing on a very contentious matter.*"

David R. Askew, Esq.
CEO and General Counsel
National Association of Minority and Women Owned Law Firms
NAMWOLF

The African-American Guide to

DIVORCE & DRAMA

PART ONE:

The Personal Dimension

In this section, turn inward as you read.

Spend some time exploring

the nature of what is happening and how you feel about it.

Chapter 1

Your Personal Legal Guide

Handheld Divorce and Drama Resolution

As an African-American divorce attorney practicing matrimonial law since 1985, I have handled hundreds of divorces and custody cases for couples married as short as a few months to those married over 40 years. Through my firm, The Barclay Law Group, I have not only helped scores of married couples obtain a "drama-free" divorce, but I have also saved many more failed marriages and breakups from becoming complete legal and relationship bloodbaths. In many instances, I have prevented a couple's breakup from breaking down their lives. I'll say more about my experience later. First, let's discuss your marital situation.

I have a good idea about the emotional swings and feelings of most divorcing spouses. You suffer deep wounds from a bad marital relationship, whether the breakdown is due to dishonesty, betrayal, rejection, abandonment, meanness, selfishness, abuse, or all of the above. Most times, whatever the cause, a breakup or divorce simply leaves you devastated. I feel you. I've seen too many crushed victims of broken marital relationships not to feel some of your pain. Trust me; you're not alone. On a weekly basis, many African-Americans contact a divorce attorney. In my firm, 70 percent of these clients are females, while only 30 percent are males. Their average age range is 40 to 50, their marriages have lasted from approximately 7-12 years, and they have 1 to 3 children. These divorce-seeking clients work in professional and semi-professional occupations, yet one characteristic ties 98 percent of these clients together: they are all on an emotional roller coaster. They are up one day and down the next. Psychologically speaking, they are scared, angry, and frustrated. Why? They cannot control the drama of their relationship.

When we are hurt, angry, bitter, torn within, and confused, we often don't make decisions that are best in the long run. Hastily made decisions may initially cover an injury, but seldom are sufficient to heal deep wounds. Catch yourself before acting irrationally. An impending and bitter divorce, or its aftermath, can provoke you to make decisions and pursue actions you may regret later. The way you choose to divorce or deal with its drama can destroy you, just like a dysfunctional marriage. In other words, "Don't be a double-failure." That's my advice for couples headed for divorce court. If you are failing at marriage, don't fail at divorce, too. Give yourself a fighting chance to make a peaceful separation and transition away from your spouse. Successfully undo your marriage by not letting a broken love relationship beat you down twice. I remember a local radio interview where I stressed just this point in response to the interviewer's thought-provoking question.

"Attorney Barclay, what made you concentrate your practice in the area of divorce?"

I collected my thoughts for a moment, then answered.

"Well, initially I was a general practitioner," I said. "However, after handling several divorces and seeing how people suffer in the process, my heart went out to those who experience marital breakup. Soon after, I began focusing my skills, energies and passion on helping people successfully make it through divorce. I especially had a great concern for the children of divorce. They are the innocent victims."

"I'm glad you said that," the interviewer responded. "I hear you saying something very important. You like to handle divorce in such a way that you *minimize the effects of the breakup.* Is that it?"

"Yes, that's it in a nutshell," I replied.

"Good," the interviewer said. "Now I can tell my listeners a fascinating story about the way you effectively reduced a couple's divorce drama.

"Recently I learned that a judge presiding over a divorce case appointed you to represent the parties' children. In the process of representing the children, you came to know the couple, and through your interactions with the parents, you eventually motivated them to refocus their concerns on the children's best interest, not on their own. Hence, you helped the couple deal with their failing marriage based on the impetus to help their children, and something happened in the process. When they began thinking long-term about their children, the couple made a responsible choice to reconcile their relationship. In effect, your counsel—whatever you advised—really saved their marriage and young children from damaging pain and deep sadness. You encouraged the parents to stabilize their home, and preserve the future quality of living for the entire family.

"You must admit, that is quite a story," the interviewer said. "What happened to that couple, Attorney Barclay, sounds almost unbelievable."

"I guess it does," I said. "But that reconciliation is a rare exception to the rule."

"What you did for that couple is fantastic," the interviewer said with a smile of affirmation. "If only more people knew about the great services you offer, our community could be so much better."

The radio interview that evening gave me an opportunity to affirm my purpose. I can help to dissolve a bad marriage—or to resolve marital conflicts period—without increasing vexation. I best describe my approach as **handheld divorce and drama resolution.**

Let's keep it real. Sometimes my approach works, sometimes not. After all, it takes the honest efforts of two sensible persons—more than either spouse acting alone—to minimize drama in most divorces. An attorney can represent only one of the litigants in a divorce case. So at best, the chances of successfully reducing a couple's divorce drama are 50 percent, despite the efforts of a good lawyer.

An effective divorce lawyer can help some clients dissolve a marriage without destroying their lives or the future well-being of their children. Most estranged persons I represent obtain what they initially seek—a divorce. The man or woman successfully petitions the court to dissolve the marriage, whether or not the divorce process is drama-free—either for the litigants or for others impacted by the broken marital relationship. My desire is to resolve the unnecessary drama and thus prevent a complete marital breakdown.

Drama-Reducing Guidance

Divorce legally separates marriage partners. Usually, the parties separated are husband and wife. As such, "divorce" does not apply to those who are unmarried or single. If a couple was never married, then they can never be divorced. This fact applies across the board, regardless of how long a couple has been in a close relationship or how many children a couple may have. Generally, two types of marriages exist: statutory (or ceremonial) and common-law.[1] Both types share certain characteristics:

1) the parties freely consent to marry;

2) each must be of legal age or gain parental consent to marry; and

3) neither person should have a disability preventing the legal joining of the union.

In contrast, common-law marriage differs from the statutory (ceremonial) marriage in the following respects:

1) the government issues no marriage license and the couple does not file a marriage certificate;

2) no formal ceremony of marriage occurs before witnesses;

3) each party must present themselves to the world as husband and wife; and

4) in most jurisdictions, the couple must cohabitate for a certain period of time when they first form the common-law marriage. Further, they must dwell together with the expectation their relationship is a legally valid marriage, and others will accept it as such. Intentionality and transparency are required.

When two single persons meet the above requirements of a common-law marriage in their country, social practice or geographical state, they are legally married. Subsequently, the marriage is subject to the laws governing divorce. Otherwise, divorce would not apply, no matter how long the couple enjoys "a close relationship," "cohabitate," "live together," are "girlfriend and boyfriend," "roommates," or describe their relationship by some other term. In the U.S., it

---

[1] The term "common-law marriage" is sometimes used as a synonym for "non-marital relationship contract," as well as for domestic partnership and reciprocal beneficiaries relationship. Sui juris (legally competent) marriages may be recognized as one of these other interpersonal relationships in foreign jurisdictions, especially if the parties to a true common-law marriage are not able to prove they actually did conform to the requirements to contract a valid common-law marriage in their home jurisdiction. Common-law marriage often is contrasted with the ceremonial marriage." See, "Common-law Marriage," *Wikipedia*, March 1, 2013, http:// en.wikipedia.org/wiki/Common-law_marriage. "Marriage," *Wikipedia*, March 1, 2013, http://en.wikipedia.org/wiki/Marriage.

is worth noting the District of Columbia and ten different states grant residents the right to contract common-law marriages. These include Alabama, Colorado, Iowa, Kansas, Montana, Oklahoma, Rhode Island, South Carolina, Texas, and Utah. All states recognize common-law marriages contracted in other states, with exceptions related to polygamous and same-sex marriages. However, in contrast to common-law marriage, no such thing as "common-law divorce" exists in the U.S. Hence, a so-called "ghetto divorce" or "walk away marital separation," where the couple simply breaks up and goes their separate ways, legally means nothing. A court of law must dissolve a marriage. Remember: divorce is *an ending of a marriage by an official decision in a court of law.*

This should help you clearly understand who is married and who can seek a divorce. Marriage partners get a divorce; no others. In addition, while the angst experienced on a daily basis by a man or woman in a pending divorce is daunting enough, more difficult is the idea of moving an estranged relationship toward the official status of legal divorce, the incipient dynamics of which can unmercifully tear at the guts of the most grounded litigant.

Therefore, you need the information on the following pages if you . . .

- seek resources about divorce and its processes
- look for handholding that is gentle, yet firm
- are embarrassed when talking about your situation but need to hear an empathetic voice
- value your children
- angrily defend your marital failure
- do not view your experience as mainstream
- are conscious of cultural idiosyncrasies and nuances and are sensitive to, not ashamed of, your black cultural context
- cannot bear to think of your family as a divorce statistic
- struggle with the notion that divorce is a question of spirituality or morality.

The African-American Guide to Divorce & Drama will do just what it says: it will **guide** you. In a personable way, it will talk to you without talking down to you. It will lead you. It will encourage and support you. It will help you understand your personal issues and place racial and cultural issues into perspective. It will also help you mediate disputes and issues between you and your separating partner, and I hope in the process, resolve much of your divorce drama.

My guidance provides an inside perspective on separation, divorce, and related matters. I disclose what some lawyers or judges are unlikely to tell you. My advice and counsel are both legal and practical, although I recognize divorce laws vary from state to state. I help those in divorce process information in the context of the African-American experience because we often view some divorce matters differently than the mainstream population. I help divorcing parties explore their viable options with the result being much less drama.

It is one thing to meet the rigorous challenges of divorce in a courtroom; it is quite another thing to keep living in a community when your relationship is "jacked-up" and all your drama is "hanging out." When experiencing separation or divorce, how do you keep facing your family, friends, neighbors, teachers, church members, club members, social group, and even your hairstylist? Some choose to "free" themselves by publicly decrying the "shame" of their divorce. They tell it raw and refuse to avoid the repercussions. However, this response to a tragic breakup does not always reduce drama, but in fact may increase it like pouring gasoline on a fire. If you choose not to call out the lowdown tragedy of your personal business for what it is, what are your other methods for coping with your ordeal?

For instance, how will you deal with the stress of holidays, children's birthdays, graduations, etc? How do you act and respond? How do you protect your children? How can you maintain your dignity and continually move your life forward? In what way will you, or can you, ever again reach wholeness?

Helping you avoid as much divorce drama as possible is my purpose. Step-by-step, this guide will discuss the course you should take and the things you should know when the breakup of your marriage seems imminent or finally happens. A series of "Act Now" recommendations follow each chapter. These clear directions cover a myriad of divorce-related topics aimed at lowering the level of drama in the divorce process and helping divorced parties emerge on the other side of a breakup healthy and spiritually at peace.

Withstanding Breakdown

An important question naturally surfaces. Why should court-bound, potential divorcees seek to avoid drama? After all, usually either marriage partner thinks the attitudes or actions of their spouse are to blame for the failed marriage. So why shouldn't divorce lawyers allow the estranged husband and wife to fight it out in "no holds barred" fashion and leave the spoils of their broken marriage to the victor? My answer is clear: divorce drama leads to breakdown in other areas of life.

Persons who fail to resolve relationship drama often reap dire consequences. A couple may bring pre-marital drama into their relationship, suffer unexpected drama during their marriage, or experience the drama generated by a heated and highly contested divorce. The result of failing to navigate the drama of a bad or souring relationship is the defeat and aftermath of breakdown. Marital emotional estrangement, conflict, separation, and divorce are in themselves relationship breakdowns and often further result in more damaging breakdowns in other critical areas of life. There is psychological breakdown, physical breakdown, spiritual breakdown, personal breakdown, and family breakdown. Added to these are values breakdown, financial breakdown, social breakdown, cultural breakdown, and more.

Simply, the disruption of relationships and the degeneration of life, whether we use terms such as "dysfunction," "disorder," "failure," "collapse," "illness," "heartbreak," "trauma," "depression" or the like—in one way or another these ideas speak to the true-to-life human condition of breaking down. And experience has taught me that resolving divorce drama ultimately empowers the divorcing parties to withstand the more sinister personal, social, and financial dramas lurking around the corner.

Peace-seeking Spirit

Divorce, as such, is not the ideal in the institution of marriage. Historically, marriage is the rule and practice in countless cultures and societies across the world. Divorce is an exception to marriage (remaining single is another). Marital breakup is not humanity's model, whether viewed from the perspective of a divine covenant, cultural custom, or a simple legal agreement.

However, it is not ideal for a spouse to tolerate social, physical, verbal, mental, and emotional abuse in a so-called "marriage." Moreover, neither does the ideal sanction the kind of divorce whose process and repercussions are similar to a tsunami that follows a devastating earthquake.

The divorce drama of some couples wrecks their lives more than years of marriage, but if divorce is the necessary option for a dysfunctional marriage (and it often is), then a "peaceful" divorce or separation is the lesser of two evils. This is especially so for the sake of children and extended family relationships in the home and community. My approach to divorce and drama advocates that a humane spirit accompany divorce proceedings and its after-effects. "Peace" is the goal. However, a fair peace is the ideal. I would never encourage a wife or husband to seek peace at any price. There is a limit to how much madness and affliction a spouse should endure for the sake of peace.

Remember, we are dealing with marriage, a love and trust relationship. Every spouse has a right to fight for fairness for themselves and their children. For this reason, this conversation promotes such virtues as humaneness, kindness, personal validation, dignity, self-worth, hope, reconciliation, restoration, merciful-justice, healing, and wholeness. No matter how reluctantly we bow to breaking up, we must nevertheless do our best to stop the cycles of indifference, abuse, violence, and pain so frequently found in marriage, separation, and divorce. Divorce if you must, but peace is your choice. As it has been said, "*Blessed are the peacemakers, for they shall be called the children of God.*"[2]

Cultural Competence

In the matter of divorce, many black people need a special kind of legal and cultural handholding. In addition, simultaneously they often need the kind of assistance designed to minimize the social drama surrounding divorce and the process, and to foster peace if possible. Therefore, I have focused this informative teaching with African-Americans at heart whose divorces span all socioeconomic levels and classes, professionals as well as nonprofessionals. Doctors, lawyers, law enforcement officers, teachers, business executives, bus drivers, beauticians, trade workers, professional athletes, preachers, restaurant owners, authors, social workers, politicians, postal workers, musicians, laborers—the list of divorce litigants is diverse and long.

Unfortunately, some non-black attorneys often do not fully understand or appreciate many of the significant cultural and social experiences of black

---

[2] *Gospel of Matthew* 5:9 (KJV); Jesus' word of blessing on persons practicing a specific virtue, a *Beatitude*.

divorce litigants. Some may say, "People from all different racial and ethnic groups get divorced. What is so different about African-Americans and their divorces?" This is a valid question. Yes, we know divorce affects all racial and ethnic groups. Yet, African-Americans confront divorce with a unique set of challenges due to complexities and cultural clashes that occur in the black community among the few wealthy, the tenuous working class, and the numerous poor. Effectively communicating about the wide-ranging experiences of persons represented within these various groups is at times difficult even for culturally sensitive blacks. For instance, consider the crucial divorce issues faced by a relatively poor, black, urban high-school educated mother of three. What cultural connections or differences might she share with her divorced female counterpart—a black suburban, highly educated, corporate executive mother of one? Certainly, though both women are black, their language, values and standards, and general view of society and the world may significantly differ. Speaking to the experiences of both at one time is a challenge.

Whether in matters of divorce, or in other civil or criminal matters, many black folks need firm handholding when dealing with our society's legal system. They often need a double kind of representation. On the one hand, they need a lawyer who is well versed in the law pertaining to the case at hand. Alongside this legal expertise, they need a culturally competent lawyer who is sensitive to the special needs and circumstances of black people and the cultural values they hold near and dear.

African-American divorces come with certain distinctions and peculiarities primarily due to:

- the prominence of the black matriarchy;
- the influential role the church plays in the lives of African-Americans, even for those who do not regularly attend;
- the reluctance of black people to seek therapy for mental and emotional issues;
- the high incidences of domestic violence in black relationships and marriages;
- the number of high school dropouts and non-college-bound youth; and
- the high rate of male, and growing female, incarceration.

As authors Oscar Barbarin and Terry McCandies point out in their article, *African-American Families in the New Millennium*, these and other cultural and social challenges can affect black couples in relationships, marriage, divorce and other matters.[3] Four of these bear special mention:

1. **The Black Male Shortage (whether real or perceived):** Some black female divorcees often feel more despair about their future prospects for companionship, hence they may appear more upset and angry than their non-black counterparts. This anger can lead to an increase in emotional distress that may escalate the conflict during litigation. Black male divorcees, on the other hand, usually have no shortage of women at their disposal, and thus often need reminding not to permit their romantic interludes to interfere with their responsibilities as a father.

2. **The Higher Rate of Single-Parent (usually single-mother) Households:** Frequently, divorcing black couples come with no model of responsible fatherhood in their personal lives. Often, these parents are not reading from the same "playbook" in terms of the appropriate roles for fathers, in particular. That's because neither one of them have a playbook from their own childhood and are making up the rules as they go along. This leads to ceaseless bickering over visitation and custody. It's like walking down an unfamiliar flight of stairs in the dark: every step brings anxiety and stress. Add to this stress and anxiety the anger and fear that often accompany divorce for all racial/ ethnic groups, and we can see that divorce, as well as the preceding marriage, is that much more emotionally taxing for blacks.

3. **The Involvement of Extended Family in Child-rearing:** Grandparents, aunts, uncles, cousins and friends assisting with raising children is common in African-American families. However, this makes visitation and custody issues in black divorces especially delicate and

---

[3] See, Oscar A. Barbarin, Terry McCandies, "African-American Families – In the New Millennium." *International Encyclopedia of Marriage and Family. Encyclopedia.com* (2003). The authors state, "Historical and cultural influences, racism, urbanization, migration, discrimination, segregation, and immigration have profoundly shaped contemporary African-American family functioning." March 1, 2013, http://www.encyclopedia.com/doc/1G2-3406900022.html.

complex. For example, when a grandmother appears in divorce court to support her son or daughter, she usually has played a role in the life of the grandchildren that most white judges and lawyers don't fully understand. This lack of understanding may lead them to ignore completely the role of extended family, much to the children's detriment.

4. **The Expressiveness and Familiarity of Black Culture:** Historically speaking, black culture is expressive. When black people are upset, we tend to get louder than other racial/ethnic groups. In church, for instance, we tend to talk back to the preacher during the sermon and otherwise talk to strangers as though they're friends in a way other cultures may find rude or a violation of "boundaries." Many white judges and lawyers misinterpret this expressiveness and familiarity as excessive "hostility" toward the opposing party; however, studies have shown that blacks and whites have different communication styles that can lead to misunderstandings with each other. Since most judges and attorneys are white, during divorce proceedings they may more likely misunderstand black litigants more than they do white litigants.

When most couples break up, each party usually attempts to keep their divorce matters private without sharing painful details of the drama with others. Thus, some black people who have never been through the divorce process are simply uninformed and do not understand the great impact of culture in the courtroom. These reasons motivated me to write this divorce guide to provide assistance in this conversation, meet a real cultural need, and fill an information void. As a result, in matters of divorce and the drama of its aftermath, African-Americans need no longer suffer the disadvantage and disappointment of legal under-representation or cultural incompetence.

Experienced Counsel

The information presented here is not theory. Neither is it a scientific study based on mountains of statistical or empirical data. I have gleaned the lessons and tips provided in this book from years of firsthand and hands-on legal experience in matters of paternity, child support, separation, divorce, custody, guardianship, and mediation.

I take into account tragedies or triumphs in the areas of male-female (and same-sex) relationships, marriage, divorce, separation, "baby's mama" and "baby's daddy" relationships—with the aftermath of consequences and drama. The stories and illustrations I cite are typical—but not stereotypical—experiences of divorce litigants, courtroom proceedings, and counseling sessions. Much of the insight I offer is similar to the wisdom you might hear from your 85-year old grandmother.

A Personal Professional Touch

Some people have a very negative image of the legal system and attorneys. Perhaps you are inclined to approve this common sentiment due to a bad run-in with the legal system or a lawyer. Not all agree with this knee-jerk sweeping put-down of attorneys. My view differs from some of the negative stereotypes, due to the longtime working relationships and friendships I have with numerous lawyers. My personal experience with those in the legal profession tells me something very positive. Good lawyers—like most dogs to their owners—can be a client's "best friend." These pets are very loyal, trustworthy, and useful. They will walk with you, guide you, guard you, and stick with you 'til the very end, even when everyone else seems to desert you.

The lawyer who offers you services with a professional and personal touch gives you the best of both worlds. When confronting certain legal matters, sometimes all you really need is good legal advice, and someone who considerately communicates and represents you. When your marriage is breaking up and tearing you apart, you need legal assistance, professional counseling, and moral support. You need a "best friend" with courtroom expertise and a listening ear. You need legal handholding.

Depending on the nature of your case, hiring or retaining a good lawyer may require lots of money. However, what happens when you do not have sufficient funds for your legal cause? When your legal problems persist, what should you do if immediate access to free legal assistance or a social service agency is not available? In these circumstances, what *can* you do to avoid the drama accompanying separation or divorce?

This guide provides you with helpful answers for your troubled relationship. Working your way through these instructions will bring you nearer to your legal "best friend." Though not costing you as much as a good lawyer—only a minor fraction of the costs—this information is a great supplement to your personal attorney. The sound advice provided here will give you help when you need it most, when you are on the brink of divorce. Use it for guidance when walking the path of your drama-filled days—those days of relationship breakdown, emotional estrangement, knock-down-drag-out fights, separation, divorce proceedings, final closure, and the aftermath. This social map will help you navigate those difficult and drama-filled minefields of relationships and social circumstances resulting from a breakup or divorce.

Up Next

Marriage has its own drama. But more often than not, when a marriage ends, it simply intensifies and transfers its existing issues into the drama of divorce. Childhood trauma and the personal dramas between husbands and wives often sow the seeds of marital breakup and can escalate and destroy a couple's love and trust. When discord replaces peace, and angry words are the only things they share anymore, many couples decide it's time to call it quits and divorce. However, thinking about divorce and actually *getting* a divorce are two different things. We look at the issues involved with this life-changing decision in the next chapter.

Chapter 2

Are You Ready to Divorce?

Is Our Marriage Over?

As a spouse, perhaps you face no question more agonizing than whether or not your marriage is over. Yet, every partner who decides to divorce (whether they are the petitioner or respondent) has asked himself or herself this question and ultimately answered, "Yes." No matter how long the marriage, the decision to divorce is never an easy one, especially when children are involved. Breaking up a marriage means dismantling a home, separating property, and ending a common life with the one you once loved— often in the midst of anger, heartbreak, and extreme drama. If you could ask the average couple on their wedding day if theirs would ever be among those marriages that would eventually break up, nearly all would say a resounding, "No." The overwhelming majority believe they will stay together just as their vows promise: "till death us do part." However, the couple does a lot of living between marriage and death, and sometimes the marriage dies first, before either partner.

Unquestionably more married couples have thought about getting a divorce than have actually followed through. Indeed, most couples will admit to having had their fights and rough patches, times when they wondered if their marriage could or should survive. Yet, for some partners, "for better or for worse" means staying together even if keeping the vow requires their moving into separate bedrooms and keeping up appearances for the sake of the neighbors. They endure a slow, sad drifting apart until they are virtual strangers occupying the same house. Despite their shared misery, divorce for them is not an option. Still, a surprisingly large number of couples encounter a definite breaking point, a moment when one or both spouses realizes there is no point or apparent good in continuing the marriage. The reasons for breaking up can be, and are, as myriad as the people who marry—anger, abandonment, cruelty, domestic violence, incompatibility, infidelity, lack of trust, loss of love. Reasons *always* exist as to why a marriage falls apart, and some causes and explanations go deeper than even the couple themselves may realize.

The Roots of Breakup

All breakups have roots, and these roots come in various forms. For instance, the idea of male responsibility is difficult for some black men to grasp because they have only experienced the primary role models of mama, grandma, and sister who raised and provided for them. Is it any surprise, then, when these males get into a serious relationship or marriage, they subconsciously expect their mate to take care of them?

A child abused, neglected, or abandoned by his father may feel rejection and insecurity as a man. He may carry this rejection and insecurity into young adulthood and marriage and create some trying situations for the women in his life. His negative behavior may show up as an unhealthy attachment to his wife, wanting her to be close all the time and desiring to do everything together. Obviously, his behavior begins smothering and binding his wife. He deprives her of personal independence, and they each suffer from freedom deprivation and lack of personal space. On the other hand, a man abused in his childhood may turn his anger and pain toward abusing his wife and children.

Another person may have grown up in a home where her parents favored their younger child over her. The disfavored child became jealous of her sibling, and years later, this jealousy carried over into her marriage. Whenever her husband showed care and affection for his sister by spending extra time with her, the wife became jealous. That jealousy began to cause problems in their husband-wife relationship. She accused her husband of neglecting her and became competitive with his sister. Her spirit of jealousy made her grasp for her husband's attention. She became reactionary and overcompensated when trying to please him.

Some women can't stand to have a man "talk down to them." Due to circumstances beyond their control, they never had a significant male presence in their lives as they grew up. So later, when their male partner is speaking to them, they hear an assertive male voice for the first time that may appear as aggressive or dominant to a female from an absent-father family. Not all wives respond in this way to an assertive husband, of course. Some women from broken homes are very capable and positive responders within the context of marriage, even if their fathers were absent or they were victims of neglect or abandonment. Yet, some women, though certainly not "always looking for a fight," react negatively.

Therefore, to alleviate some marital drama, sisters of an absent father figure should consider the following: your mother and grandmother raised you. They met your material and emotional needs; they even may have sent you off to college. They were strong and well-intended women. But, in many cases, their care for you may not have provided continual exposure to a man's perspective. Something missing in your relationship and in processing the male voice of your partner may challenge you. Consequently, subconsciously it is possible to carry certain baggage into the relationship. Female strength and self-sufficiency are good things. However, the good seeds of female self-reliance in the essentials of life—qualities you learned in your upbringing—may translate into causing a fair amount of marital or relationship tension, and require your adjustment to a "strong" black man.

Fantastic Father, Horrible Husband

Due to the absence of mature African-American fathers, boys don't learn what is required to be men, husbands or fathers. We hear it often; an African-American male will confess: "I take care of my kids; I provide and spend time with them."

The man is honest about his fatherly provision. He takes care of business in a very loving way. Yet, the same brother will refer to the mother of his children in a profane manner, and even do so in the presence of his children. The man does not understand the negative influence his verbal behavior has on the children. He is poisoning their minds about the value of black women.

Children need to see their father as a "good daddy," but they also need to see him as a "good mate" and a "great husband." Your wife's perception of your fatherhood often differs much from her view of you as a husband. Some "great" fathers exist who are truly horrible husbands, and perceptive and discerning wives know the difference. However, men sometimes do not see the disparate reality between being a "fantastic father" and a "horrible husband" until someone directly places the issue in their face. Simply because the kids have a good father does not mean the wife (and mother of his kids) has a good husband. Case in point: when speaking to the lawyer, the divorcing wife says she does not need a child support order. She says, "The kids' father takes care of them, or at least is trying his best to care for them. I'm divorcing him *and* his other four women who keep calling the house!

The bottom line is he doesn't want his children to know what is really going on; that he is "doggin' around." At all costs, the brother in such a case is trying to protect his image as a "good daddy" in the eyes of the children. We call this *overcompensation*—a response resorted to by many people failing in one aspect of a relationship: they go overboard in other areas trying to make up for their failure. So, the father overcompensates for his infidelity by taking care of the children and building a bond with them, independent of a failed marriage. In contrast, some wives simply regard their husband as, "No-good, period." The ones who have earned this despised reputation are most irresponsible. Besides sleeping around, the man who fits this category doesn't bring any money home. He keeps the lion's share of his earnings for himself and his habits. He uses his money and time to treat his girlfriend better than he treats his wife. He is nothing but a marital migraine headache.

The "Ghetto Divorce"

The African-American experience of slavery and its aftermath has sown some very destructive seeds into the bonds of our families and relationships. Often, the bad fruit shows up in the legal system. My colleague, Attorney Vickie Pasley, detailed the drama and emotional turmoil she has seen over the years, the "stigma of divorce" in the African-American experience. "Somehow," she says, "married couples erroneously think separation magically merges into a divorce. So, if the couple manages to stay separated just long enough, their separation will eventually result in divorce." Based on many years of dealing with divorced couples, my colleagues use the term "ghetto divorce,"[4] a culturally and socially nuanced term that defines the practice of couples who walk away from each other in a non-legal separation for a prolonged period. Relatively speaking, it describes an experience prevalent in numerous marital breakups of African-Americans.

What are the roots of this strange social practice, the so-called "ghetto divorce"?

In America, it once was illegal for black folks to get married. So, if you were never legally married, then you could never legally get a divorce. This is the historical and cultural perspective whose roots have given text to African-American "marital" relationships. Remember, to get married we once had to "Jump the Broom." That was our culturally "legal" form of marriage. If not, "common-law" marriage was next door. If a man and woman stayed together under one roof long enough, the laws of some states gave them the status of marriage by virtue of the longevity of their relationship.

Now if we had to "Jump the Broom" to get married, what did we have to do to get divorced? I doubt rather few couples got their "divorce" by resorting to "Jumping the Broom Backwards!" (Even if such a practice ever actually happened!) No, it didn't work that way. Instead, a couple who found their

---

[4] A so-called **"ghetto divorce"** is a term that labels the non-legal breakup of black couples as such due to the high incidence of its practice among African-Americans, in contrast to whites or other ethnic groups. Historical and social dynamics in the experience of African-Americans underlie its usage. In context, the term is not necessarily stereotypical but indicative of what many continually observe in the marriage and divorce arenas of blacks whose marital relationships fail. Though objectionable to some due to its negative connotations, "ghetto" is also a fact of life (albeit often unpleasant to many) experienced by minorities in the millions, and impacts diverse ethno-cultural groups. Other groups also have "ghettos," though comparatively they do not have as many walk-away marital separations as do African-Americans—a pattern noted by those dealing with divorce matters. "Ghetto divorces" occur, not only in the lower socioeconomic class of African-Americans, but also in the higher income and class levels. Plenty of professional blacks subject a broken marriage to the practice of a "ghetto divorce." A "ghetto divorce" is not an "unlawful" divorce, for partners can break up at will without committing any crime. The practice is "non-legal" but, as they extend their time of separation, is fraught with legal and social consequences for estranged spouses and children. If the "ghetto divorce" concept instigates estranged black couples to forsake the practice and to rapidly bring closure to their marriage by legally divorcing—while reducing unnecessary drama in the marital breakup and aftermath— then the provocative term serves its purpose effectively and well.

relationship on the rocks most likely just split, walked away, or moved on. The problem today is that too many couples are still trying to "Jump the Broom Backwards" rather than engage the legal process when dealing with a breakup. As a cultural group, the laws of the land, through the courts of the land, have adversely influenced our approach to getting married as well as how we end our relationships. As many have discovered, non-legal separation can come back to haunt you.

For instance, if a "ghetto-divorced" man who owns a home dies, his estranged wife is legally entitled to a portion of the value of the home, while his live-in girlfriend of 20 years gets nothing. If the man has a pension, his wife gets his pension, while his live-in gets zero since she is not the "next-of-kin" to the deceased. So, the estranged wife has the legal right to handle all her husband's business affairs, including taking control of funeral arrangements. The live-in has *no* rights. Therefore, if you and your spouse decide to go your separate ways, you need to do it properly by obtaining a divorce through the legal system. The "ghetto divorce" does not work, and estranged couples should divorce themselves from the practice.

In the past, the legal system has exercised much control over our lives and historically oppressed African-Americans. Yet today, we can use that system as our ally for marital justice and divorce resolution.

The Storm of Drama

"You mean I have to go through all this just to get rid of that fool!" said the flustered woman who had just completed my interview questionnaire for clients seeking a divorce. She wanted a quick exit, but her failing marital situation did not qualify for a "quick fix." Doing my due diligence, I clearly saw the entanglement of her relationship, and it did not look pretty—emotionally, financially, or otherwise.

As legally defined, divorce is *an ending of a marriage by an official decision in a court of law.* On the surface, however, most people only know that divorce is the breakup of someone's marriage. Beyond this awareness, they neither understand the deeper issues of divorce, nor how these issues can sow the seeds for all kinds of drama. Under normal circumstances, any sane person would choose to avoid the drama threatening to engulf their life. (Though I must admit, some people pathetically reveal their gluttony for punishment!) Too often, a separation or divorce spins into drama. This drama can become a roller-coaster experience where the ride-of-your-life jumps off the tracks.

I must warn you at the outset. Ironically, by possessing and reading this book you may inadvertently bring additional drama into your marriage. Your spouse may become very angry, hurt, or even threaten you with physical harm if or when he or she discovers you are reading a book on divorce. When your spouse realizes you are seriously contemplating a divorce, he or she may lose it. Prepare yourself, mentally and emotionally, for the ensuing drama. Though designed to minimize the drama associated with divorce, this subject matter may produce the reverse; it may have a negative effect on an unwitting spouse.

In most cases, to alleviate some of the drama, I do not recommend a spouse hide his or her thoughts and intentions about divorce from their mate. I believe that a good marriage thrives on open communication, transparency, and honesty. Thus, when it comes to the likelihood of you getting a divorce, I advise you to find a way to tell your spouse how you feel. No one can set a time that is agreeable under any or every circumstance to divulge your intentions to seek a divorce. Timing is everything. At some point, you ought to explain to your spouse the need to think through your marital options and the course you are pursuing.

Nevertheless, notwithstanding your ability to be forthright, brace yourself for the storm of drama that occurs upon first disclosure of your move toward a legal separation or divorce. The confusion, turbulence, and violence of first-disclosure are unpredictable and may come at any time. The drama may happen when you verbalize your true feelings, or, alternatively, when a sheriff serves the divorce papers you filed. In most cases, when the word gets out and the fire hits the fan, the drama associated with divorce will quickly heat up.

Separation or Divorce?

By the time the bitterness and drama has reached a fever pitch, some couples are absolutely certain their marriage is over and the only thing left to do is divorce—the sooner the better! Others aren't so sure this is the right path for them. They may still love and care for each other too much to throw away a long-term marital relationship. Some believe a little time apart may help them work through their differences and keep their marriage together. In any case, they're just not ready to give up and call it quits. For these couples, a trial separation is generally their first—and some would say their best—alternative to divorce. In this respect, a separation can be either of two things: a simple physical parting of the couple without any legal involvement, or a formal legal separation handled through the court.

A legal separation is different from divorce in two important ways. First, it allows someone to separate from their spouse while remaining legally married and prevents them from marrying anyone else (that would be bigamy).

Secondly, in some instances a legal separation may allow a spouse to get some legal benefits of a divorce, such as the following:

- court-ordered child support;
- custody and/or visitation;
- alimony/maintenance; and
- property distribution, while retaining some marital benefits like:
  - ○ the rights to a survivor's annuity, commonly called a "widow's pension,"
  - ○ certain Social Security payments if their spouse dies, or
  - ○ the ability to be a dependent on their spouse's health insurance.

Legal separation also freezes marital assets and liability for joint debt. Additionally, some people prefer legal separation because for religious reasons they do not believe in divorce.

Legal separation can have its drawbacks. Since in most states one party can get a divorce over the other party's objection, even when a legal separation may be in the best interest of one spouse (e.g., the wife has a serious medical condition and her husband's medical insurance currently covers her), the other party can force a divorce. Regardless, the couple remains legally married until one of them files for divorce and the court grants it.

In my experience, legal separation is not a common occurrence among African-American couples, and I do not recommend it. Most couples who cannot live together serve their best interests by dissolving the marriage.

Grounds for Divorce

In the past, divorce laws tied together money with the grounds for divorce itself, and to its processes and proceedings. Typically, a person filed a petition with the court seeking to dissolve the marriage, but the need to establish grounds made divorce about marital misconduct. For instance, if a man or a woman cheated on their spouse, the court could possibly not award alimony. By the 1970's, "no-fault" divorce entered the equation, alleviating the need to establish bad behavior. Thus, the grounds of one litigant did not have to vilify the other person to obtain a divorce. Technically speaking, consequences no longer existed for being bad or out of character. The court did not penalize the "offender."

Let's illustrate the above in a common scenario. A wife exercises her right to file for divorce because her husband is an alcoholic. These are her grounds. Under the "fault" system, the judge could punish the husband by awarding more money and property to the wife because of the husband's alcoholism. However, under today's "no fault" system, the judge would not consider the husband's alcoholism in awarding money or property to the wife. The old "fault" system led to lots of drama in divorces because a spouse had a financial incentive to badmouth their partner. The "no-fault" system removes some of the drama related to money.

Divorce About Children and Money

Today, divorce is about two things: children and money, and the legal consequences of a marital breakup center on these primary matters. Generally, the issues are custody, visitation rights, child support; who gets the house, how to divide the assets, stocks, bonds; retirement accounts as well as allocation of liabilities, if any exist. Usually, litigants can resolve financial issues faster than custody matters. Divorce attorneys simply crunch the numbers. Occasionally, a dispute arises over money, and this disagreement can create additional problems. However, when the parties disclose everything and place all the assets squarely on the table, the judge can make a quick decision as to the division of assets or allocation of liabilities. Disputes over the children often get nasty, and can become time consuming, expensive, and emotionally draining.

Sometimes, third parties must get involved to voice the best interest of the children. Generally, three types of advocates potentially may become involved in divorce cases regarding minor children:

1. The *Guardian Ad Litem* (*GAL*), an appointee of the court, often serves as the court's witness. This person may interview the children, parents and anyone else necessary to make a recommendation to the court. The *GAL* must act in the best interests of the child. Either party may call for the testimony of the *Guardian* regarding his or her observations and recommendations.

2. The Attorney for the Child has the same powers and responsibilities as the attorneys for the parties. The court usually appoints an attorney for the child when the child is older and the court recognizes the child's ability to participate in the court matter. This attorney advocates on behalf of their client, the child, but does not testify.

3. The Child Representative functions as a hybrid of the *GAL* and Attorney for the Child. As appointed by some states, this person may conduct investigations and interview the child, parents, or anyone else that he/she feels is necessary. However, Child Representatives do not make recommendations to the court. The law allows them to participate in the trial as an attorney, and to examine witnesses. Like the Attorney for the Child, the litigants cannot call this advocate as a witness.

In addition to determining the children's ability to speak on their own behalf, the court can send the litigants to mediation to seek resolution of certain issues. If the mediation does not resolve certain problems, and the parties cannot later agree, the case is likely resolved after a full trial. Sometimes, the court elicits the services of mental health professionals to assess the parenting strengths and weaknesses of each parent seeking custody.

Divorce expenses in child custody cases can quickly mount. Everyone gets a share of the money: attorneys, court-appointed attorneys, professionals, etc. The divorcing parties must pay for all these fees and costs, and some expenses can run into the tens of thousands of dollars. A typical case involving a contested custody battle can range from $30,000 to $75,000 easily.

Because of the relatively high proportion of unwed parents in the African-American community, some custody disputes often take place outside the bonds of marriage. Many of these cases exist when the father has no long-term history of living in the same household with the child. Frequently, he has no historical bond and few good reference points on which to build his case. Obviously, these types of cases can become very contentious. Another area of contention and drama is "removal." That is, the divorcing parent formally relocating to another state and desiring to remove the child to that state. Moving within a state, regardless of how far away or inconvenient it is for the noncustodial parent, is the right of the custodial parent. Consider this example:

For a parent residing in New York, more problems are associated with moving a child to New Jersey versus moving the child to a remote location within the State of New York. For those who live in New York City, New Jersey is closer than Buffalo, yet a litigant must present compelling justification for moving out of state due to jurisdictional and residency issues. What other issues might motivate a request for removal? Well, the mother may desire to marry someone else from another state. Perhaps she got a great career opportunity, or her job requires that she relocate. Those are good reasons to make a progressive move. However, the biological father contends that his ex can't just up and decide to leave her resident state since this would significantly affect the amount of time he can spend with his child. The judge agrees. So, to spite the father for objecting to her out-of-state move, the mother decides to stay within her resident state. However, she moves to a location much farther away from her child's father. In this case, the father can't say a word; he does not have legal grounds to challenge the move. The judge allows the mother to make the move because she does not need legal permission to move within her home state. The father may exercise his rights to visitation, but now it may cost him more money and time, since his child now lives miles and miles away.

Hiring the Right Attorney

Since the closest advisor and confidant you will have before and during your divorce proceeding is your attorney, hiring the right attorney is of tantamount importance. Generally, I recommend three basic steps:

1. **Check Out at Least 3 Law Firms**: In an informal survey, a group of previously divorced litigants revealed their criteria for choosing an attorney. Fifty percent (50%) said they would make a choice based on the attorney's gender; thirty percent (30%) said they would seek an attorney based on race; and twenty percent (20%) said they would choose an attorney based on whether the attorney had personally experienced divorce. All those surveyed indicated that legal competency would be foremost in their consideration. Get the names of law firms through referrals or by browsing the internet, then brace yourself, and make a few anonymous calls of inquiry. Find out as much as possible about the legal professional you choose to walk you through a divorce. Ask any questions you need to reach satisfaction, especially in the area of trust. Secure an attorney who is neither afraid in the court nor the conference room. If money is tight, consider contacting legal aid or some other social service agency.

2. **Retain a Culturally Competent Attorney**: Some African-Americans who are on the verge of divorce will retain a white attorney only. Many white attorneys are excellent and work hard to learn and understand cultural issues related to the black experience. Yet, others do not understand or attempt to understand the nuances of African-American culture. In contrast, generally speaking, black attorneys have learned to adapt bi-culturally in America, and many have the ability to represent clients across racial lines. Yet, "black" does not always equal cultural competency, though in most cases of black legal professionals it does.

A prominent colleague provides this insight about the benefits of retaining an African-American divorce attorney: "Having a black lawyer on either side of the divorce can sometimes lead to a wholesome cultural understanding of their client's situation and perhaps facilitate compromise. These lawyers can do so without sacrificing the assets the client is entitled to receive. In contrast, a white attorney may deal with simply the cold facts and issues of a case. Often, black attorneys take a personal interest in making sure that fathers are involved with the children, especially the sons. Usually, black attorneys live in the community and have a vested interest in the welfare of black people." The attorney effectively makes his point.

3. **Execute a Power of Attorney:** When you are about to retain a divorce attorney, the first thing you should do is execute a "Power of Attorney" or POA. (Make a point to mention it if your attorney doesn't bring it up.) Why do you need a POA? You need this instrument in order to cover yourself by filling a time gap. That gap lies in the period between when you first file your complaint with the court and the time it takes for issuance of the divorce decree.

A lot can happen during this period. Car accidents and comas happen. Events may occur that inhibit your decision-making capacity. The last thing you want is for something to happen to you—such as your incapacitation or death—that results in everything you own being left to a spouse who will soon become your ex. Do not let the spouse you are divorcing gain control of your assets! In the absence of a will, the surviving spouse is entitled to inherit part or all of certain assets in your estate. The next of kin makes all the major decisions. Think for a moment about a spouse who is on life support in the hospital, whose fate is now in the hands of the very person he or she is bitterly divorcing. All the man or woman has to do is tell the doctors to "pull the plug." How might his or her actions affect the children, the house, the car, or the bank accounts? When considering a POA, choose a person who will protect your interests and do right by your children and your portion of the marital estate.

The Power of Attorney in the wrong hands can be disastrous. In a non-divorce related matter, a colleague cites the case of a mother who was 93 years old and had two daughters. One daughter was the Power of Attorney, and the other daughter was the caretaker. The POA daughter did not want to pay for the caretaking service. She tied up the money and stopped paying for the home care ostensibly because she did not receive the proper billing from her sister. Then the POA daughter put her mother into a nursing home trying to hasten her death in order to get all the estate assets. The caretaking daughter and other family members had to show the court some kind of fiduciary malfeasance. The judge, angered because of the injustice happening to the mother, intervened. The lessons here are simple—find someone you trust, and who really loves you, to become your Power of Attorney.

Be Sure of Yourself

Carpenters and woodworkers have a saying: "Measure twice, cut once." They make sure to make the right cut the first time around, or they will cause an unnecessary foul-up. Applying this adage has saved woodworking professionals a lot of headaches, time and money. We can apply this saying to persons on the verge of divorce: "Be sure within yourself before you make the final separation." To put it another way, "Be careful not to jump from the fryin' pan of marriage into the fire of divorce."

This reminds me of the young man who was *this close* to pulling the plug on his brief, but very trying marriage. He was so upset with his wife one night he took to the streets to walk off his disappointment and anger. He found himself walking the aisles of a 24-hour grocery store at 3:00 a.m., mulling over his situation and mapping an exit plan to put an end to the drama of his failing marriage. As the young man paced the aisles, to his surprise and shock, he spotted an elderly colleague on the other side of the store. The colleague, his trusted mentor, confidant and vocational "father," was a wise and strong man who loved his wife and family and who put up with no mess from the young men he mentored! The older man, well known in many circles, held great influence in the community and exercised a significant measure of authority in the work and life of the young man. Quite easily, he could use his vast influence to block or impede his progress.

Knowing there was no way he could justify being away from his wife and kids at 3:00 in the morning, the young man knew he would be in serious trouble if the man saw him. He ducked out of sight and managed to slip undetected from the store. He headed straight home to his wife and children. On the way, he thought about his plan to break up his marriage and changed his mind. He decided he would rather deal with the pain of marital drama than live with the more painful drama of divorce and the professional censure of his highly respected mentor!

Act Now 2 – Are You Ready to Divorce?

In the process of divorce and its aftermath, remember that a good lawyer can become your best friend. An attorney can help you navigate some of the impending drama you will face. You also need a strong support network to help you deal with the emotional minefield you face. Use the following insights as your guide to pursuing a "No-Drama Divorce."

1) **Pause for a moment to review what marriage means to you.** Also, try hard to consider the benefits of your own marital relationship. I encourage my clients, either husband or wife, to take a marital inventory of themselves and their spouse before deciding to divorce. In divorce, what do you have to gain or to lose?

2) **Get a good personal counselor.** Whether you are getting married or getting divorced, counsel is always in order. One can choose from an array of family and marriage counselors, trained therapists, and licensed and certified practitioners. Some may even choose to go the spiritual route, finding it beneficial to talk with their minister. Referrals are another method for securing a counselor with good qualifications. Ask around.

3) **Retain a culturally competent attorney, particularly if your spouse has chosen one.** In doing so, reject the myth that African-Americans receive inferior representation from African-American lawyers. This false perception roots itself in the myth of black inferiority. My advice is to seek a good, culturally sensitive attorney to handle your divorce.

4) **Execute a "Power of Attorney" (POA).** This legal instrument gives you a voice in court through someone on your behalf. Execute the Power of Attorney on the front end, immediately at the time you sign the retainer and lodge your divorce complaint. When considering a POA, give the authority to someone you trust to make good decisions on your behalf.

5) **Join a support group.** Besides professional counselors, do not forget about other support groups. Remember your fraternity brothers or your sorority sisters. You have close friends and associates who may be able and willing to offer a bit of sage advice. Someone who

simply hears your heart at the right time can be very valuable. Other potential resources are your co-workers. A trusted co-worker may be able to assist you without fear of their feeding the gossip mill.

6) **Open yourself to spiritual insight and foresight.** Sometimes men and women of God can see roots in your life you never knew were there. A good counselor, mentor, or minister can help shape your future in a meaningful way. They can help you to navigate the roadblocks that lay ahead in your path.

7) **Resist intrusive individuals.** A word of caution: do not give any person the exclusive right to pry into your personal affairs. If you need support and desire to share some of your innermost feelings, find someone who is trustworthy. Do not buy into the uninvited divorce conversation, and resist the advances of those who prod callously into your privacy. Reserve the right to say, "I choose not to talk about that part of my life or relationship."

8) **Look before you leap.** Do not separate and leave your spouse too soon. Unless your situation is life threatening, it is better to endure a bad living situation until you have thoroughly considered arrangements to support the best interest of yourself and your children.

Up Next

Sometimes a marriage or relationship that is turning foul is reaping the bad fruit of a preceding generation. Bad roots can commingle with a couple's own personal problems. When that happens, these forces can work together to undermine and destroy a once good marriage. In addition, when a relationship is breaking down, the personal lives of the husband and the wife breakdown, too. This drama manifests itself in different areas as big emotional swings occur. Divorce can be a high conflict situation where at least one pissed person lashes out in anger. Consequently, both sides end up overreacting and pouring gasoline on the flames. Let's examine some of this anger and emotional turmoil in the next chapter.

Chapter 3

"A" is for Anger—
Lots of It!

A Range of Emotions

Divorce lawyers see a lot of anger. Divorce clients display a full range of emotions and mental states—stress, pity, depression, confusion, hate, self-hatred, suicidal tendencies, apathy, hopelessness, denial, bitterness, and anger. Of this gamut of emotions, anger generally causes people the most problems and drama.

"I'm Mad As Hell"

"Wait a minute," I said. "Say that again. You did what?"

"You heard me right the first time," my female client crowed. "I took my keys, went over to his car and tried to scratch the hell out of his brand new BMW. I scratched that paint as hard as I could, on both sides, too! I was so mad at that fool I could have pissed on his car seat! If he had been around, I would have scratched his eyes out the same way," she finished, her eyes blazing.

Many women who have been "dissed" by their mate can relate to the anger of this irate sister. The lack of opportunity (and long-term wisdom) is the only reason more women do not act out their deep hurt and disgust against their "lovers."

Let's consider the example of a female client who comes seeking a divorce. She wants custody of the children, child support, alimony—the works. In the process of the divorce proceedings, her husband seeks to reconcile. If he "drops to his knees," so to speak, and begs forgiveness, she may waiver about the divorce. Whether the husband was actually at fault, or having a panic attack at the prospect of being alone, makes little difference. The woman may likely give her partner another chance. The male client's attitude differs significantly when he comes to a lawyer seeking a divorce. If during the divorce process the wife "drops to her knees" and begs for another chance, the husband usually does not waiver. Attorneys observe that a male client is generally fixed and unequivocal. In most cases, he will not forgive and refuses to change his resolve to end the relationship. He absolutely wants out.

In the above scenarios, trust and closure are the issues. The man wants closure because he resolves he cannot, or will no longer, place trust in the woman. When he initiates divorce proceedings, he has already determined his point of closure on the relationship.

In contrast, when the woman initiates divorce proceedings, she may not yet have specified her point of closure. Usually, she is willing once again to trust the man before bringing complete closure to the relationship.

Psychologists may attribute the difference between male and female clients to a number of things, like to right- or left-brain thinking, or to a socialization environment favoring male dominance.

While most lawyers possess little to no training in psychology and could not make a proper clinical diagnosis, there is no doubt anger and pain is at the root of most litigants' actions. Divorcees show much anger and rage, and the education and socioeconomic level of the combatants does not pre-determine their levels. I know doctors, engineers and high-level executives who have keyed cars or slashed tires of their estranged mates. Some have done worse. Very angry wives may seize a bat and break all the windows of a spouse's car or bleach his Armani suits. Once, an irate and vengeful husband went to the hotel where his wife and her lover were making out, got access to his wife's car and disabled the engine, preventing the car from starting. A relationship generating this kind of domestic abuse or violence is problematic. Which partner is the primary instigator of abuse? It depends on who is the "dumper" and who is the "dumpee." In many cases, each party in the divorce feels they are the aggrieved victim.

At any rate, whether male or female, the "dumpee" is hurt, upset, bitter, rejected, and angry.

All-Consuming Anger

Anger can consume a hurting man who considers himself the "dumpee" in a breakup. An attorney friend—one who himself is going through an unpleasant separation—gives personal witness. He confesses he has not done "the crazy," but he has no problem understanding why men resort to behaviors such as binge drinking, sex parties, vengeful secret retaliation, and the like. His own experience has sensitized him to the anger that results from a soured relationship.

In contrast to divorced women, why do more men do "the crazy?" Probably because black men do not have the type of supportive groups like those available to many black women. Thus, a man falls prey to other types of coping mechanisms. He immerses himself in his sports, in the bar, in work, etc. Many men try to manage their estrangement and divorce affairs alone. Their "macho" mentality drives them and their fears of weakness. Many a man who is just not handling his business affairs well may want to keep his shortcomings secret. He may not open up to receive support from those around him. As a result, he forfeits the knowledge and wisdom vital to his well-being as it relates to the breakup of his marriage and the welfare of his children.

A salesman, who separated from his wife pending a divorce, has been able to surround himself with a fence to mediate his anger. He continues to attend his church and the men's marriage support meeting where he has access to talk about his personal marital situation—if he chooses to do so. When he is alone at his home and thinks about the raw hand dealt to him by his separated ex, the experience nearly moves him to tears. He stares at the bottle of Jack Daniel's sitting in his cabinet. His mind tempts him to drink the whole bottle. Yet, despite the pressure, he resists. He knows that drinking alcohol is the path to a downward spiral that may drown him in the bottom of the pit. He knows his anger is burning. However, whenever his hurting rage begins to surface, he thinks about his plan of action. He has friends he can call. He has church leaders who will talk to him. He has colleagues at work to whom he can vent in a safe space. He has taken steps to reconnect to his own extended family. This salesman invokes his coping mechanisms to deal with his anger and moments of depression resulting from separation. His strategies are working for him. I recommend men who are in the midst of breaking up follow some of these strategies.

A colleague of mine described a particular divorce case that gave her the blues. The female judge who tried this very messy case was African-American.

So were both litigants and their respective attorneys, one who was a female. Both husband and wife were successful professionals with a combined income over a million dollars. Their marriage and breakup were very bitter and drama-filled, so much so the judge ordered the husband to vacate the penthouse condo where the couple resided. In response, the man's wife called her friends and told them she was throwing a party—a "Mr. Gone Party!" As could have been expected, the judge was most perturbed at the wife for callously rubbing her husband's face in the mud. At any rate, their divorce trial proceeded and came to its conclusion with the female judge rendering a kind of split decision in the case. After the judge's ruling, everyone left the courtroom, except the litigants and their attorneys. Almost immediately, the courtroom turned into a scene one attorney labeled, "ghetto fabulous." The whole atmosphere went buck wild. The scene would have made for great prime-time reality TV!

Because the judge was sensitive to the cultural nuances of African-Americans, her intuition forewarned her of the blowout on the brink after the ruling. That is probably why she hurriedly excused herself from the courtroom, quickly slipped into her chambers, closed the door, removed her robe, turned up her music, and set herself down in her office chair. She had done her work for the day. If those other folks still had "personal" matters to settle with one another, that was their business. Let the chips fall where they may. The judge was "outta there" because she knew the boiling anger was coming, and everyone she left in the courtroom was "mad as hell."

Generally speaking, anger is not justified in divorce. It is understandable that the anger of litigants may have some justification based on the issue(s) leading to the breakup. However, whether the anger is "justified" or not is usually irrelevant. The question is whether the aggrieved parties appropriately manage their anger, so that they can be *reflective*, rather than *reflexive*. (E.g., "Here lies the body of William Jay who died while maintaining his right-of-way. He was right, dead right as he sped along. But, he's just as dead as if he were wrong." – Anonymous).

Of course, a party may have the right to be angry, but that will not help them in court where the main concern is how to divide assets and liabilities and determine custody of the children. Often litigants end up being a 10 on the Anger Scale, even if they *didn't begin* the process that way because one or both spouses often do things to escalate the conflict. This rage often puts attorneys in a precarious position: trying to advise their raging clients against making bad choices they likely will regret later, and then suffering accusations from those same clients for being disloyal to their "cause." This, by the way, is how attorneys sometimes get a bad rap. If they merely go along with their furious client's misguided choices, attorneys know that clients who end up emotionally and financially broken will likely blame them for the outcome and consequences.

Litigants who do not control their emotions are usually a hindrance in court. On an Anger Scale of 1-10, a 5 is about where you want to be when initiating a divorce action. The emotions of a litigant usually changes during the course of a divorce proceeding. As long as your emotions never control your decision-making, and you have a support group or an outlet for your emotions, being angry should not be a problem.

Act Now 3 – A is for Anger—Lots of It!

Below are some action-responses that will help you deal with your different emotions, especially anger, as well as better understand and cope with the anatomy of your marital breakup.

1) **Sort out your emotions.** In this process, you may need someone to assist you. Express your inner state in an objective way. Don't just mull things over. If necessary, talk it out, even if you are alone. Write down specific feelings, moods, and temperaments. The freedom you gain from getting in touch with your inner-being will help as you attempt to transcend debilitating feelings. Do not allow negative feelings and emotional swings to control your actions and lead you in counter-productive ways.

2) **Write a plan of action.** I especially promote this strategy. On a day when your mind is clear, take the time to make a written plan of action. Become proactive. Think through your situation. Identify the trigger points for your anger. Decide what to do ahead of time. Be specific about what you plan to do in several different scenarios. Share your plan with someone who can become your sounding board. Prevent yourself from becoming angry beyond control.

3) **Think long-term.** Realize breaking up is a process. It does not happen all at once. Be prepared for the long haul. Take it one day at a time, realizing some days will be better than others. Anger and depression can set in when a divorce proceeding lingers or a resolution does not come quickly.

4) **Resist making ultimatums.** Find a way to retract any threats you have given your spouse. Your divorce may be on the horizon, but refuse to push your relationship over the edge prematurely

5) **Avoid counterproductive behavior.** A breakup may make you susceptible to engaging in indiscriminate sexual escapades as a type of counterproductive behavior. If you do not stay on the watch, you may find yourself having sex, not in true love, but simply in emotional anger and a spirit of vengefulness against your ex. Beware: this type of activity will not cure the roots of anger in your life.

Up Next

Certain hints and clues reveal breakages occurring in a relationship bond. What are some of the signs a marriage is dissolving? The next chapter discusses certain factors contributing to the process of breaking up.

Chapter 4

Bond Breaking Anatomy

When the Marriage is Broken

What causes marriage bonds to break? Some divorcees confess their marriages began to dissolve right before their very eyes. They were startled at the rapid degeneration of their formerly loving relationships. Many questioned and blamed themselves for the break that occurred in their marital bonds.

"Maybe it was my fault entirely." "What did I do wrong?"

"Why didn't I see this coming?"

"Things would have turned out better for us if only he would have tried a little harder."

"Why was his mother always in our business?"

"What in the world is happening to our little group? First it was my friend's marriage that broke up, now it is mine."

"Maybe that is why a lot of couples skip getting married in the first place; it just isn't worth the trouble."

"Why can't she save some money? Seems like the harder I work, the more she spends. That's why we are broke."

"Society just puts too much pressure on married people."

Questions and statements like these run through the minds of persons whose marriages are breaking up. It is natural for them to try to figure out what happened to their relationship.

In light of the exceedingly high divorce rate among African-Americans, this is a legitimate question. From my vantage point, however, most marriages end because one or both spouses are myopically selfish. This selfishness can take several forms: infidelity; verbal, physical or emotional abuse; control of finances; mismanagement of money; excessive ambition, or a lack of motivation. Consequently, I believe it is helpful to understand certain dynamics that can precipitate a couple's divorce. Let's jump right in.

"I Want to be Free"

A lawyer friend cites the case of a man who decided to take a walk-away non-legal marital separation ("ghetto divorce"). He had separated from his wife 15 years earlier, but now wanted a divorce in a few weeks having now found someone he did not want to lose. Divorce for him had been just a piece of paper. However, his new woman cared and pushed the divorce issue. He had found himself a "church woman," and she was pressing the spiritual issue with him. She wanted to live right and her conscience was troubling her. She knew it was not right for her, as a church member, to date a married man. So she wanted to correct the situation.

When a black woman wants a divorce, usually she has yet to find a new partner. She simply wants her freedom. However, a separated man may have already found another woman. I can affirm this analysis of certain motives and the point of closure that drive men or women who seek divorce. On average, men seem to take marital separation harder than women do because support groups for women differ from those of men. A woman's support system may be her mother or her girlfriends. Of course, men give advice to other men, and while they may disagree, a male respects the boundary of another male. In contrast, the friends of a woman may place more pressure on the sister to do something.

Typically, close friends of a mistreated sister will make the following kind of remarks about a man they know is treating the woman wrong: "I wouldn't put up with that crap." "Not on your life. I'd tell that m- - - - erf- - - er to kiss my ass, and hit the streets."

"If I got the chance I'd try to scratch his face, scratch his eyes out."

"You ever thought about putting sugar in his gas tank? Let him see how it feels to take the bus for a minute. He loves that car more than he loves you anyway."

"I'd fix him good, real good." "You need to quit being a pushover and speak up for yourself. You're a good woman. That fool doesn't even know the kind of woman he got."

"All he's interested in is your pocketbook...both of them: the one with your money and the one with your honey!"

Friends operating as a cadre place pressure on the woman to take a stand against male mistreatment. Is it fair to say that some women don't want to see others happy? No doubt, as some women purposely escalate issues and tensions to drive a wedge in their friends' relationships.

Professional friends can interfere with marital relationships, too. Every marriage has problems. However, office gossip around the water cooler or during coffee breaks can make a co-worker fair game. One divorcee ran into an old professional friend who had heard his marriage was in trouble. Initially, she told him she would pray for his marriage and family, but just in case the brother's marriage failed to make it, she said, "Here's my card if you ever need me." A couple of weeks later, the same sister gave the brother a phone call! She was hot on his trail way before his marital situation had played out one way or the other.

Many couples who seek divorce never had counseling in their marriage, pre-marital or post-marital. For those couples who did receive post-marital counseling, many sought advice much too late to save their relationship. Too much water had gone underneath their marital bridge, washing out its foundation. These couples are usually going through the motions. They already know it is over. We can liken their marriage relationship to milk left out on the kitchen counter all night. Once the milk has soured, no one can reverse the process.

Counseling Over Ultimatums

Counseling can assist many couples if they get good advice early on. Consider the case of a woman who worked for a Fortune 500 company and was new to the single parents' group at her church where she shared her tragic story. The woman confessed she was upset because she had been married to a man who was a workaholic. Both she and her husband made six-figure salaries. He was decent and did not run around chasing skirts, but the long hours he worked upset her even though it contributed to their high standard of living. In a moment of frustration, she protested her husband's work-over-family priorities and threatened to leave if he did not change. After hearing this a few times, he responded by saying, "There's the door." Her pride got the best of her, and she filed for a divorce. Regretfully, she told the group, when she made her ultimatum, she thought he would be frightened by her threat to leave and start spending more time with her and their son. However, the threat backfired, and he did just the opposite.

Shortly after her divorce, the woman's employer laid her off from her six-figure job. Her ex, however, received a big performance bonus from his employer. With his extra cash, he traded his sedan for a convertible, moved into a larger place, and found a new, younger woman. His first wife now found herself tearful, regretful, and broken. The turn of events nearly destroyed her entire life. What might have been the outcome if she had sought marital counseling before she sought legal counsel? A good counselor might have wisely advised her not to make threats, and probably would have encouraged her to lower her expectation of marriage and standard of living, not her core values. In this way, the couple could have worked less and enjoyed themselves as a family. They would not have had to work so hard to support an over-the-top lifestyle. The counselor may have encouraged her to look on the brighter side of her situation.

Ultimatums do not hold true marriages together. Giving an ultimatum to your spouse will usually result in serious trouble for your relationship. Nevertheless, some unwise folks use ultimatums and the threat of divorce as a power play to manipulate their relationship.

I recall a client who, along with her husband, had several young children. The lion's share of the housework fell on her. She did everything, despite the fact she and her husband worked full-time jobs. When they came home from work, her husband loafed, watched TV and movies, and did other things that were non-essential for maintaining the household.

The wife found herself whining and complaining, though she never made an ultimatum.

Finally, she put her husband out of the house, and filed for divorce, immediately seeking child support. In response, her ex begged his wife to reconcile, promising he would change. However, she would have none of his promises. Though not yet divorced, she was finished with him, and her living situation was much better. As a mother with young children, the woman did what she had to do. Nevertheless, she did not make an ultimatum before she made her move. She was wise. Ultimatum makers usually rob themselves of time and energy, and certainly do not enhance the genuine love of a marital relationship.

When your marriage is at stake, you and your spouse should do everything possible to give your relationship a fighting chance. This means you must avoid the counsel of certain folks.

Some would-be counselors suffer from a lack of objectivity because they have too close a relationship with you and your spouse. Instead, find someone who is more objective and will shoot straight and tell you the truth, even if the truth and their frankness hurt your feelings.

Always consider the source when you talk with someone about your marital troubles. Most of us know an older couple who has been married a long time, but when asked if they would do it again, they say, "No." Though this couple has managed to maintain a long-term relationship against their true desires or better judgment, I would not advise a younger couple to emulate them. Marriage should create joy, not the bondage that makes a couple grit their teeth in the presence of one another. Think about the couple from whom you would seek marital counsel and consider the kind of model they represent. How knowledgeable are you about different aspects of their lives? What are the significant roots of their relationship?

What other kinds of supportive services should a couple having marital problems employ? Professionally trained counselors, psychologists, and psychiatrists are helpful. However, you may not know of a professional person who fits the bill. On the other hand, you may know someone who does know the whereabouts of a professional. Check around; ask a few questions and get some leads.

Typically, black males will not do counseling. Initially, they are reluctant. However, some change their minds and relent after discovering their wife is serious about ending the marriage. These husbands tend to get in a hurry to see if counseling can save the marriage before it completely fails. Pity the man who refuses the pleadings of his wife to join her in counseling, particularly in sessions focusing primarily on her, as she seeks to gain assurance her own thinking is sound. The man who refuses is acting senselessly. He will eventually kick himself for his stupidity of letting a good woman get away by not supporting her in a time of need when she is crying out. When this woman reaches the point where she feels her husband is rebuffing her peace-making efforts and no longer cares, their relationship is over.

Why are African-American men so stubborn in this area? Perhaps they act this way because, historically, black men have had to battle a whole cadre of issues society imposes on them. Consequently, they put up a façade or defense and strap on the macho armor to do battle. They react against racism and discriminatory behavior leveled against them. In many social situations, black men are afraid to take down their barriers; their guard is always up. But through marriage and other types of counseling, the same males who remove their barriers can find some form of relief and release.

Heading to Court Too Soon

Some persons contact a divorce attorney prematurely. I always give my clients the following advice: *Settle your emotional issues prior to settling your legal ones.* A person who seeks a divorce must be finished with their marital situation. Prior to filing, you should have completely exhausted yourself of the marriage. You should make up your mind. Before you make any definite moves, I suggest you ask yourself these important questions:

14 Important Questions for People Contemplating Divorce

1. What are all the reasonable things I have done within my power to make the marriage work?
2. In what *specific* ways do I think my life will be better if I get divorced?
3. How have I prepared myself psychologically for this? /What are my sources for emotional support?
4. How will I prepare my children for this? /How will the divorce affect my children?
5. Am I prepared to support myself without my spouse's support/ assistance (both financial and emotional)?
6. Should I have gone to counseling even if my spouse refused to go?
7. What percentage of my counselor's advice have I followed?
8. In what ways have I sought the advice of other married couples?

9. How will my friends/family react? / How should I prepare myself for their possible responses?
10. What is my capacity level for seeing this process through to the end, knowing it may take a long time?
11. What specific challenges/disadvantages will divorce bring me?
12. If I get a divorce, what are the odds and reasons that I will end up alone for the rest of my life?
13. What are the indications that my marriage is worse off than the marriages of my other friends?
14. What should I expect my dating/romantic life to be like after the divorce, and what might be the evidence for my expectations?

When you are wishy-washy, you increase your exposure by opening the door to your partner's manipulative behavior. Lawyers encounter manipulation all the time. Dealing with manipulative parties is part of their professional territory. They have seen enough manipulative behavior to know instinctively when a litigant is taking unfair advantage and when one partner is playing on the emotions of the other. The point made here is that someone seeking a divorce must be capable of transcending his or her emotions. Unhealthy emotional attachment to an errant spouse leads to indecision. Indecision leads to weakness and manipulation by others. Sadly, he who hesitates loses.

Recognize when your marriage is a square peg you are trying to force-fit into a round hole. Save yourself and your children unnecessary drama. An open-ended marital relationship that should have closed a long time ago is torture for the children. Also, do not discount the insight of your children. As it relates to the ups and downs of your marriage, they probably know and understand more than you think. The children say to one another, "Mom and Dad are on again...then off again...then on again." These vicious cycles and mixed-signals can become emotionally destabilizing for them. On one hand, they see mom and dad sleeping together. Then, on the other hand, when mom and dad are angry, they won't even speak to one another. As a result, the children become confused and tentative in their relationship with their parents.

Some lawyers have divorced some couples twice. These lawyers have all experienced the time when some aggrieved marital party (usually a woman) shows up prematurely at their office seeking a divorce right away. The husband complies with his wife's wishes and facilitates the process. The court quickly grants the divorce. However, only a few weeks after getting the final decree, the woman realizes she was not completely finished with her relationship. Though she successfully broke legal ties with her husband, her emotional ties with him are holding fast.

When it comes to divorce, emotional indecisiveness sometimes will wreck your life much worse than the breakup. When you finally reach the point that you are done for good with your marriage, say it, mean it, and act on it. Save yourself and your children double drama. Of course, many lawyers will tolerate your drama, as long as you've got money! With an air of very professional courtesy, the attorneys will most willingly find a way to be of gracious service to you by finding a legal way to perform whatever your heart's desire leads you to have done...just keep paying the bill!

Think about it: when your marriage is over, it's over. Don't waste your time and money, and don't waste the time and money of others. Don't pay the lawyers twice for your unnecessary drama! In instances of divorce drama, the lawyers are the only ones who make money! Everyone else pays.

Act Now 4 – Bond-Breaking Anatomy

Most persons who contemplate divorce need someone to be a sounding board and experienced guidance in making good decisions. Your emotional and psychological attachment in a close relationship is difficult to sever. The following tips may help you get a better handle on your situation and understand the emotional pains and process of separating from your spouse.

1) **Read the handwriting on the wall.** List your marital problems, values, primary grievances, and a record of the times your spouse has violated you. Discern an objective message. Does it indicate your marriage really has been over for a while? Are you in self-denial?

2) **Talk with a divorcee.** Preferably, speak to someone whose divorce occurred long enough in the past for him or her to appraise what honestly happened in his or her situation. Ask a few key questions: At what point did you truly know your marriage was over? What were the signs that made you realize the failure of your marriage was real? Keep in mind, however, every divorce is different. Your experience

and outcome will not be the same in all particulars as the divorcee who speaks with you.

3) **Seek professional help.** Sort out what is taking place in your marriage. A trained counselor can quickly spot underlying marital problems and personal problems that are negatively affecting your relationship.

4) **Guard yourself from emotional manipulation by your spouse.** Learn to recognize your partner's pattern of control. Develop an appropriate means of response.

5) **Avoid indecisiveness and inaction.** Decide either to make your marriage work or to quit it. Do not take forever to decide one way or the other, or procrastinate doing what you ought.

Up Next

When and how to separate are important decisions you must make when you decide divorcing your spouse is the path to pursue. A separation often precedes a divorce. You must prepare yourself before separating from your spouse. A mate who contemplates separating from a spouse must prepare for the kind of unexpected drama that happens when the spouse takes up with someone else. The next chapter will help you to think through some of the consequences of separating.

Chapter 5

Separate Lives, Separate Beds

Shackin' and Sexual Shock

A shackin' relationship is one where a man and woman agree to live and function together as a household but without marrying. Shackin', also referred to as *cohabitation*, plays out in two ways. Some folks shack without ever getting married or ever intending to do so. Other folks shack when they are estranged or separated from their marital partner. So, one form of shackin' is on the premarital side, whether or not the couple eventually gets married. The other form of shackin' is on the post-marital side of a breakup or divorce. Either form of shackin' influences issues relating to marriage and divorce.

A growing number of individuals prefer shackin' to marriage. In society, more couples are choosing a shackin' arrangement at a higher rate than past generations. Some couples who shack test the waters with the intention of "taking the plunge" if the relationship is suitable. For others, marriage is not even on the radar.

They resist the restraints of a relationship and enjoy what they see as their "freedom." However, we might better translate the so-called "freedom" as fear or weakness in the areas of accountability and true commitment. According to a University of Chicago research study, black professional men commit less frequently to a relationship than do other men and maintain overlapping relationships with different women.[5] At any rate, we find them shackin' with their partner. The relationship may last for a month or for many years.

[5] See, Edward O. Laumann, Professor of Sociology at the University of Chicago,

When a person has experienced a very damaging marriage and life-altering separation or divorce, there is reluctance to enter into another relationship quickly. The person needs time to assess the trauma, rethink mistakes, and heal wounds. Adopting that posture is wise and keeps the person with the marital casualty from "jumpin' from the fryin' pan into the fire" of a more destructive relationship. Marital rejection can create a personal vulnerability in one's life another "partner" can easily exploit. In this case, shackin' often becomes the testing ground for any new relationship.

Some couples find the shackin' arrangement quite beneficial and manage to maintain a wholesome relationship. In some instances, the success of the shackin' arrangement invites the envy of some "married" couples, a fact confirmed by researchers at the Pew Research Center who in 2011 reported a steep decline in marriages among U.S. adults. Despite the unacceptability of shackin' by some groups (for moral or social reasons), shackin' is an embedded relationship reality of the diverse American cultural landscape.[6] Some think the practice is detrimental for African-Americans overall, while others tout its feasibility. Serious discussion may occur around the following question: "When, if ever, is a good shackin' arrangement better than a hellish marriage?"

The Shackin' Drama

Some couples discover their shackin' arrangement turns very sour. Thus, divorce lawyers increasingly find themselves dealing with the drama created by shackin' relationships.

Consider the following scenario of a couple whose marriage is on the rocks. Amidst other "incompatibility" problems, the woman suspects her husband has been cheating on her, and following a heated argument, the partners decide to separate. In this situation, the woman, whose corporate job requires her to travel frequently, vacates the house. She leaves their young child with her father so he can take her to school and other activities.

"Sex and marriage in the City of Chicago," A *University of Chicago research study,* March 1, 2013, http://www.citymayors.com/features/sex_chicago.html.

[6] See, D'Vera Cohn, Jeffrey S. Passel, Wendy Wang and Gretchen Livingston, "New Marriages Down 5% from 2009 to 2010, Barely Half of U.S. Adults Are Married – A Record Low." 14 December 2011. *Pew Social and Demographic Trends.* Pew Research Center.

With his wife gone from the household, the dad quickly finds himself a new girlfriend. Naturally, yet unwisely, he introduces his young daughter to his new female friend. After awhile, the father and his lady desire to become intimate, but rather than going to his girlfriend's home for their trysts, he invites her over to his place. Actually, he wants to make things very comfortable for his new love and soon arranges for her to move into the house. Then, rather than trusting his young child to the temporary care of a close relative or his mother, he allows her to remain in the house with him and his girlfriend. Without any sense of shame, the father boldly exposes his young child to all the sights and sounds of his fresh new sexual relationship.

As could be expected, when the girl's mother discovers her husband's new social relationship, she becomes furious. She confronts him with all the rage of a female jungle cat. "Don't you have any decency!" she screams. "How could you do this with your own daughter in the house! Don't you realize she is still just a little girl?"

Equally irate, the father fires back, "Don't blame me. You get what you deserve. I remember the words you told me the day you decided to get your stuff, move out of the house, and leave the girl with me. You said, 'I don't care who is screwin' you. F - - k any b - - - h you want, anywhere you want! I'm outta here.' That's what you said, and that's exactly what I'm doing!"

The wife begins to have a meltdown.

Her own words—the ones she screamed in a torrent of pain and rage against her spouse—have come back to haunt her. She is experiencing a case of shackin' and sexual shock.

Grim realities like these often accompany the relationship of shackin' following a breakup. Such a scenario may cause some to reconsider the blanket approval of shackin'.

Adding certain exceptions to the position of approving all shackin' relationships may prove beneficial. Certainly not all shackin' relationships are created equal. Some arrangements are extreme, and those with sound judgment avoid them for good reasons. Consider the welfare of everyone involved in the family relationships.

You can be sure that the mother above lodged her protest with the divorce judge at the earliest opportunity—like on Monday morning. Divorce statutes charge the courts and attorneys to sort out the intricate (and intimate) drama of breakups. They must decide whether and under what circumstances shackin' is permissible. They must determine the "best interests" of the children according to state laws.

Should the parents receive joint custody of the children? On the other hand, should one parent receive sole custody of the children while the other parent receives visitation rights?

Lawyers astutely know current divorce laws do not (and cannot) anticipate every scenario possible in a breakup. Since the area is "gray," the ruling of judges comes down on different sides of the issue. When children are involved, some judges say shackin' is not permissible for either separated party until they receive their legal divorce. They allow no overnights with the child and the other friend. (Neither do they allow disciplining of the child by the other friend.) Some judges think differently. They say the litigants have their rights and can do what they want. Others who sit on the bench say shackin' is okay if untoward acts do not take place in the home and in the presence of minor children. Others say there is no problem with the shackin' arrangements so long as no one is abusing any child. The varied judicial perspectives on the law as applied to shackin' and children leave litigants frustrated and lawyers working overtime. In this legal environment, judicial discretion, when interpreting divorce law and settling related practical matters, rules the day.

What's Hair Got to Do With the Shock?

It is unnecessary to make enemies for yourself like the divorced father whose new girlfriend made it her business to do his young daughter's hair. She gave the young girl a beautiful look, but there was one problem: she did not ask permission from her boyfriend's ex, the girl's biological mother, to do the child's hair. The biological mother became furious when she noticed how her ex's girlfriend had styled her child's hair, and quickly went into the drama of a spurned ex. "How could you even allow your girlfriend to touch the head of my child!" she screamed at her ex. "I dare you to violate my child! And I dare your hussy to violate me and mine! I can't wait to get in her face. She has gone one-step too far. And I thought she was my friend! I knew I should have been watching the 'b - - - h' all along. When I get through with her, she will never again put her filthy hands on the head of my child. The child is mine! I'm her mother!"

Black women have well established the issue that "hair" and the doing of it are of high importance. By throwing mothers, exes, girlfriends, and young girls into the hair equation, you can create a tinderbox of drama that will easily ignite. I recommend the biological mother in the above situation calm down before she blows a gasket. She should remove herself from the turf war and think on the bright side of the situation. After all, her daughter looks beautiful with well-styled hair, and the girlfriend is showing some love and affirmation to the child.

I admit the catch-22 situation. The fact that the daughter's hair is styled well is the very problem. Nevertheless, the biological mother should think about the possible downside. Out of spite, the ex's girlfriend could do something sinister to the child and then feign innocence. She could also leave the young child alone, exposed to playing with some potentially dangerous chemicals that "just happened" to be around the house and accessible to the child's curiosity. An experimenting child could use some hair product with chemicals that could permanently damage her hair and scalp!

So divorced or separated mother, be thankful for the good things. Don't force your ex or his shackin' friend into becoming your enemy. Few of us can afford to treat any friendships in a cavalier manner.

Panther Shackin'

In another shackin' scenario that is prevalent, the divorcing father takes his child to the paternal grandmother's house. However, the grandmother has a live-in boyfriend. While there's no question that most grandparents love their grandchildren, today's "grandma" may be only in her late 30's or early '40's. Forget about the bygone images of the saintly senior grandmas in their 70's or 80's! Most of them have passed on. On the other hand, many older female "Panthers" are also grandmas and may be sharing living arrangements with their young male prey! Whatever the case, grandma's relationship with her live-in boyfriend causes complications for the biological mother of her grandchild. Mama in no way likes her shackin' arrangement. The "immoral" issues hit just too close to home for her comfort, not to mention the jealous streak it raises. "Grandma" seems to get any man she wants! However, daddy sees no problem with his child paying a visit to grandma under her romantic live-in arrangements. Actually, he encourages grandma to do her thing! The result: shackin' and sexual shock take place and may impact the children.

Act Now 5 – Separate Lives, Separate Beds

Ultimately, the courts must sort things out in the area of shackin' and help to settle the drama. Meanwhile, I offer the following tips to help you avoid this troublesome issue entirely.

1) **View the broader picture.** Rid yourself of tunnel vision in a time of separation or divorce. In a breakup, you may become so immediately focused on your undesirable partner that he or she is the only one you are capable of "seeing." Instead, give yourself a wider scope than the perspective and traps of your tunnel vision.

2) **Anticipate possible shackin' arrangements.** Inform your divorce attorney about all possible scenarios and relationships you or your spouse could develop. Think through your situations. Do not repress your inklings, suspicions, or embarrassments. Put nothing past "the devil." Remember, your attorney also knows how the judge in your case may think about or view certain shackin' arrangements and can steer you accordingly.

3) **Compromise with your spouse.** If the partner you are separating from or divorcing maneuvers the situation (legal or otherwise) in a way that places you over a barrel, plead for a little mercy, especially on behalf of the children. You may need to sacrifice some of your time and pride for the greater good of your children.

4) **Speak with your children.** Alert young children to the "stranger dangers" they may encounter in a situation of shackin'. The danger may not come from your ex's new love interest, but from his or her unfamiliar associates. The friends of your ex can potentially be a problem, too. Talk with your children on their maturity level. You may need to get counsel about how to communicate adult concepts to their young minds.

5) **Report illegal actions or indiscretions immediately.** Report to your attorney or the appropriate criminal authorities any suspected or actual abuse or endangerment of children (yours and others) a shackin'

situation poses. When it comes to the welfare of the children, it is better to be safe than sorry.

Up Next

Having regular sexual relations with one's spouse is a normal dimension of married life. Things like the sudden death of a marriage partner or physical impairments and illnesses of a spouse will immediately disrupt a couple's sexual activity, in addition to their companionship. In a similar way, so do separation and divorce. In these cases, a couple who once enjoyed the sexual satisfaction and security of each other finds a breakup has abruptly squelched their immediate source of physical, emotional, and social gratification. However, the normal human drive for social and sexual companionship and love does not cease, despite divorce. How then should a divorcee respond to the drama of their ongoing friendship and sexual desires? The next chapter will provide some direction in this area.

Chapter 6

Sex and Companionship After Separation

"I Need a Man"

"So what do I do now?" she asked.

"My husband dumped me. It's over. He's paying alimony and child support. He has found another woman. Our divorce is final, and now I'm free. But I've got one problem: I still need a man."

Divorce and separation cause a certain loneliness and aloneness.

That's drama, and the drama especially increases when the divorcee asks, "Where do I go from here?" "What can I do to fill this void in my life?" "Will anyone want me?" It seems African-American women experience a lot more of this drama than men.

The shortage of responsible men in the African-American community is a definite reality for black women. Especially due to unemployment and under-employment, drug and alcohol use, incarceration, mental illness, and homosexuality, black men are in short supply. No matter how you cut it, looking for a suitable or "good black man" is sometimes more challenging than looking for the proverbial needle in a haystack.[7] Then, other issues complicate the matter.

---

[7] African-American women outnumber African-American men. "The chances of ever getting married are dramatically reduced by the overall sex-ratio imbalance among African Americans and the relatively low percentage of available marriageable males." See, Oscar A. Barbarin, Terry McCandies, "African-American Families—In the New Millennium." *Encyclopedia.com* (2003), March 1, 2013, http://www.encyclopedia.com/doc/1G2-3406900022.html.

See also, Ralph Richard Banks, "A Shortage of Eligible Black Men," March 1, 2013, http://www.nytimes.com/roomfordebate/2011/12/20/black-men-for-black-women/a-definite-shortage-of-marriageable-black-men.

Consider for a moment the prospect of remarriage (or a new relationship) for divorced men versus divorced women.

Look at it this way. A couple met in high school, started a relationship, got married at age 27, and stayed together for 10 years. They have three children born prior to the marriage, who now are in their teens. After awhile, the couple runs into relationship problems, because the husband wants some "freedom" to see other women. He feels the marriage has tied him down to one woman for too long. So they get divorced. Both of them are 37 years old. Right away, he attaches himself to two younger women who like his maturity and the fact that he makes good money. He does not have a problem meeting new women. Good-looking women are all over the place.

On the other hand, his ex-wife has custody of the three children and all the drama of their teenage lifestyles. Even though he pays court-ordered child support, she has to work overtime to make ends meet with her family's new economic status. Plus, she has the drama of how she looks. That once fantastic cheerleader body has lost its shape, and gained a few pounds. Some may even say a whole bunch of weight. Compared to her female competition for getting a man, she considers herself a 6 on a scale where a 10 is off the chart. She thinks, "Nobody will want me with all this baggage!" Candidly, considering the inordinate emphasis numerous men sometimes place on a female's physical attractiveness, she's not far off point.

Comparatively speaking, making or enjoying a new relationship is smooth sailing for her divorced husband. For her, however, getting into a serious relationship is like running a marathon with her feet tied together. His prospects for remarriage are much greater than her chances. Professional men have even more options with women. Frequently, divorce drives many a black woman to bitterness. Her list of standards for qualified replacement candidates is exhaustive. She needs a guy to:

1) support her, not just financially;
2) accept and respect her children and become a father figure to them, if necessary;
3) embrace her insecurities and understand her reluctance to allow a man to move in with her, even if he does want to get serious, seeing she has a thirteen-year-old daughter; and
4) soothe her pain.

In contrast, the man who does not end up with custody has no problem finding another woman. He just picks up where he left off. For the woman, the children often become a substitute for male companionship. Her kids become her priority. They also may become her cover. She says, "I don't know if I can find and trust a man to come into my life and safeguard the interest of my children." In actuality, many times she really does not know whether in fact she can find a man, period. She is insecure.

Toilet Versus the Tub

Some men have a crass psychology about getting married and dealing with a responsible relationship. I can liken their mindset to a male who must make the choice of being either "the toilet" or "the tub" in the women's bathroom. To clean up this metaphor a bit: "the toilet" gets the crap along with the cuddle. But "the tub" gets the cuddle without getting the crap. When it comes to making a choice about marriage (or a lasting relationship), many men want to be "the tub" in the women's bathroom. They want the cuddle without the so-called "crap."

Most women find this male attitude very reprehensible and depressing. Simply, divorced black women have a hard way to go when facing men of this low caliber. Also, other black women can be most critical in this area. They may say to a sister, "You say you got a good black man! Then you had better hold on to him. If he gets away, that means something is wrong with you!" Such talk becomes a psychological assault on the worth and self-esteem of a black woman—as though she has the ability to control all the craziness of her male partner. It is unfair, but in many instances, it is a reality of female socialization in the black experience.

How should divorced or separated black women respond to the drama of seeking a male? Marriage and a meaningful relationship remain highly important for many. Here are several issues they encounter:

- their changing anatomy and physical attractiveness, and the high probability they will not find another man to marry;
- the validation of their sexual selves, especially if they are educated and have good jobs, but are still single and suffering—"counting their money in bed by themselves"; and
- their nagging personal thoughts that their sexual incompetence caused the breakup of the marriage. Some women torture themselves

thinking, "I should have tried some of that other stuff in bed with him, but that stuff was kind of freakish to me. I didn't think I could do that." Or, "Maybe I should have tried harder, and he would have stuck with me. I just don't have it in me to give him what he needs."

Divorced women face this drama, especially in the area of sexuality. Many think of themselves as sexual "failures" because their relationships did not work out. They then lower their expectations and become a mixture of a failure and a fool, untrusting and insecure. Self-blame sets in: "Was I too emotionally rigid? Were my romantic standards too stringent? What did I do wrong in bed the first time around?"

A woman who accounts for a broken marriage due to her supposed "sexual failure" may not be a failure at all. The idea that "sex sells" pervades American culture. Pornography via computer, television, and movies is rampant and influences all sectors of our society, including respectable upper middle-class families. Divorce attorneys note the strain a porn-practicing husband places on his wife. Though married, a man may indulge in pornography and pressure his wife to duplicate the sexually licentious acts he sees. He may also demand that his wife perform the sexual techniques of a prostitute or want her to try "swinging," visit sex clubs or engage in orgies. A normal and sexually reasonable wife, nonetheless, is not happy about her husband's new sexual tastes. However, he may be so deep into computer porn that he glues himself to exotic sites and screen images. She is unable to pull him away from his digital fantasy world and to the genuine physical and spiritual fulfillment waiting in their bedroom.

Porn-related sexual rejection by a husband has driven some wives to alcoholism or self-medication with legitimate drugs. Nothing is "wrong" with the wife; she is not at fault. Her husband has changed significantly. Furthermore, the husband's porn attitude of sexual "entitlement" becomes extremely offensive to his well-meaning wife, fomenting sexual drama and leading to divorce. A divorcee whose ex engaged in pornography should not blame herself for an inability to meet his sexual "needs." She should understand that pornography is a bottomless pit. To recover from the aftermath of her broken marriage, the sexually rejected wife may need therapy to regain a sense of sexual balance and self-appreciation.

The Pregnancy Trap

Sometimes, when a divorced woman says, "I need a man," she may be asking for security. However, her avenue for pursuing security can result in her getting pregnant prior to marriage with the man she thinks can give her security. She traps her male prospect by conceiving and giving birth. These sisters feel more secure if they have a child with a man. On the other hand, a married woman likewise may seek to secure a husband by having additional children. She reasons her spouse is less likely to leave her because he "loves his children too much to leave me." Thus, similar motivations of single and married women take place under different circumstances.

Sometimes, the pattern of seeking security shows up differently. There are times when a girlfriend has a child with the boyfriend (or husband) of woman #1. Woman #1 begins to feel threatened or uneasy.

Why? Simply, the newborn child creates a tighter bond between the man and his girlfriend, the mother of his baby. Ironically, some women, even mothers who "want a man," shy away from a relationship when the male already has children. This is hypocritical drama. She rejects the man because he has an ex with whom he has children. But she has children also! In contrast, it is my feeling that few black men have this insecurity. Generally, if a man's woman has a child from a previous relationship, the man, for the most part, does not feel threatened or insecure.

Some desperate women need a man so much they will steal another woman's husband. As the saying goes, "Stolen waters taste sweeter." The man-shortage in the African-American community exacerbates this problem. To their shame, some husbands are all too willing to accommodate single black women on the hunt. These husbands take advantage of the seemingly desperate plight of these attractive young women. They exploit the situation by availing themselves of sisters who pursue irresponsible men when they find themselves in need of sexual companionship. Such "two-timing" husbands pander to the "pity-party" of these single females. They take care of their mistresses by providing them enough money to do their fingernails and hair, to pay a monthly light bill, or even take care of a car note. Others demand so much more. If the man's wife discovers the affair, she may simply tolerate her husband's behavior, hoping he will eventually return to his better senses, or she will take steps to separate or divorce. Either way, the situation fuels the drama of marital separation or breakup because a divorced woman needed a man, and chose to take another woman's husband.

Changing Prerogatives

We have all heard the saying, "It's a woman's prerogative to change her mind." We may appropriately apply this saying to male-female relationships. By the time a woman reaches her 30's, she probably has quickly changed her perception of what she is looking for in a man. When she was in high school, she may have clamored for the attention of the popular high school "jock." Perhaps she dated the captain of the basketball team. Never would anyone catch her dead with a member of the chess team! However, at a more mature age, she now prefers the person she once ostracized when he was in high school. That "nerd" is now a business consultant making a great salary. He could as well be a successful accountant or a powerful lawyer. He may even be a high-tech genius who created a new smart phone app for millions of users. In his later years, the brother now has status and stature in the community. All of a sudden, he has become a very serious option for this male-seeking sister. To her surprise, she evokes her prerogative and changes her mind. She has acquired a new taste in men.

In the African-American community, the stature of the man becomes important for a woman in her middle years. In contrast and generally speaking, at age 30, a black man wants the same thing in a woman he desired from girls at age 21. The keen observation has some merit: whether young or old, many black men want a woman who sexually satisfies!

"I Need a Woman"

Of course, we all know that men, too, have the need for sexual companionship. When a separation or divorce disrupts a man's sexual activity, he often finds himself searching for a woman. However, one main difference between the divorced man and the divorced woman is that the man generally has more options. Yet, exploiting these sexual female options is not the same as gaining emotional, physical, or social satisfaction. A black man's need for a woman goes far beyond the sexual dimension.

In contrast, though not as apparent as the needs of divorced women, divorced men are hurting, too. They also have needs of companionship and the other kinds of blessings a good woman can bring into their lives. Divorced men need help as well to face issues of rejection, loneliness, sexual fulfillment, child-rearing, housekeeping, making ends meet, etc. How does a divorced man overcome the pain of his broken relationship? Does it seem to take longer for a black man wounded by his ex to trust a woman once again? Why? In what way can he regain a healthy view and respect for women? These areas and more reveal challenges faced by a divorced man seeking to maintain a functional family and a meaningful relationship with the next woman who becomes part of his life.

Negative Roles Husbands Play

Very few men get divorced because of desertion by a wife. This old-school experience is real, though atypical. In the current generation, not many black women abruptly desert their offspring. Not many African-American husbands experience desertion by their wives or remarry for the primary sake of their children.

Sometimes a man's arrogance, cruelty or antisocial behavior causes a divorce. Such a man shares a dual experience of being hurtful and culpable for his marital breakup. He is culpable because he has played the role of the "bad" black man. He just didn't do right by his wife or his children. If he worked, he wasted the money. If his earnings were exceptional, he bought and owned his wife with material things while leaving her to raise the children and fulfill the household duties. If he didn't work, he failed to share the household responsibilities with his wife. If he played the role of the "man of the house" or the "king of his castle," he dominated his mate and oppressed her personal freedom, creativity, and self-expression. If he was a sexual tiger, he used her as a concubine without providing her mutual sexual satisfaction. Then he prowled the social circles for other extra-marital female prey. These are the negative roles black husbands play. Others may exist as well. These issues often become the impetus for a woman to seek a divorce when she finally realizes the relationship she shares with her husband is not really a "marriage." We may describe their living together as an unequally yoked companionship, an onerous partnership, a dominant-passive relationship, an oppressive working agreement, or a convenient household arrangement. However, living under these conditions is not a "marriage," not of respect, trust, loyalty, honor, or love.

Some bad marriages leave wives/mothers in an emotional and mental shipwreck, besides depleting their finances and livable earning power. Adding insult to the injury of these often abused and rejected mothers, the court awards custody of their children to their ex, the same ex who has lived very badly. Sometimes it is a real tragedy when, in the mix of strange occurrences, a bad husband somehow walks away from divorce court with papers awarding him primary custody of the children.

Divorced men, whether they were irresponsible or respectable husbands, have the need for a woman. Especially for the sake of their children, we must do all we can to reduce the drama in the lives of these divorced fathers. The goal is not to sanction bad behavior but to empower responsibility and growth for the sake of innocent children.

Reasons for Remarriage

When I consider the 21st century black male who is divorced, I discover he shows a variety of reasons for seeking to remarry. Sexual companionship is prominent. However, the needs of divorced men have dimensions in other areas beside sexual satisfaction.

Separation causes the drama of emotional heartbreak. When a breakup happens in the relationship of a man who really loves a woman, it messes up his heart. Despite the black male macho image, the brother is hurting because the relationship has soured. Some social analysts overlay the love relationships of black men and women with a growing social phenomenon of female dominance, a status wreaking havoc with the male psyche. In this context, some black men get emotionally hurt, and hurt badly.

Drama heightens when the relationship of a hurting black male enters the divorce arena. If his wife is the initiator, he is angry and bitter. He realizes he is unable to maintain his marriage or keep his wife. If he grew up without a father in the home, he knows divorce may result in him being separated from his children on a daily basis—something he promised he would never allow to happen. Now he joins the ranks of black fathers who are absent from the household. He feels he is the "dumpee" in the relationship. (Of course, she probably feels that same way about herself.) The hurting brother also may cover up his hidden faults. Underneath, past negative behavior and dirt mix with his desire to do right, causing him much emotional turmoil.

Such a deserted and hurting man may lash out, becoming vengeful and vindictive during the divorce proceedings.

He may also seek to make his partner miserable, to make her pay dearly for her decision to walk away from him, their marriage, and their children. The black man whose spouse has hurt him and broken the relationship needs healing. Nor will his need for healing end with a divorce decree or cease when he finds himself another woman who "understands" him. An African-American male burned by a broken relationship will keep up his defenses to protect his vulnerabilities. He becomes gun-shy about making any new intimate relationships.

Will he have sexual relationships? He will, probably. Will they be up-close relationships? No, they will not, in most cases. The broken-hearted man will guard his heart with utmost care. He determines never again to experience heartbreak by a woman who dashes his love for her. The broken trust shatters his sense of male identity. Broken trust also impairs the good decision-making capacity of some men. Such blurred vision for the opposite sex may lead him to form irresponsible friendships or unworkable relationships. He may make a bad choice in his next mate or spouse if he does not receive healing from the broken trust of his first marriage. He may become a two-time loser. Broken-hearted men need to rebuild decision-making capabilities in this area.

Divorced African-American men need a woman. Why? Reasons vary according to divorce attorneys. Back in the day, most marriage-aged persons needed a reason to stay single. Today, most single persons need a good reason to get married, and most divorced men are in no hurry to settle down. So why remarry after a divorce? Some of the most common reasons include:

- Desire to have a successful relationship
- Sexual satisfaction
- Falling in love
- Unexpectedly meeting a great woman
- Desire for more children and another family
- Companionship

- Not wanting to grow old and die alone
- Tired of chasing skirt-tails: it gets hectic, expensive, destroys moral reputation
- Enhance life by sharing the finances, benefits of status
- Needing a helpmate to share household responsibilities
- Seeking to redeem reputation of being a failure in the eyes of parents or others
- Securing a partner to help care for the children.

A divorced man may find himself seeking a woman for any of the reasons listed above. He believes in the wisdom of King Solomon, to paraphrase: "The man who finds a real wife discovers a great treasure, and gets favor from the Lord."[8] Until a brother discovers his divine treasure, he goes it alone. So let's explore the single father dimension.

Becoming a successful parent as a divorced father is a major challenge. Divorced women appear to do better in this area than male counterparts. Yet, a number of men rise to the call of being a single parent. These fathers make resources work for them, and seek to gain the favor and confidence of the court on behalf of their children.

It is possible for independent single fathers to deal effectively with the problems of child-rearing, despite the drama caused by spiteful wives and intimidating in-laws. Most of these men manage to secure the help of a trusted female who will give them a hand with the children. That trusted woman may be a relative (e.g., his sister, or aunt), another female companion, an older woman in the church fellowship, or a concerned neighbor.

The custodial male parent who is a consistent financial breadwinner needs help. He needs to stay focused. Often, the demands of employment and the need for adequate finances compete with the responsibilities of raising the children. No one can be in two places at the same time. Neither can one person serve two masters. As a sole financial provider for his family, the divorced man must maintain a good balance between the drama of work and

---

[8] Paraphrase of Proverbs of Solomon, 18:22. Hebrew *Wisdom Literature, The Holy Bible.*

of being there for the children when they need him. He does not want to lose the children while he works to provide for their financial livelihood.

Neither does he want to lose his job by becoming lax in his work because of the demands placed on his time and by his young family.

Divorced Daddies and Dating

Most divorced men need sexual love, and most find it somehow, somewhere, in some woman. Some divorced men are more discreet about their sexual escapades and seek especially to shield their young children.

"Where are you going, Dad?" the kindergarten-aged child asked as she saw her divorced and single father getting ready to leave the house, decked out in his deacon's Sunday best. But it wasn't Sunday, and he was leaving his youngest at home under the care of her older siblings.

"Can I go with you?" she asked innocently. She knew his taking her with him was a common occurrence.

"No, you can't, and don't ask where I'm going! I've got to take care of some business," he responded with embarrassing uneasiness. "I'll be back home tonight, and I'll bring you something when I return." Having made his peace, he donned his Dobb's hat and his fine overcoat. Saying, "Goodbye," and "You all stay out of trouble," he spryly hit the door.

When the young girl got a little older and reflected back on her childhood experience with her divorced daddy, she put two-and-two together. No wonder her father and custodial parent couldn't tell his innocent child where he was going. Daddy was tippin' out on an intimate date with one of his lady friends! His sexual hormones were calling, and he didn't think it was fitting to let his young children know! "At least he gave us some respect," she said with a laugh.

Act Now 6 – Sex and Companionship After Separation

Being divorced doesn't end your need for companionship or sexual fulfillment. But getting back in the dating game, especially for those who are custodial parents, can be a little tricky. Here are some tips to help you deal with this drama and keep your mate search on track.

1) **Maintain your physical appearance.** Divorce takes an emotional and psychological toll on men as well as women. Stay healthy, maintain

a diet and exercise routine that keep you physically well and fit. This should boost your energy and self-esteem. Your prospects of getting a mate are much better if you take care of your body.

2) **Socialize where positive males gather.** If you want to establish beneficial relationships with well-meaning males, go where they gather. Know the type of man you are looking for and proceed from the general group to the particular choices.

3) **Give yourself permission to be sexual.** The thought of having sex with someone other than your ex is both exhilarating and scary. You are curious and drawn in a daring direction. You can now attend social gatherings and make eye contact with a person without feeling guilty. You can also accept a compliment without anguishing over the need to inform your spouse of someone's flirtatious attentions. Your divorce gives you a new sense of freedom and curiosity.

4) **Be sexually responsible.** Guard your sex life. Others may consider you vulnerable prey. When considering your sexual options, think not only of yourself but also of your children. Be good and healthy role models for them. When age-appropriate, clearly explain to your children the sexual choices you decide to make. Ultimately, they will follow your pattern.

5) **Procure a surrogate mother for your children.** Custodial male parents usually need assistance with their children only a woman can provide, especially very young children. Develop a short list of potential and available surrogate mothers. Then get help from someone you trust to determine which one or two would be a good fit and complement your parenting style. Take care; a surrogate mother is not your lover. Make a contract (yes, a *legal* and financial contract!) with the surrogate mother of your choice, and get on with raising your children.

6) **Cry sometime.** It is human to express emotions. Refuse to allow predominant social images to dictate how you should feel or emotionally respond to a breakup in your relationship.

7) **Don't bring women into the lives of your children unless it is a serious relationship by an "objective standard."** It may be helpful to make a timeline specifying the date when you will free yourself to re-enter the stage of forming a new relationship. Protect your young ones. Shelter them. It is natural for a woman who is interested in you to take an added interest in your children. However, sometimes a woman will use your children to worm her way into your life, or your pocket.

8) **Do a non-sexual activity.** Choose something that gives you personal satisfaction. Consider an activity you've never done before such as biking, dancing, roller-skating, etc.

Up Next

Some divorces stem from circumstances or relationships outside the "normal" patterns we see in society. The category includes those of domestic violence, interracial couples, homosexual unions, and the incarcerated spouse. Whether regarded as marriages actually, technically, or legally, these extraordinary relationships introduce more complex dimensions into the marital equation, in addition to the expected drama a breakup and divorce proceedings bring to the table. In the following sections, let's examine the dynamics of divorce concerning relationships of domestic violence and of other infrequent relationships.

Chapter 7

Divorce in Different Circumstances

Overcoming Domestic Violence

Domestic violence is a major cause of divorce, and it is much too prevalent among African-Americans. Women especially need protection from domestic violence. In a case where a woman is the subject of physical abuse, she must make a quick move to ensure the safety of herself and the children.

"I can't believe he hit me!"

An astute divorce attorney who listens well can discern the real story of a client, as in the case of a professional-looking female who walked into a colleague's office one morning with her young daughter. She was upbeat and asked the receptionist to see an attorney. The receptionist took the little girl into a playroom while the attorney escorted the woman to a conference room to discuss her situation. He seated her and offered her something to drink—coffee, tea, water, or juice. She took the water. He asked how she had heard about the law firm. She said she found it online.

My colleague queried the reason for her visit, and she said she would like to explore getting a divorce. He asked a few general questions to gain a clearer picture of her situation, one being why she thought divorce was best for her. The woman responded that she and her husband of six years were no longer compatible. She was a successful professional, as was her husband, but he was a stick-in-the-mud. He showed little initiative in bettering himself and seeking new opportunities. He was coasting, and his career had stalled. He occupied most of his time watching reality TV and sports programs. He drank a bit, but she could tolerate some of his alcohol.

What about their children, my colleague inquired. She said the daughter with her was their only child, and she would be starting kindergarten in the fall. Then he asked how she had tried to get her husband to improve himself. Had she tried convincing him to get a higher degree or to seek an executive position at a new corporation? She responded positively, saying she had attempted to communicate with her husband without getting pushy, suggesting his career could be on the fast track or booming. By simply surfing the internet, she always saw opportunities he could use to his advantage. Nothing she tried, however, seemed to work. She thought her husband had some kind of mental block as this situation has been going on for quite some time. Now, she felt herself getting tired. She thought it might be time to separate from her husband or end the relationship, but she wasn't sure. She had avoided mentioning her feelings to anyone since she could not afford to risk gossip and gain a bad reputation for her family. They lived in an upscale community where a successful social image was important, especially for a black family. The socialites could turn any negative news about her family against her and stalemate progress. So, she tried keeping them out of her personal business.

My perceptive colleague was interested in what triggered this woman to come into the office at this particular time. Was her husband wastefully spending money? Was the corporation where he worked on the verge of a major change or restructuring? Did she find her husband drunk when she returned home from work? Did she suspect or know that her husband was having an affair? Was she pregnant? Did she and her husband recently have an argument? What exactly had motivated her to come in today?

Pensively, she looked down and began softly, "The other day we had an argument, and he hit me. He hit me hard and hurt me." Then she reached for her purse, removed her tinted glasses, and fumbled for some tissues to wipe the tears that had begun welling in her eyes.

"I understand," my colleague said. "Tell me, was this a one-time incident, or has he hit you before?"

"Yes. It has happened before, more than once."

"Tell me about it."

"It all started about two years ago; that was the first time he hit me. At first, I thought his hitting me was some kind of temporary, stress-related phase he was going through at the time. I hear that lots of men hit their women at some time or another in life. I figured he would get over what was bugging him, pull himself together, and change. I actually thought things would get better, but they only got worse. Now after two years, I'm scared to death and really don't know what to do. I'm scared for my daughter and me.

"When my husband gets into his mood and goes off on me, my daughter is usually away at her grandparents' house.

"But this last time my daughter was at home when he erupted and saw everything. She cried and screamed. You should have seen the fear in her eyes. And to make matters worse, in a rage to get at me, her daddy pushed her away and knocked her against the wall. He just lost it. I tried my best to protect myself when he lit into me, but he is so much stronger than I am. Look at me! I only weigh 135 lbs. He is pushing the scale at 255 lbs. The man threw me all over the place. He grabbed my face with his hands, banged my head into the refrigerator, threw me on the floor, slapped me and punched my arms and stomach. He treated me as if I was some kind of punching bag.

"Then he grabbed me by the neck and told me he better not hear a peepin' word about what takes place up in his house.

"He said I had better not tell anybody—not one living soul—whatever he did, and whatever was going on in his 'castle.' He threatened that I better not call the police if I loved my life and my daughter. He cursed me out and told me I had better stay off my phone."

"Whew," said my colleague. "You've been going through a lot."

"I'm ashamed to say it, but the man just treats me like a piece of shit. He treats me like trash. I don't deserve this. I take care of the house. I go to church. I bring home good money. My career is solid...at least now it is."

She paused and removed her jacket. "Look at my arms," she said. My colleague observed the battle-bruises on both her arms. She then slightly raised her blouse for him to see the bruises on her back. "With all these horrible marks all over my body, how can I keep working in the fashion industry?"

"That's enough," he said. "I've seen and heard enough."

The distraught and broken wife continued. "I'm scared to death for me and my daughter, and I am so confused. I can deal with a whole lot of situations, but I don't know how to handle this one. This thing is beating me down. I'm sorry to tell you all this, but I had to talk to somebody."

"That's okay," my colleague assured her. "We clearly understand your problem, and the situations of many other women who face the same thing. You're not alone. Let us handle the matter, and I think you'll be all right.

"We will definitely take your case. Today you have done the right thing and taken a step in the right direction. Without question, you certainly need to file for a divorce. No woman deserves a beat down. No wife deserves any man kicking her around, much less a man who calls himself a 'husband' trashing her. Physical abuse is unacceptable under any circumstances. No one in a marriage should tolerate physical abuse or other forms of domestic violence. A wife must put up with many things, but spousal abuse is not one of them. It's time for you and your daughter to get out. You should get out before your husband does something worse, and you may not live to regret it."

"Thank you so much," she said, fighting back sobs. "You are confirming some things I really did not want to face. I really need your help in a hurry before I completely lose it."

"Here is where we will start," he said as he summoned his assistant. "Let's make a plan to get you and your child free from the environment destroying you. We understand your weaknesses at this time. You find it difficult to decide what is best and to stand up against your abusive husband. Though your situation is tough right now, we'll work with you to make things better. Know for sure you have our complete support. We're here to help you the best we can."

"First," the colleague said to his assistant, "file an 'Emergency Order of Protection' for 'Mrs. Jones.' Let's file the papers this afternoon. Today—not tomorrow—Mrs. Jones needs to get from under her abusive marital relationship, immediately. Find me the number of the Women's Welfare agency in her community, and get Sergeant Brown on the line. He's my contact over there in the local police district where she lives. I want to let him know personally about the violence that is happening in her home and have her make out a police report of this most recent incident. I need them to put a close watch on Mr. Jones. And most definitely take pictures of the injuries sustained. A picture is worth a thousand words."

All Socioeconomic Classes

As my colleague told "Mrs. Jones," marital physical abuse is "much too common." Many believe physical abuse in marriage is mostly the problem of lower socioeconomic classes of people in the country. Any divorce attorney can quickly dispel the lies in this portrayal. Physical abuse happens often in marriage. Whether those partners are blue or white collar; rich, working class, or poor; black, Hispanic, white, or other; straight or gay; Catholic, Protestant, or Jewish, Baptist, or non-denominational; left wing, centrist, or right wing politically; citizens or immigrants—whatever the social, economic, or religious class—physical abuse happens in marriage and is a major impetus for spouses to seek divorce. Parenthetically, a serious problem of marital abuse happens in the lives of many military veterans who have returned home from the wars in Iraq and Afghanistan.

Draw the Line on Physical Abuse

The drama of domestic violence is nothing to play with.

Legal, criminal, civic, and social workers approach domestic violence cases as serious and unacceptable crimes. They deal with the perpetrators of domestic violence to mete out effective consequences that are "swift, clear, consistent, predictable, and meaningful."[9] The collective authorities dealing with domestic violence include the following: 911 personnel, police officers at the scene of the crime, police investigators who look further into the details, prosecutors, victims' advocates, and probation officers.[10]

---

[9] "Achieving Accountability in Domestic Violence Cases: A Practical Guide for Reducing Domestic Violence," p. 26, Illinois Coalition Against Domestic Violence; Springfield, IL:2005.

[10] "Creating a Safety Plan," The Peel Committee Against Woman Abuse, April 2006: Mississauga, Ontario, March 1, 2013, http://www.pcawa.net/uploads/1/4/7/1/14711308/englishsafetyplan.pdf. http://www.pcawa.org.

Additional resources for victims of domestic violence appear below.
National Domestic Violence Hotline http://www.thehotline.org
Hotline #: 1-800-799-SAFE (7233)
"Domestic Violence and Black Women," March 1, 2013, http://blackdoctor.org/13338/domestic-violence-signs-statistics-black-women/.
"Domestic Violence: When Love Becomes Hurtful," March 1, 2013, http://

Many couples pledge to remain married, "till death us do part," a phrase appearing in many traditional marriage vows. In the black community, this faith commitment can weigh on an abused wife like a ten-ton gorilla. Most marriage counselors draw the line of separation at the onset of physical abuse. Usually, the victim is encouraged to leave the relationship and get out in a hurry. They do not regard as "marriage" a relationship where either spouse physically abuses the other, or the couple abuses one another. No marriage certificate or license justifies physically violating a marriage partner or other members of the household. No "common-law marriage" justifies a man's actions (or, in fewer cases, a woman's) who physically beats and batters his wife or their children.

Occasionally, a wife abuses her husband.

I recall a divorce case where the wife accused her husband of abusing her, and sought an order of protection. Actually, the charge was true. During one of their arguments, the man lost control and physically assaulted his wife. However, the order of protection took an unexpected turn during the proceedings. Under intense questioning, the husband revealed his wife was the real abuser in the relationship. His abuse of her was incidental; her abuse of him was consistent and often. The humbled man testified to the many times his wife physically assaulted him, scratching, biting, kicking, and emotionally attacking his maleness. He showed photos of his scarred body as evidence of her maltreatment.

The man responded to his wife's abuse as some men do: he took it and kept quiet.

His upbringing taught him a man should never hit a woman, so he let his wife pour out her anger on him. Time after time, she abused him until he could no longer take it. He snapped. That single incident was the only time in their marriage he had ever physically retaliated against her.

After the man's testimony, the tone of the divorce case shifted. The judge realized the man's wife orchestrated a game to entrap her husband. She, not he, was the real perpetrator. The wife was the clear abuser in their relationship

www.blackwomenshealth.com/blog/domestic-violence-when-love-becomes-hurtful/.
   Women's Resource Center, March 1, 2013, http://www.wrcnrv.org/helpingYou/dv_3phaseCycle.shtml.
   "Cycle of Violence," March 1, 2013, http://www.domesticviolence.org/cycle-of-violence/.

and the guilty party in the marital breakup. Thus, the court found he was simply defending himself against her aggression and denied her request for an order of protection.

"Abuse"—Its Wider Dimensions

Let's be clear about the wider legal meaning of "domestic violence" or "abuse." Often, these terms are interchangeable. Domestic violence may be physical, verbal, financial, psychologically manipulative, controlling, and sexual aggression. Depending on the particular circumstances, in most jurisdictions, "abuse" may include any or all of the following: *physical abuse, harassment, intimidation of someone who is a dependent, interference with personal liberty, or willfully depriving someone.*[11]

Some examples of spousal physical abuse include sexual abuse, using physical force, confining, or restraining one's partner. Or, it may involve doing things such as causing your spouse sleep deprivation. Then again, it may entail a spouse engaging in the kind of "reckless conduct which creates an immediate risk of physical harm" to a partner.

An abuser may be guilty of "harassing" the spouse by phoning or disturbing them at their place of employment, school, or residence; by repeatedly following or keeping the spouse under surveillance; by improperly concealing their minor child, or threatening to do so; or by threatening physical harm to the spouse or minor child.

Violence and Domestic Violence in Black Communities

Generally, a great deal of violence occurs in black communities. Period. Some of the violence is domestic violence. Law enforcement and the legal system deal with disputes and altercations. If you have a confrontation with your neighbor, the system treats the problem a certain way. In contrast, the system treats an altercation between husband and wife, girlfriend and boyfriend, differently. Some attorneys note domestic violence, in contrast to other types, is "quasi criminal," meaning that sometimes the authorities do not enforce the law consistently, and in the same manner as they would for other crimes.

[11] "Illinois Domestic Violence Act Order of Protection in Civil Court," March 1, 2013, http://www.ilcadv.org/dv_law_in_il/idva_booklet_1-2009.pdf.

Too much domestic violence occurs in the African-American community, and overwhelmingly black males are the abusers. Exceptionally, some women are batterers. In contrast to how the court treats domestically abused white women, when black (or Hispanic) women come into court, some do not receive fair treatment and due process. Women of color do not receive the high level of attention they deserve. Often, these "low-class" and "low-status" women of color have rights and remedies that the legal system may fail to recognize, pursue, or enforce. Your attorney can supply the facts and pertinent details.

The children of an abused mother are a special area of consideration. When an abused wife/mother cries out for help, so do her children. When she needs protection and security, so do the children. When she must quickly escape to a secret safe house, the authorities must also scurry her children to a place of refuge. This often impacts the education and socialization of a child from missed school days, having to adjust to living in a temporary shelter or having little to no contact with relatives and friends, and the shame of a battered household.

Children of a parent victimized by domestic violence need special counseling. They need emotional, psychological, and spiritual help. More likely than not, there is a fast link and correlation between the children who have witnessed domestic violence and the youth and young adults who currently terrorize our community with senseless shootings and other forms of violence. Abuse fosters abuse. Frequently, a young girl from an abusive home sees abuse as a sign of love and is attracted to the same type of man who abused her mother. A young man who saw his father abuse his mother and siblings is more likely to abuse his girlfriend and his own children when he grows up.

Protection and Remedies

You should know that legally, a "spouse" is at the top of the list of those persons protected as victims of domestic violence. Other persons protected from domestic violence may include those who are minor children, disabled persons, dependent adults, or any resident at a private home or public shelter. The list also includes former spouses, parents, children, stepchildren, blood relatives, in-laws, sharers in a common dwelling, unmarried parents, dating or engaged couples, disabled persons and their assistants, and caregivers.

An abused wife can receive protection and help through certain "remedies" available for her use. She has both civil and criminal options at her disposal. For example, one woman received an order of protection against her ex for posting nude pictures of her on the Internet.

Domestic violence laws in most states may cover any of the following:

- Prohibiting specific abuse that is physical, verbal, harassment, stalking, intimidation, and the like
- Granting exclusive possession of the marital residence
- Issuing a Stay-away order
- Counseling
- Determining the care and possession of minor children
- Getting temporary legal custody
- Prohibiting concealment of a child
- Getting exclusive possession of personal property like cars
- Granting payment of support and for losses
- Disallowing firearm possession
- Requiring payment for shelter services
- Other things that the law and the court deem appropriate.

The filing of a "Petition for Order of Protection" may trigger any of the above remedies. A judge may issue an *ex parte* emergency order of protection for a certain period of days or until the court hears all the facts. The victim of abuse, or, in some cases, a third party, can always file for an order of protection when domestic violence is at issue.

A wife/victim who petitions the court for a protective order need not fear her attorney will disclose vital information about her intentions or whereabouts. The law protects the *confidentiality* of any information she tells her attorney or a domestic violence counselor. In other words, laws provide for the safety of an abused wife who reports the domestic violence perpetrated by her husband.

Separating Myths from Realities When Abuse Happens

Sometimes an attorney or family counselor must help a victim of domestic violence to separate myth from the reality regarding an abusive relationship and experience. For instance, it is a myth for a victim of abuse to believe she is responsible for her husband's violent behavior or that the situation will get better on its own. The reality is that the perpetrator of abuse is the one to blame. Wife beaters never improve without the threat of consequences. Trying to appease them will not work. Winston Churchill said, "An appeaser is one who feeds the crocodile hoping it will eat him last." Aside from outside intervention, seldom does an abusive situation improve for the victim.

It is also a myth that a victim of domestic violence who leaves the home will forfeit everything, including her rights to custody. The reality is the rights of a battered mother to seek alimony, custody, and child support will remain intact even if she leaves an abusive situation. In this case, "If you move, you *don't* lose." Take your children if your life or the lives of the children are in imminent danger. In all instances, leave and return with the authorities. In some extreme cases of domestic violence abuse, the Department of Children and Family Services (DCFS) or a state agency will take custody of your children. Discuss these matters with your attorney. He or she knows which laws apply to your situation based on the state or jurisdiction where you reside. Your lawyer can successfully guide you through the legal maze when you deal with domestic violence, and the grounds for and process of divorce in that context.

The Degenerating Cycle of Domestic Abuse

Any marriage partner who suffers abuse from a spouse (or who suffers abuse under the sanction of a spouse by someone in the household) should make note of the degenerative "cycle" of an abusive relationship. A legal colleague notes physical abuse starts with "control," and then digresses from there: "control, to verbal abuse, to intimidation, to threats, to stalking, to physical contact." This downward cycle is the main reason a victim of abuse should seriously consider getting a divorce.

Based on the experiences of many victims of domestic violence, if the abused victim hesitates to leave the relationship, she loses. Some of these women lose dearly, while others lose their lives. Never think you are above an abuser's attack or imagine you are strong enough to change the craziness of an adult perpetrator. Usually, abuse gets worse as time goes on. Abuse is like a toothache; it only gets worse with time.

Think about the worsening condition of domestic violence the following passage captures.

➤ Provocative and hurtful words lead to arguments, arguments lead to insults, insults lead to intimidation, intimidation leads to threats, threats lead to fights, fights lead to physical beat downs.

➤ Dependency leads to manipulation, manipulation leads to emotional control, emotional control leads to physical and social control, physical and social control leads to domination, domination leads to despising, despising leads to oppression, oppression leads to enslavement, enslavement leads to abject submission.

➤ Disrespect leads to dehumanizing, dehumanizing leads to demonizing, demonizing leads to emotional destruction, emotional destruction leads to physical death.

Do you see yourself in this picture? Is your spouse abusing you? Where is your abusive situation leading?

Therapists and counselors note four specific phases of domestic violence against a wife (or husband). These phases cycle downward.[12]

1) **The Tension Building Phase** – stress increases between the partners; a war of words ensues; the wife tolerates the situation.

2) **The Acute Battering Phase** (or **Acting Out**) – stress and tension between spouses are extreme; the man batters the woman because he chooses to do so. He blames her when, in reality, he is the abuser who really is to blame for the physical violence and his own irresponsible behavior.

3) **The Honeymoon Phase** (or **Reconciliation**) – after the abuse, the husband responds in appeasing ways like crying, apologizing, or promising never to hit her again; or he physically or romantically pleases her when in fact he is getting off on the abuse and control.

---

[12] The domestic violence cycles, developed in the 1970's, trace to Lenore Walker. The modified concept is widely accepted in diverse circles. Some use slightly different terms to describe each phase, but the substance remains intact.

See, "Cycle of Violence," *Wikipedia*, March 1, 2013, http://en.wikipedia.org/wiki/Cycle_of_violence.

See, "Cycle of Abuse," *Wikipedia*, March 1, 2013, http://en.wikipedia.org/wiki/Cycle_of_abuse.

See, "Myths and Realities of Domestic Violence," March 1, 2013, http://www.law.arizona.edu/clinics/child_and_family_law_clinic/Materials/myths_and_realities_of_domestic_abuse1.pdf.

He seeks to pacify her in order to maintain control and domination; seldom does the abuser keep his promises. He pleads for his wife not to call the police so he does not lose his job, a fear she may share since it might compromise her financial situation.

4) **The Worsening Cycle of the Next Tension Building Phase** – the drama starts all over again, and gets worse. She recognizes the signs and seeks to appease him so he does not get angry. But no matter what she does, he finds fault and resumes degrading and abusing her.

Domestic violence is not a plaything. Police officers know from experience answering 911 calls about domestic violence and disturbances present the greatest risk of harm to all involved. Usually, an abusive husband becomes more angry and violent when he gets wind his wife is going to leave him. The simple knowledge his wife is reading a book on "divorce" may trigger and justify in his own mind his maltreatment of her. His sensing of something out of the ordinary, strange, or "funny" going on in the home or with his wife may be enough to raise his suspicions and throw him into a rage.

If an impending dangerous situation requires you to leave your home in a rush, don't try to dot every "i" and cross every "t." Place your safety and security on the front burner. Let the proper authorities and your lawyer handle the abuser and all the rest.[13]

When You Can't Leave or Divorce Immediately

Not every woman who is in an abusive relationship can immediately divorce her husband or change her current living situation. Some can. Others, for any number of reasons, cannot. Some women must remain married and continue where they live until the time is right. Each victim of abuse must carefully consider the obvious facts, listen to her conscience, and make the best decision for herself and her children.

---

[13] See, "How To Escape An Abusive Spouse," March 1, 2013, http://www. livestrong.com/article/93228-escape-abusive-spouse/.

See, Rebecca, "The Last Straw," "Making an escape Plan – escaping domestic violence with your life – Escape Plan," March 1, 2013, http://thelaststraw.wordpress. com/2010/07/04/making-an-escape-plan-escaping-domestic-violence-with-your-life-escape-plan/.

See, Dr. Phil, "An Exit Action Plan: Guidelines for Leaving an Abusive Relationship," *Health*, March 1, 2013, http://www.drphil.com/articles/article/543.

If you cannot leave your abusive situation or divorce your spouse immediately, I recommend the steps below, especially when you fear for the safety of yourself and your children. Remember, timing is everything. These steps may take days, weeks, or months to accomplish. The goal is to escape successfully and safely.

1) **Look up the phone number and address of a domestic violence shelter for women and children.** Plan to register with a false name. Alternately, think about a relative or friend you can stay with, or an unsuspecting safe place away from your spouse who will seek to detect your whereabouts. For your safety and security, it may be necessary for you and the children to go to separate places for the time being.

2) **Be secretive about all your moves.** Take photos or video of the abuse your spouse inflicted. Secretly record threats and abusive conversation. Hide these items from your spouse. Get the evidence out of the home. Have a trusted friend hold the evidence. Don't leave a trail of your actions for your abusive spouse to discover. Erase the browsing history from your computer. How? From your browser, click "Tools," "Internet Options," on the "General" tab, find "Browsing history," select "Delete." You may need access to an outside computer to do your research.

3) **Make yourself a plan for the actual escape.** Develop a plan "A," "B," and "C," where "C" is the emergency fire-exit plan. Though a checklist may prove helpful, keep as much of your plan as possible in your head. Be prepared, whether day or night, good weather or bad, do what you planned to do. Make things difficult for your abuser to chase you by deflating tires, disconnecting battery cables, or jamming door locks.

4) **Save, or get your hands on as much cash as you can.** You will need some emergency money. Find someone whom you trust to hold the money. A safety deposit box might be useful. Once you leave, immediately close any accounts you have with your abusive spouse so he can't easily track you. You should also, save up your vacation and sick days in case you need to take off work for a while.

5) **Make copies of licenses, birth certificates, titles, tax returns, and other legal documents.** Safely store them or mail them to yourself at a private post office box.

6) **Write down important numbers.** Numbers of your phone, bank accounts, his social security, date of birth, etc., fit this category. Get an unlisted phone number for your personal communication, and block your phone number from caller I.D.

7) **When you obtain an emergency order of protection, keep the papers with you at all times.** Let your friends and important associates know about the restraining order against your spouse.

Interracial Interference

American society is more open for blacks than it was prior to the Civil Rights Movement. The movement led to the abolishment of segregation and Jim Crow laws, which denied African-Americans our equal and fair share and access to America. At one time, American laws in many states made it illegal for blacks to marry whites. Legally, those days are over.[14] An African-American man or woman can choose to marry across racial and ethnic lines.[15] Some do.[16]

---

[14] The notes below give current trends in the area of interracial marriage and divorce. Nationwide, consider the following information from US Census data as reported in "Interracial marriage in the United States," *Wikipedia*, March 1, 2013, http://en.wikipedia.org/wiki/Interracial_marriage_in_the_United_States.
   • Only since 1967 has interracial marriage been fully legalized in the U.S.;
   • Multiracial Americans numbered 9 million in 2010, and are growing;
   • Interracially married couples totaled 2,340,000 in 2008, or 3.9% of the total couples married in that year;
   • In 2010, 168,000 White husbands had a Black wife; while 390,000 Black husbands had a White wife.

[15] See, Hope Yen, "Interracial Marriage in U.S. hits new high: 1 in 12," (February 16, 2012), *Associated Press & msnbc.com*, March 1, 2013, http://www.msnbc.msn.com/id/46409832/ns/us_news-life/t/interracial-marriage-us-hits-new-high/#.UMkYqG_AcnQ.
   US Census Bureau data support the following:
   • In 2007, 4.6% of all married Blacks in the US were wed to a White partner, and 0.4% of all Whites were married to a Black partner.

[16] See, "Barely Half of U.S. Adults Are Married – A Record Low." PEW studies cited support the following, Pew Research Center, March 1, 2013, www.pewsocialtrends.org/files/2012.
   • In 2008 among all newlyweds,16% of blacks, married someone whose race or ethnicity was different from their own; and White-Black interracial pairings totaled 11%;
   • Between 1980 and 2008 rates of interracial marriages among newlywed blacks

Today, more black men marry interracially than do black women, though the gap is closing.[17]

For a person to have legal access to marry interracially is one thing. To be socially accepted in an interracial relationship is quite another. Many social pressures come to bear on an interracial marriage. Besides the personal factors, some of these outside dynamics help to create fissures in the relationship of an African-American with a spouse of a different racial group.

The historical, sociological and racial context of America has created an environment that sometimes makes it more difficult for a couple to sustain a successful interracial relationship. We call factors affecting these marriages *"interracial interference."* Unfortunately, interracial interference sometimes can significantly impact some marriages and cause couples to get divorced.[18] Consider the story of a young black man who married a young white woman back in the 1970s. Both were professionals. Neither of their families fully supported the marriage, and due to social pressure, the couple decided to have a private ceremony. Still, most members of both families—black and white—boycotted the small wedding reception. For the most part, only the bride's closest white friends showed up while the groom could count his African-American friends in attendance on one hand. At the reception, male friends of the bride openly flirted with her despite her new black husband's presence, actions that were inappropriate, distasteful, and signaled that relationship trouble lay ahead.

nearly tripled;
• Regional patterns of intermarriage are stronger in the West (22%); compared to 13% in the South and the Northeast, and only 11% in the Midwest

[17] See US Census Bureau data. In 2009 there were 354,000 White female/Black male marriages, and only 196,000 Black female/White male marriages, a ratio of 181:100. In 1981 this ratio was 371:100. In 2010, 4.6% of married Black American women and 10.8% of married Black American men had a non-Black spouse; and 8.5% of married Black men and 3.9% of married Black women had a White spouse.

[18] See, Jenifer L. Bratter and Rosalind B. King, "'But Will It Last': Marital Instability Among Interracial and Same-Race Couples," *Family Relations*, 57. (April 2008), 160-171. Blackwell Publishing: National Council on Family Relations, March 1, 2013, http://onlinelibrary.wiley.com/doi/10.1111/j.1741-3729.2008.00491.x/pdf. When it comes to marital instability, as reflected in divorce rates, by the 10th year of marriage, White wife/Black husband marriages show twice the divorce rate of White wife/White husband couples. In contrast, during the same period, Black wife/White husband marriages are 44% less likely to end in divorce than White wife/White husband couples.

Despite the personal love the man and his wife shared, the anti-interracial influences of their social and religious context were working overtime to destroy their relationship. Their budding marriage faced the stark reality of interracial interference. As one might imagine, the couple could not withstand outside influences of friends and family that drove an emotional wedge between them. Their differences grew sharper as they discussed and debated matters of race in society, social dealings, and their marriage. Eventually, despite their good intentions, the couple succumbed to the social and emotional pressures; they divorced.

The main issue is not so much how an interracial couple feels about their relationship. Rather, the primary issue concerns what others feel about their relationship, how their family and core friends treat them, and the prospects of them successfully navigating the minefields of a prejudiced and racialized society.

Sometimes, differences exist in the negative dynamics faced by black male/white female relationships versus black female/white male relationships. Nevertheless, in either combination, the racial demons of American families and society often tragically assault an interracial relationship, marriage, and the children of these unions. The drama of interracial interference complicates marriage, and these complexities spill over into cases of divorce.

Divorce Complications of Interracial Marriages

Some jurisdictions collect statistics on divorce in racial groups. Cook County, IL, is the second most populous county in the U.S., second only to Los Angeles County, CA. Its divorce cases are numerous. The form that the county provides for initiating a divorce has boxes to check for appropriate information. One of the boxes asks whether the person seeking a divorce is white or black. This question focuses on the interracial context of divorce in society.

Interracial marriages or relationships can complicate matters of divorce and separation. For instance, in one interracial divorce case, the judge ordered that in the best interest of the children, no smoking of marijuana by the white father should take place. The next time the case came up in court, the African-American female litigant brought up the issue of the father smoking marijuana. The judge questioned the white male litigant about his behavior. He answered by contending the judge had ordered him not to smoke marijuana in the presence of the children, but he hadn't thought the judge's order prohibited him from smoking marijuana when he was in the home alone by himself! In this instance, the California style mentality of the white male did not translate properly in the judicial system of the Midwest.

Who initiates divorce proceedings in the case of interracial marriages? Usually the male, so say a number of lawyers. Whether African-American or white, usually the male is the one who makes the first phone call or takes the first step into the lawyer's office. Thus, the black male wants to end the relationship with his white wife, and the white male wants to get away from his black spouse. In contrast, with an all-black couple, the wife usually initiates divorce proceedings.

The trend reflects the cold, hard facts of American social and cultural reality. On the one hand, the moral consciousness of American idealism tells us persons who love each other should be married. We say, "People are just people. We should encourage interracial mixture." However, the word on the street is that socially and racially conscious people know better. The street reality differs from the American ideal. The pressures on interracial relationships and the children of these unions are immense in our society.

Besides these husbands making the decision to divorce for strictly personal reasons, I suspect they also buckle to family and social forces. What man can emotionally sustain a long-term war over his chosen mate with his father and mother, sisters and brothers, grandparents, uncles, aunts, and cousins? What male can withstand the constant pressures against his marital union in the social situations he encounters at church, in the neighborhood, in his career or profession, or with the fellas? How does a father continually cope with the development of his biracial children? How does he handle their struggles to integrate themselves simultaneously into two, often opposite, worlds—one black, the other white?

Some attorneys handling the divorces of interracial couples observe a disheartening pattern. Despite how long an interracial couple stays married, they still face the intolerant rejection of several racial die-hards in their family. These individuals never fully accept the interracial couple. Further, they reject or disown the biracial children who were born to the couple's union.

Any African-American or white male who marries interracially may soon realize he is committing social suicide. In a male's America, the interracial piece is very difficult. In my practice, the men in interracial relationships are more likely to file for divorce than their intra-racial counterparts or their wife. The male analyzes his situation, and finds the mountains and pathways before him formidable, both inside and outside the union. In every major decision, and down every path that he ventures, he encounters roadblocks and obstacles of the racial variety. Something is always in the way of his relationship, a hitch always happens as he seeks to advance. Complexities and concerns bombard his interracial relationship from every angle. Repeatedly, American racial reality painfully reminds us the interracial marriage relationships of good people, at times, do not make it. Racism is the fabric of American life and society, and its dynamics may either greatly influence or destroy an interracial relationship.

Homosexual Heartbreak

Another extraordinary circumstance that brings drama into a divorce is homosexuality. Some states sanction marriage between same-sex partners. Consequently, these legal jurisdictions must also provide for persons in these unions to receive legitimate and fair representation and a divorce. A person who chooses a same-sex relationship does not forfeit his or her humanity. When their relationships break, they feel pain and hurt just as we all do. Perhaps they are hurt more because often their loved ones and the larger society never fully accept these relationships.

Some divorce clients finally get the nerve to keep their appointment with an attorney only after three or four attempts. Such a client may make an appointment and then break it; make it, then break it again. She is ambivalent and doesn't quite know how to express her problem to the attorney. Many lawyers are good listeners and show sensitivity, but sometimes a client is not transparent. They may feel shame and embarrassment, and their lack of candor only makes it more difficult for the lawyer to give sound advice.

On one occasion, I interviewed a client who was pursuing a divorce. After about a half hour of back and forth discussion about her marital situation, she finally disclosed the real reason for her visit. She was seeking a divorce because her husband was gay. He had recently "come out" by breaking the news to her. He was no longer interested in making love to her. Instead, he preferred to sleep with younger males. This new knowledge devastated the client who saw her marriage of thirteen years going down the drain. Her now openly gay husband shook her personal identity to the core. When he broke the news of his newfound sexual identity, he also broke her heart.

Divorce and the "Down Low"

Unfortunately, the situation also nearly gave the woman a panic attack when she faced the crisis of talking to her children about the matter. She wrestled intensely with how to break the news to the children about their father's "coming out." What would they think of their father? What would they think about their mother? In what way could she keep her family together? Increasingly, more lawyers are servicing clients whose homosexual partners bring strains into the marriage relationship. Many commonly call this practice the *"down low."*

Homosexuality is nothing new. Some believe it dates back thousands of years in black civilization to Africa and ancient Egypt, where archeologists discovered the first historical record of a possibly homosexual couple, Khnumhotep and Niankhkhnum, who lived around 2400 B.C. A portrait of the Egyptian male couple captures them in a nose-kissing posture—a position regarded by some scholars as the most intimate of poses in Egyptian art.[19] In contemporary society, estimates vary for the percentage of African-Americans who are homosexual. The numbers fall somewhere between 10 and 15 percent, the same rate existing for other racial groups in our society. However, the number of openly gay African-Americans may be lower. No one knows with certainty the exact numbers.

As the lesbian, gay, lesbian, bisexual, and transgendered population increases in visibility in our society, so does its impact factor into issues of divorce and separation. One law practice dealing with divorce figures 5 percent of its cases fall into this category, and it is growing. The flavor of their legal practice reflects changes in sexual attitudes taking place in the general society.

Heartbreak and Fair Treatment

Statistics are one thing; relationships are another. Heartbreak experienced by a homosexual person is just as bad as the heartbreak of a person who is heterosexual.

---

[19] See, "Homosexuality," *Wikipedia*, March 1, 2013, http://en.wikipedia.org/wiki/Homosexuality. In contrast, some critics argue that both men appear with their respective wives and children, suggesting the men were brothers, rather than lovers. See sources in "Khnumhotep and Niankhkhnum," *Wikipedia*, March 1, 2013, http://en.wikipedia.org/wiki/Khnumhotep_and-_Niankhkhnum#Proposed-_homosexuality.

Supporting the fair treatment of homosexuals carries over into how divorce attorneys handle the legal cases of this population. Some divorce cases concern a marriage partner who is a non-admitting homosexual. The client tells the lawyer the spouse loves someone else. Sometimes, they couch their situation by saying, "My spouse has found someone else." Whether a man or woman, they cannot bring themselves to say their spouse has found a more suitable partner of the same sex.

Sexual choice by one of the marriage partners (and sexual curiosity to a lesser extent) is affecting more and more marriage relationships. A spirit of going public and being transparent in this sexual area is much more prevalent than before. A heterosexual marriage may evolve into a homosexual situation. Some persons are married and bisexual. On the one hand, they value family and seek to hold on to it. On the other hand, they live a separate life from their spouse and enjoy an open relationship with another person of the same sex.

In one instance, a competing law firm represented the father in a divorce case. The court awarded custody of the 13-year-old child to her bisexual mother. The child's maternal grandmother was bisexual also. The father became upset because he did not believe in alternative lifestyles. More and more lawyers encounter this issue: a once heterosexual wife changing her sexual preference.

Years ago, the laws did not protect the legal status of homosexuals as a class. However, many jurisdictions are increasingly giving legal protection to homosexual unions and marriages. The same legal umbrella that protects persons from discrimination based on "race," "gender," "ethnic origin," "religion," "age," etc., also affords protection for homosexual persons who are unfairly treated because of their sexual preference or choice.

As society goes through its changes on issues of homosexuality, so do individual relationships. For example, a man romanticizes about his woman, the mother of his children. He forms a mental picture of himself and his beautiful wife in their intimate relationship. As the image evolves, however, it takes a 180-degree turn. Suddenly the man's beautiful wife transforms herself into a "boyfriend" who still seeks intimacy with her mate! Obviously, the case creates a love and moral dilemma for the man, especially in the bedroom. Legally, however, no clear set of rules applies to the relationship. Any legal questions in their relationship quickly become complicated. What should the heterosexual father do in such a situation?

When Daddy's Gone to Jail: The Incarcerated Spouse

The U.S. has more prison inmates than any country on the face of the earth. The criminal authorities incarcerate African-American males in numbers far above the population percentage of black people in the country. Some black couples, and those who divorce, face the added drama caused by the prison system. When Daddy has gone to jail or prison, the same absence enters the marriage and family. Incarceration shares the same characteristics associated with divorce and breakups. It brings about the drama of separation.

Sometimes, imprisonment leads to divorce. The woman simply desires to get on with her life. She cannot overcome the hurdle of waiting years for the release of her man and his return to "normal" socialization back into society. She refuses to continue her association with a brother who has ruined himself, his marriage, and his children by committing a crime—for whatever reasons. So, she pulls the plug on her marital relationship.

Far too many black men find themselves in the "The New Jim Crow"[20] of the prison system. (However, the number of incarcerated women is increasing rapidly.) The separation of a man in prison presents its own set of challenges for his wife and the children. The challenge of explaining the "What?" and "Why?" of Daddy's absence to your children is emotionally tricky. The reality of your "invisible man" hits home and hits hard. Explaining prison is one thing. Going on with life when your mate is serving time is quite another. Though, as a woman with good reasons, you may choose to "stand by your man" by not divorcing him, you still must deal with a prolonged absence and the drama it creates.

Pressures of Prolonged Absence

✗ **The social reputation drama is present.** Everyone knows your husband went to prison and why. Maybe your neighbors read the Internet story about what happened. Maybe they saw something on TV. Now you and your children face the stigma of what happened. Your husband is

---

[20] See, Michelle Alexander, *The New Jim Crow: Mass Incarceration in the Age of Colorblindness*. New York: The New Press, 2010.

a criminal. Your children's Daddy is in prison. A good marriage and family have gone sour. By association, and depending on what crime your partner committed, some folks will bring your personal character and judgment into question. At school, your kids may even become the subject of taunts and bullying.

✗ **The sexual drama is present.** Your sexual partner is no longer immediately accessible. Conjugal prison visitations, if any, may be few and far between. So what is the agreement you have made with your incarcerated spouse? Do you have the freedom to do sexually what you feel you need to do? Do you give your spouse the freedom to do likewise in prison? Then, how do you prepare yourself to deal with a man who may become bisexual through his prison experience?

✗ **The loneliness drama is present.** Sexual fulfillment is one thing. Companionship is another. It is hard on a woman to be alone, away from the man she loves. If a woman has to choose between having a regular physical sexual relationship or a regular companion, my bet is she would choose a companion. She desires to share her life fully with a man, not just the blessings of her body. When the system has imprisoned her man, it has bound her companionship in shackles. The sister must now find ways to fill the void.

✗ **The distance drama is present.** Most times, the prison holding your partner or spouse is not geographically close. It may take hours to travel for visitation. Between work and school, church and other social and business functions, visiting with your imprisoned partner may become a major event for you and your children. In addition, contrary to a noted saying, separation does not always "make the heart grow fonder."

✗ **The communication drama is present.** Before your spouse's imprisonment, you two discussed all matters and made decisions together. You talked daily, using email, text, as well as the telephone. Now communication is not immediate; you can only communicate at certain pre-determined times. Your communication is restricted, and often monitored. Sometimes your communication will come through your partner's attorney. However, this occurs only while the trial and appeal process remain pending. Now you must make decisions on your own. You must find a sounding board in someone else. You raise questions in your mind about whether or not you are doing the right thing and making the best choices.

✗ **The money drama is present.** Often, prison separation cuts off any financial support you are getting from your spouse. Actually, money begins to flow from your limited pocketbook into the prison system. Your spouse needs your support and help for legal or other necessities as he serves his time. Depending on the crime, the state uses any money the inmate earns while in prison for bringing restitution to the victims. You find yourself financially alone. The dollars you earn must make ends meet for you and your children. You carry the whole load. All the bill collectors are calling you. They place his debts and yours on your limited income table.

The drama of preserving reputation, sexual fulfillment, closeness, companionship, communication, and money occur because "Daddy has gone to jail." Imprisonment creates a separation akin to a divorce or breakup, making "Daddy" an absentee father.

Act Now 7 – Divorce in Different Circumstances

If you are a victim of **domestic violence**, I cannot more seriously urge you to follow these steps. You must take charge of your situation to save yourself and your children.

1) **Leave your abuser at the earliest time possible.** We strongly recommend you consider a divorce, more so if your abuse is physical, frequent, or severe.

2) **Secretly meet with an attorney, and relate you are a victim of domestic violence.** Tell him or her you want out of the abusive marriage. Don't hold back from sharing the slightest details, no matter how embarrassing. Perhaps you need a restraining order against your abusive spouse. Ask your attorney to advise you about getting an emergency order of protection. Also, pursue the possibility of getting exclusive possession of the marital residence, or relocation expenses if you have to leave the marital home.

3) **Don't quickly change your mind about divorcing your abusive spouse.** The experts tell us within three weeks after you file an emergency petition for order of protection, your husband will make you every promise in the world. He does this to regain control and domination over your life. Therefore, you must resist the temptation to withdraw your petition from the court. Instead, we advise you to press on with your plan.

If you are involved in an **interracial relationship** that is breaking apart, here are some ways to lessen the negative impact of the drama on yourself and your children.

1) **Get special counseling for your children.** Remind yourself: the experience of American social reality is testing your interracial union. When it comes to the lives of your children, you cannot simply toss out the bad results and start over. To give your children a fighting chance, you need to enlist the help of someone who can make plain to them the realities of a racially divided America and the personal failures of a husband and wife relationship.

2) **Engage a therapeutic counselor.** Find one whose theory and practices takes into account racial realities. You need a holistic approach that deals with personal and group identity.

3) **Prepare yourself mentally for a potentially biased court system.** Depending on where you reside, more often than you think, the judicial system may favor white litigants. Get ready for living in a divorce social system where your former spouse with his or her "white privilege" may become the beneficiary of special treatment. In contrast, sometimes the court system appears to favor money over race.

Court cases involving issues of **homosexuality** can become very dynamic and traumatic. These guidelines can protect you as you navigate your divorce under these circumstances

1) **Affirm your beliefs about sexual choices.** If you believe heterosexuality is right, stay that way. If you prefer the freedom of a homosexual lifestyle, follow what you believe. Don't hurt people with false pretenses. Be who you are. Do not allow the swinging tides of social

and sexual evolution to carry you along. If you are confused, seek out a counselor who can help you clarify your values in this area.

2) **Be honest and transparent about your chosen sexuality.** Is it wrong for a secretly gay person to enter a marriage as if heterosexual? Should a spouse have enough love and respect for a partner not to set them up for a major marital disappointment? Should those who find it necessary to change sexual preference once married be straightforward? I recommend you have some heart for your spouse. Whether gay or straight, know your grounds for divorce. If you must divorce, do so with a clear conscience and honorably.

3) **Encourage your children to keep a loving and respectful relationship with the other parent, regardless of his/her sexual preference.** Create opportunities for them to do so. If as a parent with inquisitive and impressionable children you have moral or ethical objections to homosexual behavior, share your honest feelings. When speaking to your children, be sure to affirm the right of your spouse to make their own moral choices.

When the system **imprisons** your spouse, you must make major adjustments in your marriage and in how you handle a divorce. The following guidelines may assist you.

1) **Determine the level of commitment you will make to your children to keep their father in their lives during his incarceration.** You may change the focus of the relationship with your husband. However, the connection of the children to their father can remain strong.

2) **Resolve in a reasonable amount of time whether you will seek a divorce.** One consideration is whether your spouse is able to maintain the earning power of his present employment when he finishes his prison term. How will you prepare to deal with a lower standard of living? Communicate your decision to your spouse. If divorce is your choice, do it quickly. Do not procrastinate with your decision. Indecision on this matter usually complicates the relationship.

3) **Make yourself a plan for living without your spouse.** Prepare yourself to live without the presence of your imprisoned spouse for

a significant period. Prepare also to deal with any rights of visitation your spouse has to see his children. Your schedule will alter.

4) **Tell your spouse the truth if you decide to move on.** Though the whole "prison ordeal" may hurt, you owe it to your spouse to let him know the relationship is over. Acknowledge you will do your best to keep the children in his life. However, recognize the children may need to sort things out on their own, as they get older.

Up Next

The next section covers **the legal and financial dimension** of divorce. What kinds of legal moves should you first make? How should you rework your financial budget as a divorcee? What mistakes should I avoid when going through the divorce process? How does support for the children enter the equation? In some of these matters, you will be able to provide input and help shape the outcomes of these areas. In other related matters, the judge will make decisions based on the current laws and statutes and require you to obey the ruling. In these areas, you will have no room to determine the outcome. The court will have the final say. What I can do is help you prepare for the full discovery process of all your assets and liabilities during the unfolding divorce proceedings. As a result, you will be better able to deal with the emerging financial realities of your breakup drama.

PART TWO:

The Legal and Financial Dimension

The legal and financial steps of divorce

are the focus of this section.

Chapter 8

Your First Legal Moves

The Divorce Lawyer's Role

Lawyers get involved in all kinds of issues and in almost every phase of our lives. Do you remember when you first met a lawyer? Did your parents get a lawyer to represent you as a teenager in a misdemeanor? Was your first encounter with a lawyer in traffic court when you tried to beat a speeding ticket? Maybe you used a lawyer at a closing when you bought your home. Maybe you sought a lawyer to represent you before the IRS on some tax matters. Sooner or later, it seems everyone needs a lawyer for one reason or another. Our society is civil. The legislators base the society on governing laws designed to administer justice, although that "justice" is not always equal. Whether our society rises to this noble cause is debatable, especially in the eyes of African-Americans and others who have not always experienced liberty and justice.

The responsibilities of lawyers are numerous. However, in all lawyers do, they seek to keep the society legal and civil. An attorney practicing divorce law plays a unique role in the legal profession. First and foremost, a divorce attorney handles matters related to marriage and family, the foundational social group in society. They also influence the way their clients value their greatest commodities: their children and their spouse. Material assets are often secondary.

A divorce attorney touches on every aspect of their client's life—children, real estate, taxes, retirement, sexual practices, psychology, finances, employment—you name it. A divorce attorney, in one way or another, has his or her hands on the very pulse of the day-to-day realities of their client. Since divorce, by its very nature, affects so many vital areas of life, a competent divorce attorney keeps abreast of the law in order to represent the litigant effectively. A litigant should be careful however about what they expect of an attorney. Some clients mistakenly think the lawyer handles all their issues. However, a client should expect the attorney to handle only those things that are specifically set forth in the retainer agreement, no more, no less.

When it comes to divorce, a competent and empathetic lawyer will seek justice and a stable outcome for the client. In this way, a lawyer will seek to limit the drama often erupting during the divorce process. A considerate client will avoid misinterpreting the attorney's objectivity as indifference. A disinterested attorney is not the same as an uninterested attorney. A client may passionately report some issue about a spouse, only to hear their attorney respond, "I know how you must feel, but the issue is not relevant to the outcome we are seeking. Instead, you need to focus on. . ."

Divorce attorneys note their clients often reach a high level of anxiety, depression, and frustration during the litigation process. A client wants the divorce and wants it now. However, the court, or the other spouse usually does not move with such expediency. Sometimes the spouse doesn't show up for a scheduled court date. This may happen for various reasons. The substance of the documents provided during the documentation exchange process required to commence trial is inadequate. The other side may need a continuance or witnesses are unavailable. Sometimes the lawyer of a divorce litigant stops a client from communicating with their spouse. Perhaps the attorney doesn't want the opposition to get a leg up on the client. Perhaps the attorney wants to drag things out so he can make a little more money. Unfortunately, sometimes both motives are in play. Whatever the case, such delay tactics can frustrate a client. They can wreak havoc with the litigant who wants a quick and final disposition, and desires to get on with life.

The Process: From Counsel to Court to Conciliation to Closure

So, what can you expect to encounter as you move your divorce from your consultation to the court and to the final disposition? Though it varies from state to state, the process is generally similar throughout the country. Briefly, here is the divorce process step-by-step. It moves from counsel, to court, to conciliation, and to closure.

1. **Step One: Counsel**
   a. Arrange a meeting with your attorney.
   b. Attend a detailed interview about your marriage and related matters.
   c. Decide the course of litigation. Remember, no-fault divorces are the rule, not the exception. (In 2010, NY became the 50th state to enact no-fault divorces)
   d. Execute a retainer (contract) for services anticipated and a Power of Attorney.
   e. File a petition or complaint to dissolve the marriage.
   f. Have your spouse served with the divorce petition.
   g. Have your initial court hearing and address issues such as temporary alimony, child support, visitation, allocation of payments for household expenses and orders of protection, if necessary.
   h. Enter the discovery phase of disclosing all assets and liabilities.
   i. Confer with your lawyer about what you should expect in a divorce settlement.
   j. If child custody is at issue, prepare for third parties to assist the court in assessing the strengths and weaknesses of each parent and determining the needs of the children. This process can take significant time and may include the appointment of a *Guardian Ad Litem*, an attorney for the children, psychological evaluations and home assessments.
   k. Consider a meeting for you and your lawyer with your spouse and his/her lawyer. Try to reach a meeting of the minds to ensure no drama.

2. **Step Two: Court and Conciliation**
   a. As the gap narrows, go back into court and offer the agreement of the parties to the judge, informing him of any remaining areas of disagreement.

b. Be open to the direction of the judge who may offer a recommendation on how to resolve issues short of a trial.

c. Have another meeting for the litigants and the lawyers to try to reach a full settlement.

d. Go back to court to present the settlement to the judge or to submit the unsettled matters to him/her for possible resolution short of a trial.

e. Reconciling with your spouse is always an option. If you and your spouse decide to make a last ditch effort to patch things up, the judge may place your case on a "reconciliation calendar" and agree to suspend proceedings, if both sides agree. If the couple works things out, fine. If not, the judge will continue the process and resume the case from where it left off. The divorcing parties will waste no time in the legal system if attempted reconciliation fails. However, the lapse of time may present other financial ramifications.

3. **Step Three: Closure and Trial**

a. Mentally prepare yourself for going through a trial lasting a day or two, to possibly a month and even longer depending on the complexity of the issues. Laws of individual states may also impact the length of trial.

b. Hear the judge's decision. Agree to abide by it or discuss issues of appeal with your attorney. The divorce will be final, but certain aspects of the decision may be appealable.

c. Receive your divorce decree. It will likely include "Judgment for Dissolution of Marriage," "Property Settlement Agreement," and possibly (pertaining to minor children) a "Parenting Agreement" or "Custody Judgment." The court will retain its jurisdiction over your case in order to enforce the final decree.[21]

---

[21] For a cross-referenced process, see, "What are the Steps to Getting a Divorce?" March 1, 2013, http://www.wisegeek.com/what-are-the-steps-to-getting-a-divorce.htm.

Patience in the Process

Be patient! Usually the divorce process can take from six months to more than a year or two, depending on the circumstances. When fighting over custody of children and substantial assets, the process can become very difficult and even messy. That's why your best source of information is your attorney, and you should seek to educate yourself as well as you can when going into the divorce arena.

Act Now 8 – Your First Legal Moves

Below are several things you should consider as you prepare to make your first legal moves to obtain a divorce.

1) **Control your anger.** Do not transfer to the court the angry feelings you harbor toward the spouse who has treated you badly. Focus any anger you have toward justifiable targets rather than against the court, the judge, the mediator, or the lawyer. Better yet, channel your anger into making the right decisions that will help you transcend the plight of your divorce.

2) **Maintain control of your case.** Never allow a lawyer to persuade you to file for a divorce. Further, make certain that you remain thoroughly involved with decisions made in your case. Stay empowered. Remember, the client is the boss. This is not to imply that your lawyer is distrustful. However, at the end of the day, you have to live with the consequences of your choices, not your lawyer.

3) **Be prepared to spend money on legal fees and court costs.** A good attorney and the divorce proceedings will cost you. In most major metropolitan areas, you can expect to spend at least $3,000 for a relatively simple divorce. However, if you don't settle your disputed issues early on, the amount can increase tens of thousands of dollars, and the case may take years to resolve.

4) **Retain an attorney to file for your divorce.** Avoid the "do it yourself" approach. If unable to pay, determine whether you qualify for assistance through an agency or legal clinic that offers help to low-income or indigent persons. Do not discount the quality of such

representation, as many recognize that legal aid attorneys are some of the best-trained lawyers in the divorce business.

5) **Consider mediation.** These services may help you avoid expensive and time-consuming litigation by resolving issues of custody, visitation, and division of property.

6) **Stay focused and prepared for the long haul.** Talk to trusted friends or family who can help you remember that your divorce proceedings will not last forever!

7) **Never close the door on communicating with your spouse.** Stay open except where there is a history of abuse or issues of dominance, control, psychological manipulation, or browbeating.[22] In most instances, you will want to keep the door of communication open because you and your spouse are family and the major stakeholders in your relationship. Couples often are able to work out issues, even as they part ways.

Up Next

Sometimes a divorce client needs specific advice and guidance. After all, this is the primary reason a person whose marriage is breaking up consults with an attorney. In the next section, I give special advice, *pro bono*. What questions should you ask a divorce attorney? What are the biggest pre-divorce and post-divorce mistakes clients make? What kinds of behavior should you avoid while in court? I give sound advice and answers for these questions and more in the following pages.

---

[22] Browbeating is the practice of making someone agree to do something by constantly asking or threatening them.

Chapter 9

Ask Attorney Barclay: Wise Counsel

Some clients are too lazy or too intimidated to ask a lot of questions, preferring to assume their attorney will handle all the necessary details to their satisfaction. Do not fall into this trap. Remember, the only dumb question is the one you *don't* ask. So ask all the questions you want. The following 25 are a good core list.

25 Questions You Should Ask Your Divorce Attorney:

1. How long will the process take and what factors affect the process?
2. What is your fee, and how much will the process probably cost me?
3. How much of what I "want" will I likely get if the case goes to trial (as opposed to settling)?
4. What lifestyle changes should I expect to make in the near future?
5. Will I have to move out of the house/downsize?
6. How much child support will I pay/receive?
7. How much in maintenance/alimony will I pay/receive?
8. Under what conditions will I have to give up one of the cars?
9. What things could cause me to lose custody of my children?
10. What is likely to happen to the marital debt?
11. What debt must I consider marital?
12. What are marital assets?
13. How does the court decide to divide the assets?
14. How does the court decide custody and visitation?

15. In what way will my children be involved in the process of deciding custody and visitation?
16. What should I do with any money that I have in the bank?
17. What should I do with any stocks/ investments/ properties?
18. What documents will I need to proceed?
19. How do I keep my spouse from getting all of the assets?
20. What do I need to communicate to the court to obtain the best result?
21. What assets will the court likely award to me?
22. What am I likely to have in terms of assets when the divorce is final?
23. What happens to our assets while the divorce is pending?
24. What happens to the children, in terms of custody, while the divorce is pending?
25. How should I respond if I believe my spouse is hiding assets?

Divorce attorneys see it time and time again: clients who end up being their own worst enemies because of the numerous mistakes they make in handling their marital problems. In fact, many clients make their biggest mistakes before they even set foot in a lawyer's office. Below, I've listed some of the biggest pre-divorce mistakes in the hopes that you will avoid some of these same pitfalls.

11 Biggest Pre-Divorce Mistakes You Should Avoid:

1. Not going to counseling early on when problems arise, and not following the counselor's recommendations
2. Not viewing the relationship/marriage as needing to be reciprocal/ mutually beneficial
3. Not thinking through/planning for the financial consequences
4. Not thinking through/planning for the emotional turmoil
5. Filing for divorce too soon
6. Filing for divorce too late
7. Not putting aside necessary funds
8. Not telling your lawyer important information until the 11th hour
9. Not gathering information regarding assets
10. Drawing down pension

11. Discontinuing support/contribution to the children, household expenses, and marital debt.

Many divorce litigants continue their string of mistakes once they get into court. Some African-American clients especially can be guilty of bad or disruptive behavior that can negatively impact the desired outcome of their cases. African-Americans need coaching on the proper way to present themselves in a court environment. They need guidance on the appropriate style of dress, courtroom demeanor, communication style, and other tips for fighting a successful court battle. Other clients may experience problems because they are unfamiliar with or distrustful of the legal system or because of their excessive anger toward their spouse. Regardless, when in court, a certain level of decorum is expected. The list below should help you stay on your p's and q's.

9 Things You Absolutely Should NOT Do in Court:

1. Bring your boyfriend/girlfriend to court.
2. Bring your children to court (unless the judge or your attorney specifically instructs you to do so).
3. Interrupt the other litigant or opposing counsel while they are talking.
4. Argue with the judge.
5. Interrupt your attorney when they are paying attention in court to what the judge or opposing counsel is saying. (Your attorney can't listen to you and someone else at the same time. Write down your thoughts. Before your attorney responds to the judge or opposing counsel, pass the note to him or her.)
6. Fail to respond to the questions asked when testifying. (Answer the questions asked, not the questions you wish were asked.)
7. Come to court looking disheveled.
8. Visibly react to what your spouse says.
9. Focus on "what a bad person" your spouse is.

Once the court finalizes the divorce, you might assume both parties are through tormenting each other and are ready to put the past behind them. If so, you would be wrong. Reality is generally just the opposite. Due to lingering anger, custody issues, and other personal maladies, clients often make their biggest mistakes post-divorce. This only leads to a continuation of the drama, and delays the healing process. Consider the list below of biggest mistakes to avoid.

14 Biggest Post-Divorce Mistakes That Can Hurt You:

1. Mismanaging your anger or letting anger consume you
2. Viewing the children as "property" rather than accommodating them as human beings with their own needs, thoughts, and feelings
3. Badmouthing the ex to mutual friends
4. Being emotionally unprepared for the "identity crisis" that often occurs after divorce
5. Failing to get enough emotional support from a network of friends and family
6. Excluding from your support network all those who disagree with you and are able to give you a reality check
7. Stewing too long over the failed relationship, not realizing forgiveness means giving up all hope for a better past (If you think you really are the hottest thing since sliced bread, then the breakup was your ex's loss. Why are you so upset?)
8. Forgetting that the more the parties fight, the more the attorney fees accrue
9. Rejecting counseling/therapy to help you cope with mixed emotions
10. Neglecting the terms of the divorce decree and being unprepared for the consequences for violating the decree
11. Procrastinating about removing your ex as a beneficiary on insurance policies, retirement plans, bank accounts, and annuities
12. Avoiding compliance with entry of "Qualified Domestic Relations Order" (QDRO) and payment of the marital portion of retirement proceeds
13. Failing to comply with the court-ordered transfer of items such as personal and real property, and quitclaim deeds
14. Refusing to pay postsecondary educational expenses for children.

9 Sticky Problems and Straight-Up Answers

At every stage of the divorce process, there are two things—drama and questions! Below, I've addressed some common problems clients typically run into pre-, mid- and even post-divorce that I hope will provide some illumination into your own situation.

(1) Husband Refuses to Sign Divorce Papers

After ten years of marriage, I finally had enough of my cheating husband and filed for divorce. Problem is, he's had the papers now for almost three months, but still hasn't signed them. I know he's stalling in hopes I'll change my mind, but I won't, and I'm getting tired of all his little games. Can I move ahead with my divorce anyway, whether or not he signs the papers?

P.K.

Yes, you can. In order to file for divorce, you should have filed a Petition or Complaint for Dissolution of Marriage. If your husband never filed an appearance (officially entering into the case and letting the Court know he has received a copy of your filed request to commence a divorce proceeding) or an answer to the allegations in your Petition or Complaint, you can file a motion requesting a default judgment. Basically, a default judgment asks the court to grant you all of the relief that you requested in your Petition or Complaint for Dissolution of Marriage. The judge signs it, and the signature of your husband is not necessary.

However, your husband may file a document called a *motion to vacate* the default judgment. If he files these papers within **the number of days allowed in your state after the entry of the default judgment**, the court will most likely grant the petition. If your husband has filed an appearance and answer, or if the court grants his motion to vacate the default judgment, you may initiate discovery (send questions that you want your husband to answer regarding property, bank accounts, investments, assets, debts, etc.) You may also file a motion requesting the court to schedule your case for trial. If delay has happened for an extended period because of your husband's inaction, do not hesitate to request an early trial date from the judge.

(2) Man Unsure if He's Divorced

Me and my wife split up about 17 years ago. I stayed in Philadelphia, and she took the kids and moved to Atlanta. When she left, she said she was gonna file for divorce. I assumed she went through with it, even though I never got any legal papers to sign or recall seeing a decree. Besides, I've moved a couple of times, and maybe she didn't have the right address. Anyway, I've met a real nice lady, and we want to get married. She knows I was married before, but she keeps asking if I'm *sure* I'm divorced. I told her, yeah, because I heard somewhere that when a man and woman haven't lived together for 10 straight years they're automatically divorced. Am I right?

T.N.

You are not divorced until a court with jurisdiction enters a Judgment for Dissolution of Marriage or divorce decree. There is no such thing as an "automatic divorce." You should find out whether your spouse has filed for a divorce, or a court in Philadelphia or Atlanta entered a judgment. If your spouse has not filed for divorce, you will need to file for divorce, and you may need to do so in the state where your wife currently resides. *Never* assume that your spouse took care of the business of legally ending the marriage through divorce. Know for yourself. Many court systems now have computerized records that you can easily access. Therefore, you have no excuse for not knowing whether you are legally divorced or still married.

(3) Client Assumed Fee Was Free

My divorce became final about three months ago. I had an excellent attorney who got me a terrific settlement. He cost a small fortune, but he was worth it. Well, a small issue cropped up with my ex over some joint property we share, and I called my attorney and asked him to handle it. He drafted a short letter, sent it to my ex, and resolved the problem. Three weeks later, I got a bill from him for $800! I admit I was shocked. Since my divorce is settled, and I've already paid him a huge sum, I feel he should have handled the letter as a courtesy and not charged me. Shouldn't he have done this for free?

A.S.

No. Whenever you speak with an attorney, make sure you are clear on exactly what the attorney intends to do and what charges there will be, if any. Never assume that the attorney will take an action for free or without charge (*pro bono*).

(4) Deadbeat Dad's in the Doghouse

I'm a divorced dad and my ex-wife has custody of our three kids. I have visitation every other weekend. The last time I stopped over to see them, my ex wouldn't let me in the house because I was late with this month's child support check. She said, "No money, no visitation." I got mad, and we got into a shouting match. I ended up punching a hole in the wall, and she threatened to call the cops if I didn't leave. So I left to keep from catching a case, but I'm fed up with this mess. Can the court help me with this, or should I just send her the check and steer clear until the kids are old enough to come see me?

M.L.

You can file a motion explaining there is a judgment granting you visitation on alternate weekends and that your ex-wife is violating that order. Your ex may file a similar motion stating that you were late with the child support in violation of the judgment, but the court will decide each matter separately. You do not pay child support so that the court will allow you visitation with your children. Many states allow for an automatic deduction of child support from your paycheck or wages to facilitate sending the funds to the primary custodial parent. As a result, the primary custodial parent won't be "upset that the check is late." As well, having the money come directly from your employer to a state clearinghouse is great for accounting purposes. There will always be a record of what you paid in child support.

(5) Soon-to-be Ex-Hubby Wants Her Heirlooms

My husband and I have decided to divorce, and we live in a community property state. I recently inherited some valuable antiques from my grandmother's estate that have been in my family for generations. My husband has already said he wants two of these items in the divorce property settlement. I said, "Over my dead body!" I don't want him to have any of my family's heirlooms. Can I do anything to prevent this?

F.T.

Even in a community property state, the law considers as separate property any items received through inheritance. Neither party has a right to claim any portion of property obtained through inheritance during the marriage.

(6) Moral Mom Says "No" to New Honey Tucking Kids In

After 15 years of marriage, my husband came home from work one day and told me he wanted a divorce. Just like that. After a long and bitter battle, I got the house, car and custody of our two kids, and he got his freedom and overnight visitation once a month. To make a long story short, my ex now has a new live-in girlfriend ten years his junior! That means she's there on the weekends my kids sleep over. This really bothered me, so I talked to my pastor, and he said it was my responsibility as a Christian woman and mother to protect my children from willful sinners. He said as long as my ex and his girlfriend are living in sin, I should not allow the children to stay overnight at his house, no matter what the court decrees. I'm a God-fearing woman, and I want to do what's right. Can the court force me to put my children in a morally unsafe environment?

C.V.

Yes, it can. Unless you can show a specific harmful effect that your ex-husband's cohabitation is having on your children, the court, most likely, will not force your ex-husband to make certain that his girlfriend does not stay overnight when your children are visiting and will order you to comply with the visitation schedule. However, you may be able to negotiate with your ex-husband regarding visitation. Even though you may not have enough evidence to win your argument regarding the girlfriend, the process itself may be lengthy enough and costly enough that your ex-husband may rather avoid the fight altogether and comply with your wishes regarding the girlfriend.

With regard to your religious beliefs, moral and legal issues often clash. In the African-American community, church pastors often have significant influence over members of their congregations, so it is understandable that you would want to heed your pastor's counsel. Though you may feel the example your husband is setting for the children undermines your moral teachings, as a Christian woman you should also learn to step back and let God handle the situation. Remember that when you avail yourself of "Caesar's court," you get "Caesar's results" which may be morally inconsistent with your personal and spiritual views.

(7) Good Christian Sister Wants Ex Kicked Out

Does the Bible sanction divorce? My husband and I divorced last year after 21 years of marriage. He didn't attend church much before we got married, but has since become a regular and active member. I was really happy about his move, as this has been my church home since I was a little girl. When we got married, I really expected it to last until "death do us part," but my husband had other ideas. When he left, of course, people at the church took sides, with the majority making me feel our breakup was all *my* fault. It's gotten worse now that my ex-husband is newly engaged, and has started bringing his new fiancée to the same Sunday service I attend. It galls me to the bone when I see them sit together and other church members who know what he did to me greeting and talking to them as if nothing ever happened! I feel totally betrayed. I was a member here long before he was. I think the church should support me, and my ex-husband and his new honey should find a new church. Am I being unreasonable?

L.D.

Theologians may argue about why Moses granted bills of divorce. Therefore, I will leave the theological questions for the scholars to debate. The problem posed is a common one, and it has no legal answer. No judge can order your friends to remain loyal to you. The bottom line is that the church is open to everyone. So you will have to decide whether you want to remain at that church or go somewhere else. It also sounds like you might benefit from some counseling.

(8) Divorce Has Son Spinning Out of Control

My husband and I got divorced three years ago. Our son was 13 at the time, and the court awarded me custody. Because his father travels extensively on business, my son only sees him one weekend a month. Since my ex-husband moved out, my son has been increasingly hard to handle. He talks back and is very disrespectful when he's not holed up in his room playing video games. His grades have slipped in school, and he's started hanging out with some older neighborhood boys whom I'm afraid will get him into trouble. Now my son says he wants to go live with his father. In truth, my ex always was the better disciplinarian, but I know his work schedule isn't conducive to him being a full-time parent. I know my son blamed me for his father and me getting a divorce, but he can't still be brooding about that after all this time, can he? I'm at my wit's end. What can I do to alleviate this situation?

G.W.

This situation is not uncommon in the African-American community. There are no scientific reasons for when and why it occurs, but it happens a lot with teenage boys. Your son wants to be around his father more, and it sounds like you would be open to him living with his father if dad's work schedule permitted it. If dad cannot take him on a full-time basis, then talk with him about spending more time with your son. Ask him to suggest other family members or trusted male friends whom he would feel comfortable serving as role models in his absence. If your ex won't or can't change his work schedule, and he's unable to talk your son into behaving better, then your only realistic option is to find more effective ways to discipline your son. His father may be able to help you with this by offering suggested boundaries and punishments.

(9) Daddy Wants DNA Tests

My husband and I are in the process of getting a divorce, and he's demanding paternity tests for all four of our children to "make sure" they're really his. He says he's not paying child support for some other man's bastard. I thought since his name was on all their birth certificates as the father that was significant proof of paternity, but he's insistent. The only problem is, he *isn't* the father of my second child—his brother is. You can imagine the effect such a revelation would have on the family, not to mention the damage it would do to my husband's relationship with his brother! Besides, I'm afraid he'll follow through on his threat not to pay child support for a child that's not his. Can I do anything to prevent the paternity testing or force him to pay support regardless of the results?

B.R.

Laws vary by state, but generally speaking, the legal question here is whether your state permits the father to demand a DNA test under these facts, and whether the law in your state will recognize the results at this time. You need to seek the advice of an attorney in your state. However, regardless of the legal result in your case, you have a big non-legal issue: how will you repair the relationship between you and your children? I think the best approach is humbly to acknowledge your mistake. It is inevitable that there will be damage done to your family. Do you feel you owe your husband an explanation about your affair with his brother? Your focus seems to be more on hiding the truth than telling the truth. Understandably, who would want a court to mandate them to support a child they did not father?

Up Next

Divorce is about two things: child custody and money, though not always in that order. In the discovery phase of your divorce, you will have to disclose your assets and liabilities—including debts and current expenses—and your spouse will have to do the same. This helps the judge gain a true picture of the litigants' financial state with regard to the property settlement. As such, any assets you fail to disclose can cause you untold drama in the thick of a heated divorce. In the next section, I discuss the division of marital property and show you some practical ways to identify and appraise your personal assets.

Chapter 10

Dividing Your
Marital Property

A Financial and Asset Accounting

How much money do you have? What do you own? What is actually yours? What things do you own, of which your spouse is unaware?

Occasionally, nearly everyone faces questions of financial accountability. The student who applies for college financial aid; the budding entrepreneur who approaches a bank officer or venture capitalist for a loan; a single parent who applies for food stamps; the uninsured medical patient who seeks admission to the hospital; the homebuyer who seeks prequalification from a mortgage lender—any of these occasions requires a person to present some measure of financial accountability.

Your Range of Assets

The divorce process requires the parties to disclose fully all assets acquired before and during the marriage. In fact, the scope of financial accountability required of divorce litigants is extensive and extremely detailed. The process is sweeping; it gets *all up* in your financial business. It exposes you totally—both your assets and your liabilities. Further, you must become transparent... as though the FBI or the IRS were investigating you. Divorce is synonymous with financial drama. So prepare yourself for how vulnerable you will feel during discovery.

Let's get into the specifics of the type of financial accounting the divorce process will bring to bear on your life. You will likely be required to provide the following information about yourself and your spouse:

1) Personal Information (name, addresses, birth date, etc.)
2) Employment history
3) Education
4) Marriage and marital history
5) Your children with your spouse and other children
6) Income from all sources
7) Joint assets, owned by both husband and wife, including a description and value of all assets
8) Retirement accounts
9) Husband's assets, owned by the husband alone
10) Wife's assets, owned by the wife alone
11) Assets transferred (normally within 3 or 5 years; whatever your state requires)
12) Related documents (Tax Returns, Payroll, W2s, Deeds, Mortgages, Auto Titles, etc.)
13) Inheritances
14) Insurance policies
15) Business interests
16) Vehicle titles
17) Trust documents
18) Checking, Savings, and CD's
19) Jewelry and Furs.

Methods of Gathering Information

Refer to the Assets Form of the Financial Affidavit in the Appendix (p. 258) for a related form to use when gathering your asset data. The discovery forms may differ from state to state. However, they all attempt to accomplish the same goal: provide a comprehensive and detailed analysis of the financial state (and potential future earning power) of divorce litigants. You will have to disclose this information in accordance with the state laws where you filed for divorce. Once you survey the financial forms, you will immediately realize the process of financial discovery in divorce is no joke. The court wants you to disclose everything.

Some general thoughts are in order. A good divorce attorney will carefully question a client about the money and assets in the marital estate. Make yourself a running list of everything. Sometimes couples accumulate a lot of things over the years of the relationship. Most do not even know or remember all of their possessions. Parenthetically, it is why insurance companies encourage policyholders to videotape everything in their possession. Shoot the pictures, describe the belongings and assign a dollar figure to the current value of the assets. Record everything inside and outside the house. Think about big things, small things, obvious things, and inconspicuous things. Think about items having a sentimental value and items you would rather just throw away. Go through every dresser, drawer, and closet. Review all your papers and documents. Keep monthly statements of all your bank accounts and credit cards. Do not forget to check your safe deposit box. Think about retirement plans on the job and that extra $50,000 life insurance benefit the employer has set aside.

Gathering this kind of information will help your attorney gain a true picture of what is going on in your life. During the divorce process, put everything on the table. As the process equitably divides the assets, you may surprise yourself with some useful bargaining chips. A small piece of very sentimental jewelry, or an almost forgotten, rusty antique car your spouse stores in the mechanic's garage down the street, can make a great difference.

The Drama of Discovery

Upon initial consultation with a divorce attorney about the requirements of discovery, some clients may have second thoughts about going through a divorce. Is the intrusive financial invasion worth it, especially when you probably will have to relinquish some of your assets? You must decide the best course to take for you and your children.

The discovery process is major drama. For instance, not many women understand why they must reveal how often they get their hair and nails done! Don't get offended when you must list every piece of jewelry you own—even the pieces your deceased mother left you. Men, don't be shocked when you have to reveal whom you lend and give money to (yes, even to other "female friends"). Also, don't forget to disclose how much money you've lost over the last year gambling every payday. Include how much you spend weekly on your booze with your buddies! The divorce court wants to know it *all*.

Of course, to avoid some of the drama of dividing assets and allocating liabilities, some couples choose the do-it-yourself route rather than place these matters into the hands of the judge, which may result in an unpredictable outcome. Before choosing this route, consult your attorney who can set the general parameters for negotiating with your spouse. For instance, the attorney can advise you about the applicable standards for property division in your state.

Here are some tips for those who choose to negotiate a property settlement with their spouse:

1) Take off the table any property you or your spouse acquired prior to getting married. Do the same with inherited property and gifts;

2) Stake your claim on any particular items you desire to retain for yourself after the divorce. Make a clear and reasonable list;

3) You and your spouse should exchange lists and review each other's wishes;

4) Discuss areas and items of disagreement with your spouse. Compromise in a simple way that is less emotionally taxing;

5) If possible, give your lawyers an agreement signed by you and your spouse dealing with property issues. The attorneys will know how to process it from this point forward.[23]

Reasonably speaking, if a couple is able to negotiate a property settlement independently, the odds are they could possibly reconcile the marital relationship. I am sure the couple would ask themselves, "If we could resolve a property settlement without all the drama, why are we in divorce court in the first place?" Divorce proceedings require negotiation and settlement. So does an "ideal" marriage.

Your Liabilities

In life, there are savers and spenders. Which one are you? Full financial disclosure in divorce deals with both assets and liabilities. Just as the court

---

[23] See, Mike Broemmel, "How to Divide the Assets in a Divorce," March 1, 2013, http://www.ehow.com/how_2302800_divide-assets-divorce.html.

Or, Tracy B. Stewart, "Who Gets What? Dividing Property During Divorce," March 1, 2013, https://www.institutedfa.com/Public.php?Articles-Dividing-Property-during-Divorce-24.

requires you to reveal what you own, it also requires you to list your debts and current expenses—all of them.

Usually, one of the divorced parties has to pay some sort of support to the other, as well as support the parties' children. The amount may vary from state to state. The judge will make the determination and will likely base the amount on factors related to income, assets, and liabilities. Thus, it is important a divorce litigant give a true picture of expenses and liabilities.

Divorce proceedings demand that each spouse present and attest to the accuracy of their financial condition. The court gets deep into your financial business. Sometimes, the discovery process gets intensely personal, intrusive, offensive, and embarrassing. This intrusive process is an added incentive for a couple to work through most of the important financial issues prior to a trial. A good lawyer who is protecting the interests of your spouse can drag you through living and legal hell during discovery and in the court. Do your best to avoid this drama.

Track Your Debts

The method of gathering information to determine a person's liabilities and expenses is similar to the process of determining one's assets. You can find a detailed **Liabilities Form** of the Financial Affidavit in the Appendix (p. 261).

Here we list the general categories related to liabilities. Both husband and wife must state liabilities and debts, separately or jointly due, which should include:

1. Mandatory and regular deductions from your paycheck
2. Income taxes (federal, state, local)
3. Monthly expenses
   a. Household
   b. Transportation
   c. Personal
   d. Miscellaneous
4. Liabilities
   a. Bank/credit union loans
   b. Charge/credit card accounts

   c. Vehicle notes

   d. Student loans

 5. Mortgages on real estate

 6. Child support

 7. Money you owe (unsecured)

 8. Judgments

 9. Contingent liabilities; co-signed obligations

10. Bankruptcy

11. Other

Each category listed above has standardized subcategories for monthly expenses. Usually, the court will provide an affidavit in the form of a Disclosure Statement for you to complete (see p. 250).

Is your marriage headed for an impending divorce? If so, it is important for you to track the living expenses of you and your spouse. Start the process as soon as you can. Review your financial records for the preceding two or three years to the present. Try to remember everything you spent and provide estimates where you lack specific amounts. If you have a separation prior to divorce, track how you spend, donate, or give away your money. Get a handle on how your finances flow as someone who is now functionally single. Avoid incurring new and unnecessary debt. For the drama coming, save and safeguard all the money you can in a "rainy day" fund. You'll be glad you did.

Act Now 10 – Dividing Your Marital Property

The following tips may help you as you work your way through the discovery process.

 1) **Review the personal information and disclosure forms.** (See the Assets and Liabilities forms in the Appendix.) Begin completing them. Remember, you must provide detailed answers; generalities will not suffice.

 2) **Give your complete financial picture.** Hopefully, you will provide full documentation in detail. If you trust the attorney you retained, disclosure should not be an issue. Full disclosure at the beginning minimizes drama later. In some states, a spouse can suffer court sanctions, which may include monetary fines or preventing a witness

from testifying at trial for failing to disclose certain information about assets in their possession or control. Also, make sure you record the full names of your spouse's family members, as some spouses hide money in the names of their relatives.

3) **Consult with a financial advisor.** Your advisor can become your sounding board for financial matters as you progress through divorce proceedings. Be sure to ask about ways to claim all legitimate expenses for tax purposes.

4) **Make a budget as a functioning single person.** Try your best to keep the budget you make. Avoid short-term fixes like borrowing from payday loan sources. Usually, they just add to your financial drama.

5) **Use a credit or debit card if possible.** The card will help you keep track of where your money goes. Be sure to pay as many of the debts as possible in this way.

6) **Do not destroy or dispose of things belonging to your mate.** Your spite may bite you in court.

Up Next

Awareness of your financial realities will emerge as your divorce proceedings transpire. Gaining keen sensitivity in this area is good because a raised consciousness about financial matters will help prepare you for your future as a divorcee. A divorce often decreases the standard of living for both parties. Some even describe it as economic suicide. Therefore, you must prepare yourself to cope with the overcast days inevitably coming when your divorce is complete. The next section will help you think through some of these dynamics, so that you, as a divorcee, can survive the drama of financial blues.

Chapter 11

Your New
Financial Reality

The Financial Blues

Abuse comes in many forms, and financial exploitation is one of them. A wife may frequently cower to her husband's overbearing and controlling demands. I recall the story of a particularly bitter divorce of Mrs. Smith. Family and friends attested to how the husband often browbeat his wife and played psychological games with her. Even though each party earned a six-figure salary, the family only owned one car, and the husband refused to allow his wife to purchase a second. Additionally, he refused to let her use the car without his permission. The neighbors often saw her at the bus stop taking the children to various activities.

Well, during the divorce proceedings of Mr. and Mrs. Smith, their respective lawyers got together and worked out a fair financial settlement, one the judge considered reasonable. However, later the husband–knowing he would no longer exercise the same control over his wife–changed his mind. The judge called for a conference with the attorneys in his chambers and asked the husband's attorney to explain his client's sudden change in position. The attorney said his client was obstinate and refused to accept the proposed settlement, even upon the advice of counsel. The judge became furious. With a few choice words, he told the husband's attorney that his client better think twice about the proposed financial settlement or risk facing a different outcome at the end of a full trial and warned that if the matter ended up in his hands, things might not look too good for the husband.

Both attorneys reported to their respective clients their discussion in chambers, and the judge's agitation over the husband's change of heart. The husband dug in, and eventually the wife caved. She refused to listen to her attorney or to his report of the judge's informal sentiment.

Why did she cave? Her spouse's psychological manipulation drained her emotions and mentally burned her out. After years of repeatedly yielding to her overpowering spouse, she simply wanted out. Her lawyer tried to convince her to stand firm. He assured her the impending decision was leaning in her direction and the judge could potentially award her thousands of dollars—far more than her husband wanted her to have. Nevertheless, the wife would not cooperate and agreed to her husband's unreasonable demands for the sake of "peace." Ironically, this wife sought to avoid the drama of a single-day trial, and in the process, caused herself years of financial drama and financial blues. Though this woman needed the money, she abandoned any hope of getting her fair share. Her husband walked away with the disproportionate share of the marital estate. Perhaps the attorney should also have suggested a good therapist for his client. She needed one.

One lesson to learn from this unfortunate incident is this: divorce-seeking clients should choose what kind of drama they want to endure. Not all drama is bad for you. Another lesson warns against being hasty and unwise. A spouse should not add to their financial blues in the heat of divorce negotiations. If divorce proceedings reach the stage of an intense court battle, and your spouse is stubbornly digging in, give the fight your best shot—especially when your attorney advises you to do so, and you learn the judge is leaning your way!

Money Versus Peace

As previously stated, divorce is about children and money, but not always in that order. When it comes to how a court may divide the assets, a divorce can break you or make you. The financial blues can set in quickly, resulting in a lower standard of living for both parties. One counselor suggests it is best for a couple at the beginning of a marriage to make purchases based on only one income. If divorce occurs, the practice could help lessen the financial blow. I am certain many divorced persons, in hindsight, would agree.

Differences over money and finances also cause trouble in many marriages. In a divorce, a lot of tension may swirl around money and other assets of financial value like the family home. Our law firm once represented a wife in her 40's, married for 9 years to a husband in his 50's. The husband accused his wife of cheating and filed for divorce. Both their names were on the deed to the house. However, her name alone was on the note, which affected her credit and made her financially accountable to the lender. Due to the economic recession, the home mortgage was "upside down," that is, the balance owed on the house was greater than its appraised value. The wife wanted to sell the house so she could move on with her life, but her husband opposed selling, even though his name was not on the note. Selling the house would cost him nothing, yet he refused because he was vindictive and simply wanted to stall the sale to bring as much misery as possible to his wife.

Such behavior frequently happens in divorces. One party leverages the advantage of money and assets in order to punish the other spouse. The responsibility of your attorney is to secure for you the best possible deal in the divorce. Your lawyer will take into consideration all your interests—past, present, and future—and seek an equitable share of the marital estate on your behalf. A good attorney may not get all you desire, but he or she will negotiate with nerves of steel. Unless the negotiations begin to destroy you on the inside or have the potential of jeopardizing your health and welfare, do not cave. The fight may be worth it.

Frequently, a party who is motivated to seek more than an equitable share of money and assets from a divorce settlement may sacrifice peace in the relationship and peace of mind. Money and the peace work in inverse proportions to one another. Holding out for more money may mean you risk losing some peace. Accepting less money, on the other hand, may mean you gain more peace. (See the chart below.)

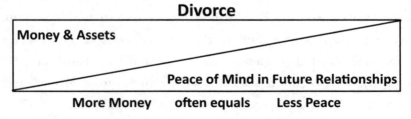

Divorce

Money & Assets	
	Peace of Mind in Future Relationships

More Money   often equals   Less Peace

Drawing attention to the above should not dissuade you from getting all you are entitled in your divorce settlement. I mean only to warn you about the drama during divorce negotiations and trials. Emotionally and psychologically, those times can unravel the best of persons.

As a formerly loving wife whose "low-life SOB" abused and dumped her—and who now feels duped, angry and vengeful—you may unleash your attorney to go for your spouse's jugular. Know that such feelings are "normal" and are expected under the circumstances. However, your attorney may know from experience that "snakes" such as your husband will use both money and power to try to "finish you off." During the divorce proceedings, your attorney may notice you are going through all kinds of personal and emotional struggles. Your demeanor is changing. Your thinking is becoming irrational, and your health is deteriorating. Your attorney is personally witnessing a downward spiral of your life, a meltdown. Her human concern kicks in, and she tactfully offers you some simple advice: "Take this latest offer. Settle for a little less, and get the man out of your head and your life. If you continue on this course, you may end up with a little more money, but wreck your health in the process. If this is the outcome, what have you and your children really gained?"

Any divorce client should carefully consider such counsel. The notion of throwing in the towel in a brutal fight may seem tasteless. However, such advice may actually save further drama and even your life. The manager of a boxer will not risk the life of his fighter by delaying the inevitable. Remember the old saying, "He who lives to run away, lives to fight another day." If your situation in divorce reduces your options to choosing either more money or more peace, wisdom might direct you to choose the latter. At any rate, listen carefully to your attorney. You are paying for sound advice, which you should not hastily disregard.

Be advised, however, that a litigant can never "appeal" a settlement because, by definition, a settlement means that both parties have agreed to the terms. Litigants often settle for terms they aren't happy with, because they wish to end the continued cost and stress of ongoing litigation. On the other hand, a litigant may *appeal* a final judgment or ruling made by the judge. Let's face it: at the end of a trial, one party may feel the judge listened carefully and arrived at the right decision—whether the issue was custody, visitation or division of property—while the other side strongly disagrees. If you decide an appeal is in order, you must timely file the papers in accordance with the laws of your state. Also, be prepared to pay more money beyond what you have invested for the trial.

Where's My Money?

The repercussions of a divorce may result in economic suicide. Divorce court reveals just how much materialism pervades life in American society. In such instances, race or culture does not matter. Usually, in the context of divorce and finances, the only color that matters is green. Despite the close relationship of a marriage, at the end of the day, all that matters to some litigants is, "Where's my money?" Some divorce parties do not care one bit that a divorce may reduce their spouse to relative financial crumbs or about the emotional well-being of the children. Yet, a divorce can significantly alter the lifestyle of all family members. Be prepared. Your kids may ask gut-wrenching questions about provisions or their needs, which you cannot answer.

In marriage, two partners once supported a single household with combined incomes. However, divorce creates two independent households. The single income of each divorced party must now primarily support his or her own personal household. The bills they once shared remain the same or increase, while the income of the whole dwindles. Such situations create financial blues! Some divorce parties must learn to live on half of their previous income. In the case of child support, one party must now seek to support two households. Discouragement and depression can easily set in.

Do not forget the IRS and your federal income taxes. Many couples submit income tax returns under the status of "Married, filing jointly." However, once you divorce, your filing status will be different. Depending on your income, the government probably will have you paying more taxes at the end of the year. If you think you need some tax advice, I recommend you consult a tax accountant. You will have to train yourself to think differently about your income and expenses.

At the beginning of this section, I told the story of the overbearing husband who dug in and the cowering wife who caved during divorce negotiations. Another side deserves mentioning here: the lawyers. As expected, the woman's attorney was furious and in a bind. By continuing to represent the wife, the attorney looked like a fool before the judge, the other attorney, and the woman's husband. However, at this late stage, he could not withdraw from the case, even though he knew his client was making a terrible mistake.

Fortunately, this wise attorney knew the lay of drama-land. Given her emotional state, he knew a few months down the road his client might have regrets. However, by then, the only party she would be able to sue would be the very attorney who had tried unsuccessfully to protect her interests. Therefore, to protect himself, the attorney had his client sign a disclaimer stating she fully understood that she was entitled to, and would likely receive, more after the trial than she was accepting at the time. Further, he insisted the client put in writing that she fully understood the financial repercussions of not allowing the judge to divide the couple's marital assets more equitably. As a condition of the attorney's continued representation, he required the client to agree to hold the attorney and his law firm harmless from any errors or omissions.

Financial Tools: Yours and Your Spouse's

How do divorcees take charge of their financial future? Avoiding the blues is an important step. Another step is learning to think differently when it comes to financial matters. Primarily it means learning to think of yourself *first*, and as a single entity. Then you have to know how to separate yourself from emotional ties influencing financial areas. Certain tools can help you in this process.

Married life directs a person to turn financial thinking from the "me" and "mine" to "we" and "ours," as financial independence turns into financial interdependence with your spouse. On the other hand, the financial thinking of a divorcee flows back toward independence. The reality is that divorced spouses are financially responsible for their own survival. Perhaps a lot of time has transpired since you last thought about yourself as a sole provider. Consequently, you now have to adjust your thinking in this area so you can keep pace with your emerging financial responsibilities. You are not alone—thousands of divorcees face the same challenge.

Managing Your Awarded Assets

Divorcee: take charge of your new financial reality. Grab the bull by the horns and prepare yourself for a rocky ride. Your money and earning power belong to you alone—from the day your divorce becomes final. You no longer have a joint relationship. You no longer have a 50/50 partner. No longer must you give your spouse an account of your finances. The family meetings are over. How you deal with your money is up to you. You and no one else determine whether you fail or succeed in your course of independence. It's time to prepare for a period of financial adjustment.

As is in most divorce cases, the judge may have awarded you certain assets, alimony, and child support. However, as a divorcee, the way in which you manage those funds is in your court alone. Your personal courage and skill in the financial arena will determine whether you fall or rise to the challenge. Give yourself a goal to thrive, not just survive. Try to use the circumstances of your divorce to explore new financial opportunities and generate some new money. Use a financial planner to assist you, if needed. A little extra cash here and there can lessen some of the drama of your divorce.

You should immediately make an especially smart move: prevent your ex from having access to your money. Change or close any joint financial accounts you had with your spouse. Do this with checking and savings accounts. Do this with credit and debit cards. Revise your pension plans, stocks and bonds, etc., to reflect your new single status. Do not forget to remove the name of your spouse as beneficiary from insurance policies. Change vehicle titles, retirement accounts, powers of attorney, last wills & testaments, trusts, and deeds. Do whatever it takes to insure you can navigate your financial world without your former married status impeding your progress. Certain kinds of financial ventures will require you to respond quickly. You may regret missing a great investment opportunity simply because you did not take the time to untangle yourself financially from your spouse. You do not want the financial baggage of your spouse to bog down your business dealings or throw a monkey wrench into your plans. If necessary, fax or mail your divorce decree to your creditors. As much as possible, manage your emotions as you seek to negotiate repayment of your debts.

Act Now 11 – Your New Financial Reality

Here are some ways to avoid the drama of financial blues in divorce.

1) **Listen to your attorney's counsel about the law and financial parameters.** Divorce settlements in your state and your specific situation may vary from those in other jurisdictions. An attorney knows the

general rules. Are you asking for too much? Are you settling for too little? Allow your attorney to keep you in the ballpark.

2) **Let your attorney negotiate when an abusive marriage has weakened your will.** Recognize you may not be able to negotiate a fair divorce settlement with a person who sees you as less than an equal. When a spouse browbeats you, tell them: "I will check with my attorney." Keep in mind that if your spouse is paying your fees, it will cost them each time you consult with your attorney. This can be a financial incentive for an overbearing spouse to stop the drama of pressuring you to accept less than what you deserve.

3) **Let the court fight the money battle.** A spouse can continue to abuse his ex by manipulating her by deliberately withholding their alimony and support. Avoid this drama. Allow your attorney to run interference on your behalf rather than engaging your spouse about money that is due.

4) **Block a day on your calendar to reorganize your financial world.** Reshape your financial reality to fit your single status. Plan first, and then execute as soon as possible.

Up Next

The court will insure the support of the children in a divorce. The judge will make the decision despite the challenging circumstances of the husband and wife. Individual states have laws, rules, and guidelines that govern the amount of support received for children of divorced or separated parents. Divorced couples do themselves a favor when they carefully consider issues related to child support in the context of their divorce. To avoid some of the drama in this area, each parent should place the welfare of their children above all else. Parents should lean toward financial graciousness rather than seeking simply to adhere to the strict construction of the law. The next section tackles the issues of child support in divorce and separation.

Chapter 12

Your Children's Support

Not Enough, Brother!

"Where there is good understanding, there is no room for misunderstanding."

This wise saying lessens the drama associated with child support in a separation or divorce. Fathers take heed since, overwhelmingly, fathers are the ones who pay child support. Right up front, I clearly advise "daddies" to avoid the drama. Get yourself a good understanding of your financial responsibilities relative to your children. Clarity in this matter is important, especially in regards to the married versus the unmarried.

If a father is unmarried, and has the slightest doubt about whether or not the child is his, he should request a DNA test in a timely manner. What is "timely" will vary according to your state or jurisdiction. On the other hand, if the father is married to the mother at the time of birth, a presumption exists he is the father of the child. Usually, that presumption is rebuttable if the father requests a timely DNA test. In any event, black men should not wait until the child is older before questioning paternity. Understand that the social and financial realities of your children link tightly with their mother. If she is without transportation, so are the children. If she has no lights in the house, the children are also in the dark. So early on, parents need to resolve the issue of paternity for the sake of the children, themselves, and the family's stability.

When it comes to child support, a father should talk to the mother of his children and agree on a budget. Consider the needs of your children and learn the child-support laws of your home state. At the earliest time possible, talk to an attorney to get the real deal. Establish your paternity, be proactive, and take the first step with the court.

The state or court system does not always initiate child support. In some instances, divorcing or custodial parties arrange for child support outside of the legal system. View the court system, however, as more reliable for accounting purposes and enforcing any agreement of the parties through an order signed by the judge. Be prepared: you may think the money you give your divorced or separated partner for your children is adequate. However, your former lover and mother of your children may think your contribution is meeting less than 50 percent of the child's needs. In reality, the true price tag may actually be more like 125 percent of what you give. In almost every instance, she will likely conclude the support you give is *Not enough, Brother.* The way economic things are going today, the money you give may never be enough. So I advise you, cover yourself and meet your responsibility head on.

Of course, advising most fathers to face courageously the challenge of paying child support is like closing the barn door after the cows have already escaped. The advice comes after the fact. Often, the deeds of some irresponsible fathers have already been committed and the social damage has already occurred. Advice given in these situations is too little, too late. In other words, it has never been the pattern of some black men to think responsibly about the consequences of fathering a child. For instance, did the man think about the consequences of having unprotected sex in the first place? Did he think about the future challenges of fathering children with different women? During the nine months of pregnancy, did he make financial preparations for his child prior to birth or responsibly care for the child's mother during the relationship? The brother who is on the verge of up-and-running from his partner should think about the adage: "It's cheaper to keep her."

In far too many cases, these questions receive negative answers. Thus, when the child support issue surfaces, the barn door has already been open for a while. Sadly, when it comes to supporting children, I usually see too many black fathers displaying the same old irresponsible behavior. Some men simply ignore the financial issue and deprive their children in the process.

I must admit, however, sometimes a responsible and well-meaning father runs into trouble. Consider the case of a certain divorced father who had remarried but was dutifully paying child support to his ex. When the brother fathered a child with his new wife, she began protesting the child support he was paying his first wife. She insisted that he return to court seeking a reduction in his child support payments. Typically, the law does not allow for such a reduction. The court refused his petition, causing financial tension in his marital relationship. Since then, the dilemma has forced the man to walk a tightrope between competing interests, acting as "peacemaker" between the females of two families. More drama ensues.

Reversing a Negative Image

Notwithstanding the tightrope walkers, our community must reverse the prevailing negative image of black men irresponsibly refusing to pay child support. We must instill a pervasive pride in our men. This dignity must begin to sweep through our community so that our men will begin to find pleasure in taking care of their children and the mothers of their children. In doing so, those men who are noncustodial parents will accept the reality that the custodial parent—oftentimes the mother—has a bit more power and authority in raising the children. When the court determines the mother as the custodial parent—absent abuse or neglect—the father should respect the boundaries and remember, "Strong fences can make good neighbors."

Some fathers refuse to pay child support, because they encounter visitation problems when complications arise with the ex about seeing the children. However, never tie visitation rights to child support. For instance, the fact that a man is unemployed and has no money to pay child support does not mean anyone can prevent him from seeing his children. His visitation rights stand, regardless of his financial condition. Some women exploit their children for financial gain when they realize the father is no longer interested in a continued romantic relationship with them. Simply put, he moves on. Using your child to get even or to "kick their father while he's down" will result in consequences beyond measure.

Another major issue in the area of paying child support arises when the ex starts to date. Even though some men can clearly see the way to support their children, they stumble over the obstacle of the new-male factor. Sometimes, an ex will object to his "baby's mama" spending a single dime of child support on another man in her life. Sometimes, a father even delays giving his ex the funds due for the children. In doing so, these fathers cut off their noses to spite their faces. In seeking to punish their exes, these men hurt their own children. It is counter-productive for a father to withhold child support from his own children, because his ex hooks up with another man. Think about it this way: if your ex is doing a good job raising your children, what is the problem? If the other man carries his weight in the family and plays a positive role in their lives, what do you have to lose? So maybe your pride gets hurt a bit. Get over it! You're the one who decided to move on. Should you interfere with her choice to move on also?

Child Support Guidelines

Remember, your state sets the guidelines for child support. Usually, you have to give a percentage of what you earn to support your children. For example, California bases the amount paid for child support on each parent's net disposable monthly income and the amount of time each parent cares for the child.[24] In New Jersey, both parents are responsible for the financial needs of the children based on the contribution of each to the combined income of the family and the relative sharing of household expenses.[25] Illinois has a flat-rate guideline requiring the noncustodial parent to pay 20 percent of his net income for a single child and 28 percent for two children. Sometimes, a state deducts the amount directly from your paycheck. Some states establish a clearinghouse for funds, prior to disbursing payments to the custodial parent. The process helps with recordkeeping to avoid any dispute about what you paid and what she received. When you make your payments in this way, you have met your legal responsibility. You are giving what you are required to give,

---

[24] See, "California Guideline Child Support Calculator User Guide," March 1, 2013, http://www.childsup.ca.gov/LinkClick.aspx?fileticket=2Mp0n3MS4Ug=&tabid=114&mid=800.

[25] See, "Child Support Guidelines," March 1, 2013, http://www.judiciary.state.nj.us/csguide/index.htm.

and your obligation is satisfied. In such cases, so long as your ex properly cares for the children, does it really matter how she manages the finances or with what man she gets involved?

Yes, I know what you are thinking. The story is different if another man is abusing your ex and the children. It is different if she is financially wasteful and doing things with the money inconsistent with the best interests of the children. This situation is a real possibility, and may call for court intervention. However, all things being equal, stay focused on making sure you do your part and everything the court requires of you. Brother, pay your money—on time. Satisfy yourself that you are meeting the needs of your own children. You do not want your flesh and blood to suffer in any way, if it is within your power and control. Then, allow room for some flexibility in the way your ex establishes her new relationship.

Some fathers have the money, but are stingy. In one case, a certain woman worked for a popular entertainer in California. A lover fathered children with her, but they did not marry. Her children attended private school, lived an upscale lifestyle, and lacked for nothing. As time went on, the sister turned bitter about the relationship and ended it. Later, she lost her six-figure job. She knew she could only go to New York or to Europe for work, but the father did not want her to take the children out of state. To his credit, the father was a warm and loving parent, but his work as an insurance consultant required him to travel around the world. On the other hand, to the man's "debit," he only paid $800 a month to support his two children. Since the mother was the primary breadwinner, she decided to seek employment in New York. The father, however, did not want the kids to leave California. When the mother asked her former partner to give her a proposal for keeping the children's quality of life intact, the brother came up empty. He could not find a means for raising the extra dollars to replace the income she had lost. Obviously, as a world-traveling consultant, the brother could have done better, but he did not. He wanted the pride of fatherhood, but he held back on making a greater contribution. The sister did what she had to do for her children. She requested permission from the court to remove the children from California to New York where she had found a job, and the judge agreed. If the father had not been stingy, he probably would have preserved easier access to see his children. He punished himself by being miserly.

Counselors notice that a "guilt factor" is often present when black-man-to-black-man counseling occurs. On the one hand, brothers don't want their children to become shooting crime statistics. On the other hand, they don't always step up to the plate with their resources. Black fathers must be honest. In the area of supporting their children, disproportionately, black mothers have done the lion's share while some black fathers are often little more than "holiday magicians" who only do something for their children on special occasions. Counselors see a lot of this guilt tripping. It should not be the State's burden to underwrite the birth of your child, provide food, housing, and medical insurance. If you are man enough to father a child, be man enough to take care of your child.

Distressed Dads

Certain "changes in circumstances" may occur permitting the court to modify child support legitimately. Such changes may include the loss of employment (involuntarily), fathering another child you are supporting based upon a "court order," or support you pay for a child not living in your household. Be aware. In some jurisdictions, the rule of "first in time, first in line" may apply to your situation. In other words, child support is often determined based upon the birth order of one's children. Each child may not receive an equal share of financial support.

In making child support determinations, sometimes judges are unreasonable. However, often fathers fall behind because they fail to return to court immediately when they have a change in circumstances that decreases their income, like the job laying them off, suffering a job-related injury or becoming incarcerated. Remember, judges do not make the law; they just enforce it. Therefore, if a father finds himself unable to meet his child support obligations, he should file the appropriate court papers as soon as possible, and ask the judge to lower his child support payment or even suspend it until he gets back on his feet.

Consequences for failing to pay child support can be severe. Laws vary by state, but generally speaking, falling behind on your child support obligations can result in wage garnishments, suspension of your driver's license, or suspension or denial of state-granted professional licenses like a barber's or broker's license, etc. Also, remember that jail time might be a possibility if a party refuses to pay child support without justification.

While we are on this money issue, some men who are financially blessed create a lot of drama when their relationships are on the verge of breakup and divorce by doing a bad thing: hiding money and other assets. When a man refuses to share his financial gains with his former and loyal companion at a time when she and the children need it most, he is cruel. He stirs up the drama of anger, hate, resentment, revenge, bitterness, and the like—in both his ex, their children and her extended family. In the midst of the conflict, these men mindlessly escalate the conflict with the spouse and the court. I warn them to take the high road leading to peace with the woman spurned.

The financially well-off husband and father should share finances fairly. If necessary, when resources allow he should provide for his wife. By every possible means, he should support his children. He should do so graciously. He should prevent severely reducing his family's standard of living or consigning them to a state of marginal poverty. He must do the right and good thing.

Some men in the black community earn their money through the "underground economy," in cash. They do so to avoid paying child support. These brothers avoid responsibility for their children by not embracing a "legitimate" job the judicial system can track and attach for child support. Surely, when the divorced man chooses the course of running and hiding from his responsibility, astute attorneys will track the assets. Justice will take a little longer, maybe even years, but it will come. Skilled attorneys will discover and uncover hidden assets. At every turn, they will seize the opportunity to stick it to such a man. On the matter of pure principle, these lawyers will do everything within their power to get justice and money for their divorced or separated female clients. They will make a brother pay and pay dearly. When the courts give you that word—*Not enough, Brother*—the days of your running and hiding are over. The court will make you pay through the nose, whether you like it or not.

Which Kids Are You Supporting?

Many black families support children who are not biologically their own. The practice has existed among people of African descent since the times of slavery. Informal "adoptions," legal adoptions, fostering extended family and neighboring kids from other families are all part of the African-American experience. Black families also support nieces, grandchildren, cousins, and other kin, without reservation of association.

In the context of divorce, the question of child support may boil down to which kids you are supporting. An in-depth analysis would reveal many black families support someone's children in one way or another. However, in the case of a man who has a bunch of dependent children in his life, he should make it his priority to support the children of his marriage or those he has fathered. The practice is primarily a correct action for the man who financially supports his own.

A married man with a "love child" outside the marriage should take care to protect the relationship with his wife. Disruption from this source may occur before, during, or after a divorce. Too many married men have allowed a "love child" to interfere with their marriage and other children. Instead, a man should protect his immediate family relationship without neglecting the outside "love child."

Sister, Make A Stretch

When it comes to paying child support, surprises do happen. Every now and then, the role reverses when the father wins custody. The court will likely order child support to the father. So occasionally, but not very often, the script flips. When it does, the litigant mother usually gets very upset when the court orders her to contribute a fair share of money to the father for the support of the children. Despite the chagrin of the divorcee, she's got to give up the cash.

Compared to her husband, sometimes the wife has greater social and economic exposure. If her marriage breaks down, she finds herself facing a court appearing less sympathetic to her than her husband, whose income and assets are lower than what she possesses. In the area of the children and assets, she faces the daunting prospect of having a judge make the determination her husband should function as the custodial parent, retain possession of the family home, receive child support, and enjoy a substantial monthly maintenance or alimony payment. Though this outcome in divorce does not happen as frequently for wives as it does for husbands, it does occur. Wives should prepare themselves for this possibility.[26]

These circumstances occur sporadically, yet are an increasing possibility in some African-American divorce cases. Times of economic recession and changing or reversed husband-wife roles within society exacerbate this social phenomenon. Numerous women of any color or culture would find it very difficult to support a man financially under any circumstances. Yet a woman would fully expect to receive her husband's financial support since historical and traditional values across our society teach that a man should support a woman. Many women experience a rather foul taste at the thought of having to support a man. The foul taste becomes extremely bitter, even toxic, when the disposition of a divorce results in the woman supporting her ex. Herein psychological, emotional, and social drama abounds.

Some circumstances warrant a wife giving financial support to her husband. Perhaps his long-term job let him go at a time in life when it is difficult for him to retool with marketable skills. Perhaps he terribly and permanently injured himself. Perhaps his physical and mental functions became impaired through the early onset of an illness. These reasons and others may justify a wife lending financial support to her husband. However, while it is one thing for a wife to support her husband under exceptional circumstances, it is quite another thing for her to support her ex due to the financial incompatibility of a marriage. In such a case, the man may turn the success of his high status wife against her. He can easily say she spends too much time away from him and the children, when they need stability in their young lives. And neither should his wife neglect his frequent sexual needs and other conjugal rights.

---

[26] Social and economic forces impact the settlement of some divorces, even in the African-American community. In this realm, something happened to the US economy in 2008 that decreased the living standard of millions in the U.S., and caused repercussions that impaired the global economy: the Great Recession. Everyone, except a small fringe of the population, suffered loss in the Great Recession. These losses affected people in every dimension and status of American life, including black families experiencing divorce. Understandably, the Great Recession increased the exposure of divorced women of a certain social and economic status.

So the husband pits his wife's career against the immediate needs of the family. At least this is his argument on the surface. Sometimes, the hidden agenda is his desire to get his hands on his successful wife's money. Further, he may desire to support the young woman he is now dating on the side when his wife is away on business. So, the husband files for divorce. He thereby forces his wife to choose either her career or her family. She thinks she can manage both, but ultimately realizes that she can't have it both ways.

The litigants and their respective lawyers see no room for compromise. The case goes to trial. Despite the wife putting forth her best legal and emotional appeal, the judge determines it is in the best interest of the children to award custody to the father. This allows him to live in the marital house for the sake of stabilizing the children, and the wife has to move. Moreover, the judge awards the husband $4,000 a month in alimony and child support. The ex-wife is now an every-other-weekend parent.

The judge's ruling shocks the wife and causes her life to crumble before her eyes. If as a divorcee you find yourself in a similar circumstance, somehow, someway, it is imperative you learn to *make a stretch*. You must find the internal resources to rise above your dashed hopes and do your best to help your children even though their father has pulled a sophisticated coup. You must take the high road, even when you think your ex is "nothing better than a dog."

Sister, you can do it.

Yes, a woman—an African-American woman—can support her children and her ex, and do it with grace and dignity. With divine help and the support from close family or friends at your disposal, you can make the adjustments these extreme circumstances dictate. Your children need to know their mother has not rejected or forsaken them, even though their young minds find it difficult to grasp the unfolding social dynamics. Mama is not an evil person, and they should not treat her as a pariah. Daddy has his faults, and hopefully he will correct them over time.

Based on the court ruling, your ex understands he has won an important battle: he got your children and your money. Yet, he must never be allowed to console himself with the perverted thinking he has won the righteous war. The character and behavior you exhibit following your divorce resolution will go a long way toward shaping the ongoing perceptions of others about the events transpiring in your family life.

Act Now 12 – Your Children's Support

Avoid the drama. Fathers, do the right thing, the first time around. Support your children and the mother who cares for them. Mothers, don't be afraid to "make a stretch." Here is some sound counsel for your unique situations.

1) **Pay your child support through the court.** Do not bypass the court by giving the money directly to your ex. Avoid paying child support in cash. If you must do so, get a receipt and keep track of all cash payments. Better still, write a check or get a money order. In court, let your paper trail document that you have made child support payments. You will be glad you did when the mother of your children says otherwise. Protect yourself, and demonstrate your full compliance with the requirements of the court.

2) **Do not involve your children in child support issues.** For example, never say to your child, "I would take you out to eat, but I can't afford to. Your mother takes all my money and leaves me broke."

3) **Do not hide assets during your divorce proceedings.** Discovery of such hidden assets may result in the court penalizing you for violating rules of full discovery regarding income sources.

4) **Secure the best parenting schedule you can.** Tell your attorney to pull out all the stops. Since your ex has custody, you must counter with the ability to visit and parent whenever possible. If you can, get visitation with your children during the summer if your ex has them mostly during the school year. Get yourself the lion's share of annual holidays.

5) **Position yourself to step in if your ex falters.** Ironic circumstances can change the equations in a divorce. When this happens, you will have done yourself a favor by staying prepared to seize the moment to head back to court. Keep yourself armed with information to request a change in the custody arrangement with your children.

6) **Use non-monetary resources to enhance your children's lives.** Not having financial resources is no excuse for not spending quality time with your children. Some activities are free. For example, take your children to the park or library; identify free days at the museum, zoo,

etc. You may think your children always want material things, but in reality, they want time with you. Nothing is more important than time spent with your children.

Up Next

A divorce experience changes family life on both sides of the couple's relationship. Issues arise in divorce affecting the ex, children, parenting, and extended families. We touched on some of these issues as we talked about the personal, legal and financial dimensions of divorce. In the next part of this book, we will explore in depth those issues related to the **family dimension** of divorce.

PART THREE:

The Family Dimension

*In this section, take stock of how family life
—including your former spouse, children, parenting, and in-laws—
will change because of divorce.*

Chapter 13

You and
Your Ex

The Former Mr. and Mrs.

Why do folks marry? The reasons vary, and include such motivations as legal, social, emotional, financial, spiritual, religious, and, very high on the list, sexual.[27] Though in some sectors of our society the idea and form of marriage are evolving, most people desiring marriage seek these things. Marriage is the foundation of family and society with most marriage partners legally binding themselves "till death us do part" in a formal ceremony with witnesses. Conversely, divorce is a main cause of social dysfunction in the African-American community. Many drama-laden social problems are traceable to the breakdown of marriage and the black family. Disrupted male-female relationships spawn all types of social maladies. Miseducation, gangs, drugs, street crime and violence, identity confusion, and other problems significantly arise from the breakdown of

---

[27] In some cultures and societies, marriage revolves around a man attaining exclusive sexual rights over a woman. In effect, the marriages in these societies serve the purpose of blunting the sharp edge of social tension and competition by men for sexual control over the females of their group. Otherwise, vying for sexual prominence exacerbates friction among the men. See, Duran Bell, "Defining Marriage and Legitimacy," *Current Anthropology* 38 (2): 237–254, University of Chicago Press (1997). In a dated and extremely unjust male treatment of females in marriage found in some cultures placing emphasis on the woman's sexual function in marriage—certainly a relationship that should be rejected by all humane persons—the author describes marriage as "a relationship between one or more men (male or female) in severalty to one or more women that provides those men with a demand-right of sexual access within a domestic group and identifies women who bear the obligation of yielding to the demands of those specific men," March 1, 2013, http://www.economics.uci.edu/~dbell/marriageandlegit.pdf. See also, "Marriage," *Wikipedia*, March 1, 2013, http://en.wikipedia.org/wiki/Marriage.

marriage and family life. We can expect such outcomes since marriage is one of society's most essential institutions. Our community needs healthy male-female relationships and the holistic and wholesome upbringing of children that a good marriage affords. We need less of divorce and its drama.

The Mid-Life Divorce

I remember the story of a 50-year-old husband who decided to trash his 30-plus year marriage to his beautiful and devoted wife. As marriages go, from the outside his marriage looked "perfect." From the wife's perspective (and to most other people looking in), the relationship was clicking on all cylinders. The couple had respectful, well-educated and successful children, a home, sufficient finance, and a well-ordered household. Besides, the wife maintained her physical attractiveness. Her gorgeous physique still turned heads in her 50's.

One day the husband came home, walked into the kitchen, and abruptly told his wife he was ending their long-term marriage. He finally found the love of his life in a 35-year-old "hottie" and wanted to divorce. Obviously, his wife became irate. As quick as she could she went to the kitchen drawer, pulled out a claw hammer, and started whacking at her husband's head. She chased him from the house flailing away, trying to "beat the hell" out of him! Her husband barely escaped destruction as he jumped into his car and hurriedly screeched out of the driveway. She never allowed him to re-enter the house. The man was fortunate enough to escape death-by-hammer, get his divorce, and get on with the rest of his life. Even though he willingly gave up most of the marital assets during the divorce proceedings, he still could not understand the continued anger of his hammer-driven wife and never considered the effect his decision would have on the lives of his children. Their response bordered on hatred for their daddy. Whatever the man's reasons for his very irrational behavior, he did a very stupid thing. As an adulterer, he was unfaithful to his wife and unfair. He violated and destroyed his long-standing marriage. And he paid for it.

A black man should ask for advice about the best way to deal with mid-life crisis. Recognize every marriage presents a challenge at some point. Seek counseling to determine whether your marriage is still viable. Making a rash move can generate much drama.

My Baby's Daddy

After dealing with a husband and wife, divorce next concerns the children. Having children by multiple women can play a big factor in marital relationships and divorce. Therefore, overcoming "baby mama drama" can be an equally big challenge.

"My baby's daddy."

Now where did this now-popular terminology come from? When did it catch on? All of a sudden, this descriptive phrase for black male partners has burst into the cultural language of African-Americans.

"He's my baby's daddy." Every woman is saying it—at least it seems that way. She doesn't say, "He's my man." Or, "He's my main man." Or, "He's my boyfriend, my date, my live-in, my steady, my roommate, or my fiancé." She says, "He's my baby's daddy." (And he says, though a little less often, "I'm her baby's daddy.") Younger adults also use this term as an endearment, and find no offensiveness in its use.[28] The term "baby's daddy" is what it is." A time once existed when our community looked askance at sexual liaisons outside of marriage. These sexual liaisons, called "fornication," often resulted in multiple children by different males. Today, the trend in this area may call for a more reality-based socially descriptive term. If I could coin a new term, I would call the practice, *"bornication!"* That is, many children being born outside of marriage. Too many men are fathering children seemingly without regard to any moral code. This is "bornication!"

A cultural shift has occurred. We replace terms we use to describe a primary relationship of female-to-male (such as girlfriend, boyfriend, partner, etc.) with terms (albeit important) referring to a derivative relationship of child-to-parent-to-romantic partner. So, the romantic or significant male in the life of a female is now, "My baby's daddy." In such a situation, divorce and breakup complicate how we view and order or reorder the relationship. So, this one significant male is "...my baby's daddy." And a second significant male is "...my *other* baby's daddy." And this former partner is "...my other two babies' daddy." The males in these relationships become "appendages" to their children's relationship to the mother. The relationship reordering

---

[28] See the video by B-Roc & The Bizz, "That's Just My Baby's Daddy," March 1, 2013, http://www.youtube.com/watch?v=2kKqfPy_cag.

works for a second. However, the kind of drama created by this reordering, or disordering, soon becomes apparent. The children and mothers begin reaping some affliction that better life choices could have avoided.

Let's keep things clear: "My baby's daddy" does not automatically mean, "My husband." Legally, a woman can be married to only one of her "baby's daddies" at a time. Likewise, a man can be married to only one of his "baby's mamas" at a time. Yet, divorce attorneys increasingly deal with parties who have multiple children outside their marriage. In this area, several issues surface in divorce and breakups. The main issue is "paternity." Who fathered this child and to whom does this child belong? Hence, the DNA tests. Paternity deals with children born into marriage or outside of wedlock. The law presumes a child is the offspring of the husband of the child's mother. However, a child may be fathered either by the husband of a wife or by another male in an extramarital relationship with another man's wife. While "baby-mama" drama is high on the list of social dissonance, "My baby's daddy" has other complications.

I often encounter a complicated and explosive drama of "My Baby's Daddy." It happens when a mother fails to identify or clarify to others the true biological parentage of the children. For instance, a child lives with his mother who lives or associates with another man who is not the biological father of the child. Whether the mother is single, married, separated, shackin' or divorced does not matter much. Drama escalates when the biological father discovers his child referring to the husband of his ex (or to her other special man) as "daddy." The biological father gets irate, and accuses the mother of disrespecting and undermining his fatherhood. A similar volatile response erupts when the scenario flips, and a child refers to a woman as "mama," who is not his biological mother.

A litigant should strive to keep in check some of the drama of "My Baby's Daddy" or "My Baby's Mama" by always clarifying to their young children and to others the biological parents of children. Make a distinction between the natural parent of the child and the person who is your special partner, whether or not living with them. And, be sure your children grow to understand the importance of making this distinction, and of using the right terms when describing the relationships.

The Absent Baby's Daddy

An interesting interview took place when the sister showed up at the office wanting a divorce. The attorney asked her a few questions.

"When did you separate?"

"Fifteen years ago."

"When was the last time you saw him?"

"Fifteen years ago!"

"Did he have any relationship with the children?"

"He called them, every now and then."

"How in the world have you been operating and functioning?"

"I thought he was going to file for a divorce."

It's a sad situation, but lawyers see it repeated too often. "Just moving on" is often a black man's issue. In some instances, when the African-American male walks away from the relationship with his wife, he leaves his "baby's mama" and his babies hanging by a thread. And he disappears. He vanishes. He drops beneath the legal and social radar. He financially survives in the sub economy of the streets. Few can contact him or find him unless he wants them to know his whereabouts. Sometimes he moves to another state or across the country. When he wants information, he has his own way of checking on things, but the communication is short and one-way.

A husband or "baby's daddy" can have a mid-life crisis. He is ineffectively dealing with personal and multiple-family issues and just wants to get out, get away from it all. He's thinking about things and going down mental and emotional roads that never before crossed his mind. The brother needs special counseling to help him work his way through the deal, but he doesn't know that. He needs emotional and mental support and some tender and tough-loving care, but the uncontrollable urges within him keep him from opening up. They foster a sense of irresponsibility and recklessness he can't manage on his own, but he's too macho to seek help. So he thinks his best alternative is just to leave and drop out of sight.

A woman whose husband or "baby's daddy" emotionally forsakes her, and who is on the verge of socially abandoning the family, faces a serious dilemma. How should she balance insecurity and shame with continued love and sacrifice? Answers to this question do not come easily. Soul searching is required. Counseling is appropriate, and compassion is always in order. No one can absolutely tell the woman in these circumstances what is right or wrong for her to do. After she has considered every possible issue, her good conscience should guide her.

Let's consider it another way.

"My baby's daddy" can sometimes turn violent. A prominent divorce attorney recalls representing a mother who wanted custody of her teenager from the father. Several years earlier, the mother had split from her husband when their child was young, and had chosen to remarry. The biological "baby's daddy," who had initially won custody of their child, did not want his son raised by the wife's new husband. Such great animosity existed between the two men that, in a confrontational altercation, her husband assaulted the child's biological father. The court convicted him of the assault, and he served time. Problem. Drama.

Now, what happens to visitation rights of the "baby's daddy"? Imagine the tension between the adults and the child on visiting days. The home life of the teen could become very dangerous or destabilized. Then, flip the script. As the teen matures and begins to sort out the history of his own family relationships, what thoughts of vindication might he harbor toward his surrogate daddy for assaulting his biological daddy? In a society of youth rebellion, the surrogate daddy could find himself becoming the victim of a teenager's pent-up emotions and explosive rage. Drama. "Baby's daddy" drama. Mama is just pulling out her hair. Caught in the middle, she doesn't know what to say or do. After all, her second husband assaulted her "baby's daddy," a man she once loved. And her child is now feeling the pain and fear.

The Secret Baby's Daddy

Attorneys tell countless stories about wives who had no clue their husband had fathered a son or daughter out there somewhere. Some of these wives were happily married until a turn of events pulled the cover off their husband's past. Sometimes the uncovering happens during a feud or at a funeral or family reunion. Imagine the shock of a wife who discovers her husband's other child when the county sheriff shows up at her front door with a summons for him to appear in court on a case of child support. So, sister, consider yourself fortunate that you know about the other children of your husband. What you should know, but don't know, can hurt you...at the wrong time.

Guess Who's Coming to the Funeral?

With death comes drama, especially in the African-American experience.

Whether drama comes with the social death of a relationship or drama results from the physical death of a loved-one—whatever the case—death creates drama. Death by divorce and death by physical expiration share similarities. In its own way, each death causes issues to come out.

At the time of a person's death (or shortly before), somebody has to make the funeral arrangements. Somebody has to pay money to bury the deceased. The folks who know the decedent get together to do the obituary. At the start of the service, the family lines up for the processional march with the nearest kinfolks first, then the rest of the family (or very close friends) following in the order of those closest to farthest in their relationship to the deceased. Now in the midst of the emotional loss resulting from a loved one's death, the social drama makes a grand appearance, and it often shows up at the church or the funeral home.

In the African-American tradition, funerals can be revealing. Often, "too much information" can put the family in grief overload. Funerals bring out a lot of trash surrounding marriage and divorce as the event can be a gathering spot for vital family information, if not the culmination of truth when all the most-guarded facts come out. How the family publicly reads the obituary it fashions often uncovers buried family secrets few knew beforehand. In addition, the remarks of friends and family, as well as the preacher's eulogy during the service, may also reveal bits of tantalizing information that sends shock waves through the pews.

This is especially true in the case of a deceased African-American male who may have walked away from a relationship without filing for divorce. This behavior, frequently familiar in the African-American context, often reveals itself at the time of death or at the "funeral." For instance, the primary male to whom the mother was married, and whom she refers to as "My baby's daddy," dies. Before his death, only a few people saw the whole picture of the man's life. Now, it's revealed that he fathered not just one set of kids, but also two or three sets. The obituary tells it all. "He leaves to cherish his memory a First Son from 'First Baby's Mama;' Twin Daughters from 'Second Baby's Mama;' and 'Youngest Son from 'Third Baby's Mama!'" The father's death becomes a social and legal mess, especially since he did not leave a written will. Legally, the courts must determine the next of kin. Socially, it's up for grabs, and the victor gets the spoils.

Suddenly, the issues of "My baby's daddy" as discussed earlier, begin to explode. Chaos erupts at the funeral home, at the church, or at the repast. Before and during the funeral, everyone usually shows up to pay his or her last respects to the deceased. Each is ready to stake a personal claim on what daddy left them. Listen to the conversations:

"Who is going to pay for daddy's funeral? Did he have any insurance? Where's the money?"

"Even though he put my name on the insurance policy, everyone should pitch in to bury him. I'm not using all my money for his funeral. He's everybody's daddy, not just mine."

"What did he leave for his children by me? Whose names should we write first on the program? I need to say something, too. He was with me before he was with you."

"This was his favorite song. His good friend and running buddy wants to say something. Also, I think we should bury him beside his brother in 'Closest To Home Cemetery'."

"No, we don't have enough money for a casket. Let's cremate him and keep whatever money he has for my kids. He really didn't take care of them, as he should have. Where's the money?"

"During the service, I think me and my mama should sit in the front closest to the casket. My mama is the oldest. Did he take out an insurance policy for my kids? Did he have a will? Where's the money?"

"His son, 'B-like-Em' wants his car. He deserves it. And my baby, his favorite girl who always sat on his lap, wants his computer."

"By the way, where is that nice piece of jewelry he used to wear? I want to wear it to the service in his memory, and I'd like to hold on to it so I can always remember him. Anybody find his debit card? He gave me his number."

"What you doing here, girl? . . . He's what?! Did I hear you right? You say he's *your* daddy, too?! You mean, you're my *sister?!* Well, what in the world! I can't believe this! Lawd, have mercy! Tell me something, what did he leave you? You know these folks. Are they going to give anything to you?"

We all get the picture of this African-American experience. Before the body of the deceased has turned cold, and the family lays it to "Rest in Peace," the drama starts and keeps going on and on.

Even a Broken Clock is Right Twice a Day

In a divorce case, seldom is one party totally right or completely wrong. There is something good in the worst of folks and something bad in the best of folks. Divorce, however, often brings out the worst in even the best person. How often have we heard a black woman say about her husband or her children's father: "He ain't no good for nothin'!" or, "I can do bad all by myself." Many women feel this way after a divorce. The bitterness is especially vile if the man mistreated or physically abused his wife or dumped her for no good reason. A dog-and-cat type of marriage and divorce produces raw and angry feelings that can make you demonize the person you once loved. Be assured, you are not alone in feeling this way. Millions who have undergone wretched marriages or divorces share common feelings. These feelings are not imaginary; neither are they necessarily "wrong." Simply, your feelings are just that: *feelings.* I'm here to help you control and channel your feelings in a positive way, especially as this will certainly prove beneficial for you and your children while you rebuild your life following divorce.

Balance feelings about your spouse with the facts of your circumstances. What was the actual relationship you shared? Where credit is due, give it to your spouse. However, be careful about staying too long in a dysfunctional marriage, albeit for good reasons. The practice of "self-sacrifice" absent redeeming effects may prove harmful to children.

Searching for Positives Amid the Pain

It is difficult to see the good in another person through hurting and angry eyes. Yet, alleviating drama requires the one who is divorced to recognize (and even at times commend) good things in the life of his or her ex. No one should ever minimize the pain of a victim of divorce. Usually, a person pursues a divorce after recognizing irreparable cracks in the foundation of their marriage. In other words, they justifiably seek a divorce based on the negative behavior of their spouse during months or years of marriage. This rationale for divorce usually holds true whether or not one pursues a no-fault divorce.

Let's consider a few examples:

Example One: The husband has been a weekly gambler at the casino. His wife concludes the man she has committed her life to is nothing but a loser whose vice one day will jeopardize the livelihood and welfare of his family. Tired of his gambling, the wife stresses these negative character traits about her husband during their divorce proceedings. She encourages her attorney, when appearing before the judge during settlement discussions, to paint a picture of a spouse who has placed the family at severe risk. She is angry and wants him to pursue this angle as a negotiating tool to obtain a settlement for her far beyond what is equitable and fair.

Example Two: A wife has relatives who overly influence the relationship between her and her husband. The husband perceives this weakness as a flaw in her character, and concludes she does not act in an independent and mature way. Further, he resents her spending habits based on the suggestions of her sisters. She is wasteful, disrespectful to him, and more deferential toward her family. So the husband tells his divorce attorney his wife is robbing him of his hard-earned money and no longer listens to what he has to say. Because she's argumentative and self-centered, he wants to get out of the relationship as soon as he can. His gold-digging wife and her family sucked him in, and this is how he wants his lawyer to present his wife to the judge.

Each example fairly presents an accurate portrayal of the respective spouse. Essentially, one person is a "no-good gambler" and the other a "good for nothing gold-digger." However, to portray either spouse as simply a gambler or a gold-digger who has little value does no justice to a holistic view of either character. A balanced perspective would yield a clearer picture. The "no-good gambler" has some positive qualities. He works steadily at his good job and earns enough to support his gambling habit. Despite his gambling, he has managed to accumulate a sizeable amount of cash and other assets. He never stays out all night, does not chase other women, does not get drunk, fixes stuff around the house, and even attends church once a month. He just likes his gambling. The "good for nothing gold-digger" has positive traits and virtues as well. Despite at times showing deference to her family rather than to her husband, she nevertheless shows she values her family ties. She realizes family is an important part of her life and protects the relationship. It is true she spends lots of the money, but she works for the money, too. And she doesn't spend the money on things that have little value. She buys quality things, just too many of them. And the way she speaks to her husband does not so much reveal an argumentative spirit as it does her educational training and lively nature. In either example, it would be quite easy for the aggrieved divorced party to brand the spouse summarily and react with blinding anger and bitterness. Few persons deeply hurt by a marriage partner would behave otherwise. Yet such a reaction does no justice to the overall good contributions of the spouse.

Couples divorce for various reasons: out-of-control spending, disagreement on how to raise the children, sexual dissatisfaction, infertility, unwanted pregnancy and childbirth, extramarital relationships, placing childcare duties over the needs of one's spouse, in-law interference, a controlling or domineering spouse, ineffective communication, and a difference in latent core values. Upon contemplation, many of the reasons a spouse uses to justify seeking a divorce may reveal certain positive character traits. Perhaps you've heard the saying, "Any vice can be described as a virtue run amuck." Sometimes, bad attitudes and behavior simply reveal underlying or misapplied extreme values and virtues. It is important for divorced (or divorcing) parties to become more objective. Objectivity may not be possible in the middle of conflict; however, you can make the choice to listen to objective counsel, not just your lawyer, but also honest friends and loved ones. Avoid surrounding yourself with "yes men" or "yes women." You want the advice of trusted friends who are not afraid to speak the truth.

With time, you should learn how to step outside the immediate and troublesome circumstances of the failed relationship and see positive things in your ex. Add everything up. Don't be one-sided in your view. Add everything up for yourself. The challenge you face adjusting your thoughts is difficult, but you can do it. You will benefit from the way you take a better look at your spouse. Recast your perception of the spouse who divorces you, and reflect on the good side. Regardless of how the relationship between you and your spouse turns out, think about how these matters affect and benefit your children. Do not influence or force your children to take up the offence you have against your spouse. In time, they will gain the resources to sort out the details and the mess causing the breakup of their mama and daddy. In the meantime, refuse to pit them against your spouse.

Give your children some space to make their own judgments. If you perceive bitterness and hate in their hearts, check them. You can remind them of the positives your ex brought into the marriage and the making of your family. Recall the occasions when your ex was greater than anyone you ever met. Tell the kids about the good things your ex did for them when they were too young to remember. By speaking to your children in this way, you protect them from the internal venom that can destroy their relationship with their other parent. You can better lead your children in this way if first you add it all up for yourself. Spare yourself and them the drama of your breakup.

Maintain an Accurate Picture

A perfect marriage is essentially a good marriage. A good spouse is far from being a perfect spouse. Don't be too hasty about getting a divorce, neither about using the public forum to condemn and berate your spouse. Beware of such conduct because somebody's always listening. The one who hears a man degrade his ex just might be his co-worker who will jump at the chance to snatch her up for his own. Rest assured, the sister who berates her ex in the female gossip circle should know no less than ten other sisters are just waiting to get their chance to say, "Let's get together." Remember the saying, "One woman's trash is another woman's treasure." Think about it this way. Others may not agree with the overwhelmingly negative picture you present of your spouse. After all, every person has some sort of negatives and character flaws. They know your ex isn't totally "evil!" And they know you are not totally good. Constantly berating an ex is a sign of bitterness. Even your friends will avoid you after a while if your bitterness persists. Further, what potential partner will want to start a relationship with a bitter person, even if that person is the victim of a bad relationship?

Be thankful for your life. You could be experiencing some issues you never dreamed could happen to you. Challenges are not roadblocks, but stepping-stones. Learn from all life's experiences. A wise poem is worth repeating here:

"Of all that is said from the cradle to the hearse, whatever did happen, it could have been worse."

Act Now 13 – You and Your Ex

The following are some tips to help you cope with the problems associated with **"My baby's daddy."** They should be helpful as you seek to "add everything up" about your spouse or your soon-to-become ex.

1) **Be transparent with your spouse about all your offspring.** They deserve to know the truth. (A woman may also consider revealing any adoptions to her husband.)

2) **Tell your divorce attorney the whole truth about your children's parentage.** Your attorney can represent you better when you place all the history and facts on the table.

3) **Fathers, claim your paternity.** If necessary, get a DNA test, even in a case when you have doubts about whether the child given birth to by your wife is yours. Talk with your spouse, and then act responsibly.

4) **Ask someone to be your sounding board for evaluating the character of your spouse.** Use their services even as your impending divorce proceeds toward finality. You should always welcome the objective viewpoint of a trusted source whose perspective is more honest than your own. In the process, use this occasion to examine your own character flaws. Do you have immaturities hidden from you, but not from others?

Funerals can become a time of healing or a time of hating. Divorced, separated, single-but-mated, and married persons all need to prepare themselves for the inevitable. Life is uncertain, but death is sure. Prepare yourself in advance. Here are some tips:

1) **Take the high road, and nurture a tone of respect for the memory of the deceased.** This tip is the most important thing you can do. In life, the deceased might have treated you badly. Pray to show grace and mercy anyway because some younger ones are watching your example. Refuse to desecrate the deceased or funeral occasion. To avoid drama, you must not react out of anger.

2) **Protect your young children at all costs.** Shield the young ones from information they are too immature to process. Protect yourself from embedded family rancor or the venom directed at you because the occasion of death revealed a "ghetto divorce."

3) **Be preemptive in disclosing hidden information.** If you know your children will find out the truth sooner or later, you should tell them the truth sooner. However, speak to them in a place that is their "safe space." Maintain their security as you help them adjust their thinking.

4) **Make pre-death preparations with the help of a good attorney.** The attorney will help you work through all the issues and advise you about different types of wills, trusts, and pre-arrangements. Get help and avoid the drama on the front end, while you're in your right mind!

Up Next

When dealing with divorce, it is impossible to address the different family dimensions separately. Matters in one area shade over into others. Divorce impacts family life as a whole and has a particular impact on your children. How will mama make a way? How does she feel and respond when the judge awards child custody to the father? Most often in divorce cases, the courts award custody to the mother. In the African-American cultural and social experience, "Mama" is the one who rises to the challenge of taking care of the family's welfare. In this respect, she well demonstrates the matriarchal role in black people's history. In the upcoming section, we turn our focus to one of the most central issues in any divorce case—child custody.

Chapter 14

Child
Custody Matters

Children's Issues Vary

In the African-American community, children's issues vary in cases of divorce and separation. For instance, how do parents deal with illegitimacy in the context of family relationships? How do they include an outside child? How does the wife cope when she discovers her spouse has fathered a baby with another woman or has a much older child? Nonbiological children are prone to receive the least respect and care when a breakup occurs. A look at the African-American family during the time of slavery provides a historical perspective on the way we as a people deal with our nonbiological children. Routinely, black parents raised a child or children who did not belong to their spouse as "family" took on the connotation of extension beyond the "nuclear" composition of mother, father, and biological children. Slave parents merged these offspring into a socially functioning unit. Though problems still existed, they all survived together.

In an extended family, the use of corporal punishment in parent/non-biological child relationships can become an issue, just as corporal punishment itself is a hot-button issue in our society. A biological parent may in fact approve of using corporal punishment as a method of discipline. However, that same parent may disapprove the use of physical discipline by the nonbiological spouse. If the divorced mother remarries, then the father likely will not want another man spanking his son, and especially not his daughter.

Gender and gender roles become a sensitive issue in times of marital break-up. In the cultural and social times in which we live, black boys yearn for and often need their fathers. Sometimes, the courts do not fully understand and appreciate this need. Further, the courts may discount the advice knowledgeable African-American mothers or fathers offer in this area. Generally, many women see fathers as an extra pair of helping hands. In their sight, those hands do not differ much from a grandmother's or aunt's. Consequently, when the mother receives custody, a young boy may find himself predominantly surrounded by female figures. Over time, these associations may affect his personality. Debates may range about the cultural and social characteristics distinguishing black boys from black girls, but the discussion of what makes a boy a man and a girl a woman is legitimate. Though living in a societal climate that oppressively targets black males from earliest school days through the system called "The New Jim Crow," African-American parents must be alert to the dangers facing black people in general and our males especially. Black boys and young men need a healthy consciousness and clear identity. Men as protectors and providers—though certainly not exclusive of the black woman's lofty role—remain a good standard of maturity and socialization. Something is truly wrong when a mother at the gas station jumps from the car to pump gas while her teenage son continues to sit comfortably in the back seat. Or, things are out of whack when an obviously pregnant woman has to stand on the bus while able-bodied men continue to hold their seats. Something is wrong with the culture when our boys and men demonstrate behavior that degrades black women.

Yes, fathers can teach forms of aggression and risk-taking that may appear to some mothers as reckless and irresponsible parenting. On the other hand, mothers may emotionally respond to a child's difficult life situations with tender loving care, which to some fathers may seem like weakness or coddling. Beyond the stereotypes, however, a father plays a unique role in a child's life. When disagreements exist between mother and father, sometimes we discover a difference in perspective traceable along gender lines. All things being equal (and they seldom are) the cultural reality in the African-American community is that boys need their fathers to play an active role in their lives. Some would further argue that girls, more than boys, have the greater need for the active presence of a father.

Mama Will Make a Way

Motherhood is priceless, and divorce or separation often punctuates the value of "Mama."

Since the times of American slavery, African-American families have suffered trauma. The slave trade separated tribal peoples from the African continent, a geographical separation from the homeland that was very difficult for the individuals who had to survive the "Middle Passage" across the Atlantic. More devastating, however, was the separation of these persons from their close kindred. The slave trade separated Africans from their culture, their tribes or extended families, their immediate families, and even from those who spoke their same language. It also disrupted the basic institution of human socialization, the African marriage and the family unit. On slave plantations, relationships developed between African males and African females whose masters allowed them to live together. Sometimes, the slave owners forced sexual cohabitation to increase the slave population through breeding. Yet, the slave master could abruptly break a "family" unit apart on a whim. He could sell a male slave (or a female) to another owner or remove children from their biological parents. The slave owner had absolute control over his slave "chattel" or property.

During slavery, the value of Mama increased tremendously. Moreover, in the generations since, the African-American mother has continued to play a strong, resilient role in the black family. That strength is most evident in times of crises. The breakup of a marriage or relationship, when young children are present, is one such crisis. When an African-American mother experiences family desertion and disruption by her partner, or even his in-your-face disrespect, she often responds with a courage that says, "Don't worry, Mama will make a way." And she does. Whether an African-American family is patriarchal or matriarchal is an important discussion because it feeds into the social expectations of fathers. However, the issue tends to take second place to the child-focused nature of the marital union, particularly as expressed by African-American women. Time and again, courts and divorce attorneys give witness to black mothers who step up to the plate on behalf of their children.

In a divorce, where the disrupted relationship once enjoyed two incomes, now there may only be one: Mama's money. Too often, the disappearing partner shows inconsistent financial responsibility. He puts nothing on the table. In such instances, Mama must shoulder the complete financial load unless some other sympathetic relatives pitch in. African-American mothers make tremendous sacrifices for their children and carry the lion's share of the load in their male-absent families. They make up their minds: whatever it takes to get the job done, they will do it. Whether they receive honor, or thanks, or appreciation, or outside help is beyond the point. As mothers—mature, reliable and child-loving—they take total responsibility. Their creed is, "Mama will make a way."

A Word About "Big Mama"

We must say a word here about "Big Mama," a role in the African-American experience that cannot be overestimated. Often, "Big Mama" rears two or three generations of children, proving she not only can make a way for her children, but also her grandchildren. Some divorce attorneys notice that grandparents usually express more sense than anyone else involved in the divorce drama. They try to be peacemakers, and more often than not, keep the welfare of the children in mind. Consequently, more and more folks rely on "Big Mama" for assistance. She often steps up to the plate, becoming a quasi-legal guardian for the grandchildren, especially when prison is home for the father or drugs have overtaken the mother. "Big Mama," being nearest to the broken family, is usually the most qualified to care for the vulnerable offspring.[29] She can also assist the children of busy professionals whose careers demand long work hours and frequent travel. She is respected, stable, financially reliable, has a decent living environment, and the will to make things work for her grandchildren.

My firm once represented a 30-year-old father whose ex-wife had gained custody of their child while the father got visitation rights and had to pay child support. During the proceedings, the maternal grandmother became more active in her grandchild's life, a pattern she continued after the divorce when the child was living half the time with her and half the time with the mother. One day, the mother retained a lawyer to help enforce her ex husband's child support order.

---

[29] "Grandparents—particularly grandmothers—play an especially important role in African-American families in providing support for mothers and care for children. When mothers are not able to carry out their roles, grandmothers are the surrogate parents of choice." Barbarin and McCandies, "African-American Families." *Encyclopedia.com* (2003), March 1, 2013, http://www.encyclopedia.com/doc/1G2-3406900022.html.

In turn, the man argued he should not have to pay child support because his wife's mother was taking care of the kid. He raised the question: "Who should get the child support: Mama or Big Mama since the child's grandmother is taking care of her?"

Lo and behold, the judge agreed with the father! In a classic turn of events, he decided the wife's mother should receive the support since she was the party responsible for the child's day-to-day care. The wife's lawyer reminded the judge the court had given custody to her; therefore, she should get the child support, contending the judge would have to change the custody order if he did not force the father to pay child support to his client. The judge did not budge. In his own way, he expressed approval of the supportive provisions made by the child's maternal grandmother and gave her kudos in open court. In this case, the custodial mother—to her embarrassment and chagrin—failed to retain child support. But from the court's standpoint, "Big Mama" was adequately fulfilling the role of the custodial parent.

Yes, "Mama will make a way," and Big Mama will make a way, too! When they put their minds to it and stick together, they both can and do work "miracles" every day.

"I Lost My Children"

Perhaps there is nothing more serious in a divorce ruling than when the judge makes a decision about which spouse gets custody of the children. Often the decision is rather easy, especially when the children are very young. In theory, and in most jurisdictions, judges are supposed to view both parents equally without gender bias when presented with the issue of deciding custody. Most courts focus on the "best interests" of the children. However, such is not always the case in practice. Usually, the judge awards custody to the mother and grants visitation rights to the father. Every now and then, however, the circumstances of a divorce compel the judge to award custody to the father, and such a ruling can cause trauma for the mother who loses her children.

A parent places a number of things in jeopardy when he or she makes a decision to pursue a divorce. A mother in a contested case faces the possibility she may lose custody; that is, lose primary control for the care of her children. A father does also. Taking this risk is a serious matter. Yet, each year, millions of women and men take that gamble. The father or mother believes the odds of obtaining custody of the children will fall his or her way in court. Some win. Others lose. Usually one parent leaves a contested custody trial thinking the judge can walk on water. The other parent, however, feels the judge should have drowned in the same water.

The Decision-Making Battle

When the legal battle of divorce or separation comes down to who wins custody of the children, the results can be tragic. Sometimes, it's the mother's fault. The way she lives is just bad news, or her mental state is problematic. If she cannot improve her own life and make things better for herself, how will her young children have a fighting chance? Other times, a divorce judge has to make a very tough decision over custody. The difficulty becomes most acute when each parent, father and mother, are exemplary. Both have commendable characters, both work good jobs, each is a great parent, either could do a fine job raising the children. Yet, at the end of the day, the judge must decide which parent gets custody. Laws vary by state, but generally speaking, the judge has wide discretion to decide what's best for the children. Factors considered include, which parent has a deeper emotional bond with the children; which parent has better parenting skills; which parent will provide a better education for the children; which parent has a better support network for the children. Another significant factor often overlooked by parents seeking custody is which parent has the greatest ability to foster or facilitate a loving relationship between the children and the parent who failed to obtain custody.

This is the most difficult decision faced by divorce judges. Sometimes the balance tips in the favor of the parent who would best facilitate an ongoing relationship between the children and the noncustodial parent. At any rate, this kind of custody decision can cause much drama for all involved. Even if you are the "better" parent, consider that a custody fight will have a corrosive effect on your children. Are you such a good parent, or your spouse such a bad parent, that a bitter custody fight is worth the stress on your children?

A judge's decision becomes most heartbreaking when the judge tells the mother, in so many words, "Your spouse or partner is better to raise the children!" The mindset of the judge is not so much anti-mother as it is pro-child. He may say, "I'm not taking your children. I'm granting their father the right to raise them and make final decisions regarding their education, health, and religious upbringing. You will still have liberal visitation, but I'm placing the day-to-day care of the children with their father."

There is evidence that fathers win in custody cases more often than mothers do because fathers usually do not fight for custody unless they have a very strong case.[30] Most divorce lawyers who litigate custody matters would agree there is no greater visible expression of pain and anguish in a courtroom than when a mother loses custody of her children. This is heartbreaking, gut-wrenching drama. In such a case, the judge seeks to provide a father-figure "ark of safety and security" for the children. Certain instances of disputes over children (and especially over sons) beg all parties to show deference to the father receiving custody. Current social realities in the African-American community teach us never to minimize the positive father-figure role in the life of a child. Some judges, child advocates, and many mothers embrace this wisdom.

When the court denies a mother the right to raise her children, it is as though a ton of bricks drops on her. With the loss, a mother faces a range of emotions that she expresses more overtly than a father might. Some mothers become irate and break down when faced with social drama outside the normal experiences of the father. Mothers who lose custody immediately face a stigma and the drama associated with it. Some folks with little discernment automatically think that the court deems as unfit the mother who loses her children in a divorce and custody trial. As a result, these women often have to deal with:

- **Embarrassment** – How can she face her family? What can she say to her girlfriends and to the neighbors? When it's time to arrange and formally transfer the children from the mother to the father, how must the mother feel? How can she face herself?
- **Bond Breaking** – At a time in her children's lives when they need the nurture and care of their mother, she is gone. Disruption suddenly happens in the bond between mother and child. The hugs, the kisses, the care, the baths, and the comfort—things children need daily—are now gone.

---

[30] See, Attorney Joe Gitlin, "Questions and Answers: Who Is Awarded Custody of The Children?" Gitlin, Busche & Stetler, March 1, 2013, http://www.gitlin.com/pages/questions/qa_custody.html#Q1.

- **Personal Drowning** – A mother may feel she has no good reason to keep on living because she has lost her children. She feels she has lost everything.

Sometimes the drama of a custody battle begins before a spouse files for divorce. The couple may have separated, and the young children stayed with their mother. The father knows the inadequacies of their living situation; so he takes a pronounced legal step to gain an advantage in an upcoming custody battle prior to filing for divorce. He contacts DCFS and reports his wife, her living situation, her use of corporal punishment, or even her new boyfriend. All of a sudden, the department's investigators show up at the house. The department's main goal is to protect the children. In some instances, the agency removes children from the home pending the outcome of the investigation. The children could end up living with the father on a "temporary" basis, or longer, during a contested custody trial. The mother is frightened. She knows things aren't right, and the agency may snatch her children away quickly and permanently. She realizes the divorce papers are coming, and the father will use the investigative reports of Child and Family Services to enhance his chance of getting the children early on. Mother gets a gnawing fear, either of the uncertain or the inevitable.

Drama happens even after the court awards custody to a parent. The custody-losing or noncustodial parent may begin to play the game of "one-up-man-ship." It is not uncommon for a noncustodial parent to use the legal system to get back at the parent who wins custody. Often, the noncustodial parent will invent things about their ex-spouse related to the children. The ex may resort to lies and deception by reporting nonexistent circumstances of neglect and abuse. Sometimes, a spouse plays "smoke and mirrors" by blowing an innocent incident way out of proportion to truthful reality. In some instances, if Children and Family Services' investigators are not alert, the deceitful spouse becomes successful in laying the foundation for a case. When the judge feels it best for the children's safety to award custody to the father—due to accusations of child abuse, neglect, or other reasons—the mother nevertheless feels deep pangs of separation from her children. The separation is unnatural and can be emotionally destructive. Most mothers would never want to admit—for whatever the reasons—"I lost custody of my children."

However, "every dark cloud has a silver lining." It may be difficult for mothers who have lost custody to see the brighter picture, but it is not impossible. Once they get past the initial shock, they may be able to count their "loss" as a gain. A divorce judge will usually state the reason for awarding custody to one party over another based on a determination of what is best for the children. Perhaps the judge sees something in a mother's character and circumstances that raises concerns about her stability. Maybe he simply feels the father is truly better equipped to be the primary custodial parent. So mother, listen closely to the judge's decision. His awarding of custody to the father may later prove best for your children, even as painful as it may appear initially. Remember, as children get older, they will decide for themselves the strengths and weaknesses of their parents.

When Daddy's In Charge

So what are the implications for the father who gains custody? What adjustments must he make in order to raise his children successfully? What drama will he face? When a divorce judge awards sole custody to the father, the man alone becomes primarily responsible for his children's daily well-being. Since mothers usually get custody, a father who receives control may feel he has won a major victory. Yet, a father awarded custody should seek to partner with his ex for the sake of the children.

In the section "I Need A Woman," I discussed some of the drama of divorce as it impacts the man's need for female companionship and remarriage. I discussed similar dynamics and factors related to his children, but from the divorced male's perspective as a single man. In contrast to taking care of himself, the divorced or separated black male who becomes the primary custodial parent is obligated to place the needs of his children above his own.

African-American custodial fathers face automatic social pressure. First, society generally expects failure in the lives of black males. Second, not many people believe a black man can successfully raise children (especially young children) by himself. Some think a motherless home is a disaster waiting to happen. Whether you agree or disagree, this type of thinking about black men is prevalent in many sectors of society. Amidst the social pressures to succeed, the custodial father must reorder his life after divorce and make the well-being of his children the top priority. He must balance his career, his work, and his personal interests around the children. While married, the father may have been a great dad who did all the right things. Post divorce, the circumstances require this father to become an even *greater* dad.

Father, you are primarily responsible for the children under your care. You may enlist others to help you, especially in the lives of very young children. However, at the end of the day, the court holds you responsible for your children, not the other partners who are lending a helping hand. Remember, partners are not parents, and you should not expect them to be. Furthermore, not many judges can afford to give a pass to a custodial father who is irresponsible in his child-rearing. On notice of such a situation, you can be sure the judge will issue a summons for your presence back in court and may even reconsider the decision to grant you custody. The judge (and the attorney appointed to represent the children's interest in the divorce) will do everything necessary to undo any adverse situation created for the children. He will hold you accountable, one way or another.

After your divorce is settled, your list of priorities grows exponentially. Consider what you must now do (if you are not already doing so) for your children:

- feed them, clothe them, provide health care (at home and at the clinic);
- comb hair, fasten shoes;
- keep clothes clean and presentable;
- ensure the house stays livable, safe and secure;
- make sure the children have enough money;
- discipline with love;
- reward successes;
- listen to their words and their deeper needs;
- calm their fears;
- Develop their spiritual potential alongside their social growth;
- encourage excellence;
- get them to school on time, pick up report cards, help with homework;
- supervise curfew, settle disputes, monitor friends, and regulate computer and television time;

- † protect them from bullies and predators;
- † discuss sex with them, the "birds and the bees";
- † check your son when he begins to "smell himself";
- † assist your daughter in preparing for her first of many menstrual cycles;
- † attend their sports events and extracurricular activities;
- † take them to summer camp, and enroll them in summer activities;
- † teach them how to drive the car, and trust them with the keys;
- † guide them in higher education and career choices;
- † assist them with their first job; and
- † build a network of family, friends, and helpers.

The list of all-encompassing responsibilities facing the custodial father is daunting. The drama is intimidating. Your children will look to daddy for everything. For their benefit, don't be a solo act. It takes a real man to rise to the challenges of being a custodial father. At the same time, a primary custodial father should clearly understand he cannot be a substitute for mother. Each parent plays a different role in the child's life. Just as we would think it strange and unnatural for a person to function well with only one leg, we should also think it counterproductive for a child to have only one parent when they have been blessed with two. The child needs both. Nevertheless, a child from a broken home is capable of doing just as well as a child from an intact home if the custodial parent works hard to compensate for the absence of the other parent.

Of course, other causes beside a broken home underlie dysfunctional child-rearing. Sometimes, one or both parents may be guilt-laden from past behaviors, broken from tragic events in their life, or lacking essential parenting skills. A father (or mother, too) can find it quite challenging to adjust to a role reversal when there is a change in primary custody. To be sure, many fathers are capable of doing some of the things for the children their mother would ordinarily do. However, a father may be fooling himself if he thinks he can actually be both mother and father for his children. Consider the "non-chore" roles a custodial father faces. Children have psychological and emotional needs, too. Generally, men and women think and respond differently, and those thoughts and responses play out in different ways with their children.

In a primary custodial role, a father may find himself becoming an emotional ball of knots as he adjusts in vain to the non-material and inner-spiritual needs of his children. In addition, he may face the children's resentment for taking them away from their mother.

Further, the custodial father may find himself isolated from extended family as he tries to fulfill the roles of mother and father. He may face the anger of in-laws who distance themselves because they believe the mom got a bad deal in the divorce. Also, fathers typically have a comparatively smaller support network than mothers to help them with the children. Therefore, a father will usually have to make a deliberate effort to build a support network to assist him with child-rearing.

Act Now 14 – Child Custody Matters

The following action-responses about supportive resources will help ensure that things run smoothly in relation to custody matters. If you might—or indeed do—become the primary custodial parent, I suggest these tips to help you avoid some of the associated drama.

1) **Use the courts, especially those that pertain to child support.** Establish your rights. It is better to secure money you may not need than to need money for your children, but not have a way to get it. Fathers who produce children should support their offspring. Remind yourself, child support is for the "child," not the mother. If possible, budget with money you earn, and avoid dependence on child support, except for the children's benefit.

2) **Make a proactive plan.** Move away from simply reacting to situations that happen. You are making financial ends meet today and for now. However, the cost of living will continue to rise. Know the ins and outs of your budget. Deciding what you can live with and without will guide you.

3) **Save time for yourself.** Everybody, including a Mama who is making a way, needs personal time. You need time to relax, reflect, renew, and reorganize. So schedule time for yourself. Get your space for freedom at least once a week, or twice a month. Your down time will help you to keep on moving and going in a positive direction.

4) **Form a support group of other mothers.** Share babysitting responsibilities, car-pooling, and shopping chores. Form a close knit and practical network with others you trust so you can share each other's burdens. You will find added strength by supporting mothers just like yourself. Look for parents with children the same age and gender as your kids.

5) **Refuse to fall into the "anything is okay" trap of single mothers with your sons.** A mother who lets her son do what he wants is damaging his future. When the pampered son grows up and gets himself a partner, he will exhibit this spoiled and selfish upbringing. So mother, if the father is not present, don't give way and allow your sons to do whatever they please. That experience will hurt them, and hurt you, too. Seek the advice of responsible adult males when setting appropriate rules and boundaries.

6) **If you lose custody, continue to enjoy the time you have with your children.** No doubt, losing custody is painful. However, your loss should not define you and your relationship with your children. Use your custody loss as motivation and an opportunity to spend as much quality time as you can with your children. They will always need you.

7) **Read books on single-father parenting.** Get good information. Learn all you can. You'll need it.

8) **List your new responsibilities relative to your children.** Define them in as much detail as you can. Study your list, and make sure it covers all dimensions of your children's life. Ironically, prepare to adjust the list when necessary. No written manual can suffice for the everyday changes life brings. Good parenting also requires adaptability and flexibility.

9) **Protect your single parent fathering from inherent dangers.** For example, how will you counteract the advances of insincere women who pretend to help you with your children? How will you handle your moments of anger and frustrations when you want to get away from everything—including your children? When you are tired and temporarily broke, you may become resentful of your ex for getting you into this bad situation in the first place.

10) **Stay connected to some trusted mature women.** Call on them for assistance when you get into a pinch. These should be women without romantic ties or a desire to date you. Appreciate their good advice and help, but keep a respectful distance between you and them. It's about the children.

11) **Allow your children to see and speak with their mother.** Allow more opportunities than the directions set forth in the parenting agreement. Though the court establishes a visitation schedule for your ex, be sure to offer additional parenting time for your ex to be with the children. Remember, the children may have resentful feelings about you separating them from their mother. Hence, they will appreciate the extra time with her, and this will only improve their relationship with you. Re-establishing positive communication with your ex helps your efforts. Facilitate your parental responsibility by staying approachable to your ex even though she may still harbor angry feelings about your having gained custody of the children.

Up Next

During most of my legal career, I have served the court as a *Guardian Ad Litem*. Simply, I assist the court in looking out for the "best interests" of children of divorce. Symbolically, I provide an "ark" for the children, just as the mother of Moses provided for his safety under circumstances threatening his life. All children who are victims of their parents' divorce need an "ark" to protect and preserve them from the dangers brought about by a broken marriage and the associated drama. I discuss the great need for this children's ark in the next section.

Chapter 15

The Children's Ark

Modeling Noah's Ark

Noah built an ark and saved himself and his family from the destruction of the Flood. He spent a lot of time and energy constructing the ark and labored under difficult circumstances. It was a strong, durable, and sustaining shelter, and Noah recognized the importance of creating a safe haven for his family and the animals. Like Noah's flock, children of divorce need an ark of safety to protect them during the turbulence of divorce. Parents have a responsibility to look beyond personal self-serving interests to respond to their children's needs for love, security, safety, and emotional stability.

Children are the greater victims in a time of breakup, especially young children. And like other children of divorce, black children often feel rejected and abandoned. Divorce stirs up feelings of guilt within children who often blame themselves and believe they are the ones at fault for their parents' breakup. Every child of a divorced family suffers—every single one. The only fair comparison to make between one child of divorce and another is in the degree of pain each child experiences. For this reason, all divorced parents should heed this message: KEEP YOUR CHILDREN OUT OF YOUR DIVORCE DRAMA.

There is no question that when it comes to divorce, children are often the innocent victims caught in the middle between their warring parents who are generally too angry to care about the emotional effects on their children. However, a warning is in order: divorce can wreak destructive havoc on a family, leaving children psychologically scarred and wounded for years afterward. That's why I counsel my clients to approach their divorce *humanely* and to keep their children's well-being at the top of their minds. If you are contemplating a separation, or already in court, here are some tips to help you protect your children from the drama and pain.

10 Tips to Keep Divorce From Hurting the Kids

1. Remember that your children love your ex and feel a sense of loyalty to them, even if the ex is abusive.
2. Keep in mind that your children will eventually make their own judgments about your ex. It may be slow in coming, but its arrival is certain. Any attempts you make to influence that judgment will likely backfire.
3. Remember, the best gift you can give your children is fond memories of their childhood.
4. Try to maintain as much stability for the children as you can. If possible, keep them in the same church, school, and neighborhood.
5. Don't install a revolving door in your bedroom. Be mindful of how and when you introduce your children to a new love interest.
6. Understand that the children are hurting, too, but don't be afraid to discipline and set boundaries.
7. Don't overcompensate by over-indulging your children.
8. Don't use children as messengers between you and your spouse.
9. Don't assume that your children are "ok" while Mom and Dad are going through a divorce.
10. If necessary, seek counseling to help the children cope with your breakup.

In the Children's "Best Interests"

What is best for the children? Opinions vary and can be very subjective. Jurisdictions addressing custody, child abuse, and other related children's issues remove much of this subjectivity from the discussion of what is best for the children. Most states have enacted statutes for determining the "best interests" of children that jurisdictions consider in the context of the children's ages and developmental needs. Specifics may vary by state, but below are some common guidelines and standards used for determination:[31]

- The physical safety and welfare of the child, including food, shelter, health, and clothing
- The development of the child's identity
- The child's background and ties, including familial, cultural, and religious
- The child's sense of attachments, including:
  - Where the child actually feels love, attachment, and a sense of being valued (as opposed to where adults believe the child should feel love, attachment, and a sense of being valued)
  - The child's sense of security
  - The child's sense of familiarity
  - Continuity of affection for the child
  - The least disruptive placement alternative for the child
- The child's wishes and long-term goals
- The child's community ties, including church, school, and friends
- The child's need for permanence, which includes their need for stability and continuity of relationships with parent figures, siblings, and other relatives
- The uniqueness of every family and child
- The risks attendant to entering and being in substitute care
- The preferences of the persons available to care for the child
- The prevention of child abuse

Both Physical and Emotional Needs

The children's ark should provide for both their physical and emotional needs since parents are responsible for attending to all the needs of their children, even as they are facing the drama of their own broken relationship. Very few children escape deep emotional damage resulting from divorce. When the potential for damage becomes apparent, the court may appoint

---

[31] For a specific state, see, March 1, 2013, http://www.childwelfare.gov/systemwide/laws_policies/statutes/best_interest.pdf. "Child Welfare Information Gateway: Protecting Children, Strengthening Families," March 1, 2013, http://www.childwelfare.gov.

a *Guardian Ad Litem* or an Attorney for the Children. The investigation of a *Guardian Ad Litem* may shed light on issues the children face resulting from divorce or separation.

During one particular divorce case, a court-appointed attorney asked the parents how they felt their child was coping with their breakup. Both mother and father said their child was doing fine, handling the situation well. Then in a private session, the *Guardian* asked their pre-teen son how he was handling his parents' divorce. "Terrible," the boy said, confessing the divorce was tearing him apart. Contrary to what his parents thought, their divorce was destroying their son.

What can parents do to insulate, protect, and preserve their children's emotions from the complications and collateral damage of their divorce? What is the nature of the ark parents can build for their children's emotional health and wholeness? Well, they should seek to strengthen their children's emotional well-being with these considerations in mind:

Children of divorce need the ark of both parents.

Whether absent or present, all children need their father and mother. Each parent should take personal responsibility for nurturing their children's affection for the other parent, as this balance is emotionally healthy for them.

Children of divorce need the ark of cooperating parents.

Divorced parties who cooperate are a great benefit to their children; so work together in their "best interests." Avoid making them unwitting pawns between feuding parents. Parents sharing custody must make common sense decisions, together. They should agree on their children's basic routine, regardless of which parent has the children for their stipulated period. For instance, think about those special and regular events that divorced parties have to attend, some that recur year after year like birthdays, anniversaries, and family reunions, and others that happen occasionally, like weddings, graduations, family outings, and funerals of friends or family. Though it is impossible to anticipate the different scenarios of drama that may challenge your peace of mind, consider your manner of handling recurring and special occasions where the presence of children and spouses is expected. It might be helpful to talk with your ex and set some ground rules to:

- determine which parent will be responsible for the children's arrival and departure;
- decide who will exercise discipline of the children and settle disputes during the event;
- agree on the types of conversations that are off limits in the presence of the family and in-laws;
- determine who will get the gifts and how to allocate funds;
- discuss the appropriateness of either divorcee inviting a date to the family affair;
- Consult a mutually trusted third party if you and your ex arrive at a stalemate on certain ground rules.

In addition to repeat events and special occasions, everyday encounters with your ex and the children can also be a source of drama, like shopping at the same grocery store. Ditto going to the same church every Sunday, especially when you bring the children. And what about when report card pick-up happens at school? Who will engage the teacher or counselor? If your ex has different ideas than you about education and academic advancement, how will you mediate the difference? What will you do if a difference of opinion arises about the value of a particular teacher or class? How should you approach the conflict? Sure, the custodial parent is responsible. However, just one parent being in charge does not negate the valid opinion of the other. In these instances, it is advisable for the parties to use some sort of mediation to resolve areas of disagreement rather than rushing back to court.

Divorced parents who obtain joint custody should cooperate on the children's sleeping schedule. Parents create senseless and destructive drama for the children when one parent sends them to bed at 8:00 P.M. while the other allows them to stay up until 2:00 A.M. Instead, parents sharing custody must make common sense decisions together and agree on their children's basic routine. Both must ensure their well-being by providing for their proper sleep and rest.

In a highly contested divorce and custody battle, the judge kept uncooperative parents from disrupting and jerking the children around by issuing a temporary order that required the parents to move *in* and *out* of the house on alternating weeks. Thus, the judge's order stabilized life *and rest* for the children but disrupted the normal routines of the parents. His unusual but wise decision protected the essential needs of the children in the face of parents who refused to cooperate.

Children of divorce need the ark of hope for their father.

A divorcee should keep her children's hope alive for a father who is not always present. She can do this in the presence of her children by putting the best face possible on her broken relationship with their father. There are responsible ways for dealing with the problem of black fathers who are gone or missing. The black male shortage is a known fact of life. Many contend that confusion generated in black boys through lack of strong male figures exacerbates this situation. The good image of an absent father, which a divorced or separated woman presents to her children, can become their ark of hope. Negating a father who is not always present can be a double-edged sword. Mothers can reduce some drama by saying positive things to protect the absent father's image. Depending on their ages, she may have encouraging conversations like the following:

"I know your daddy doesn't come around that often, but he's probably having a hard time and needs some help. I know he's a good man. If it weren't for your father, you wouldn't be here. We miss him, but in the meantime, we are going to try extra hard to make our family better. And we will always stay ready to love and welcome daddy when we see him."

Children of divorce need the ark of belonging.

Sometimes, a child's need to belong will surface unexpectedly. The following story highlights the responsibility of both mother and father to make sure a child knows his or her real daddy. It involves the issues of paternity and the breakup of an unmarried couple who had a child. In the case of these separated parents, the mother had custody of their infant boy. She then married, and her new husband took full responsibility for his nonbiological son with whom he had a good relationship. As the child grew, he always assumed the man in his life (his stepfather) was his biological father. However, one day at school, the little boy's friend shocked him by blurting out, "Your daddy ain't your real daddy!" Obviously, this disclosure caused emotional drama in the child's life and a stir in the family. Around the same time, the boy's biological father filed for paternity rights. However, his son did not want a relationship with him. He liked his stepfather better. What course should the parties take? The situation was not very comfortable for the father. However, he would be ill advised to disrupt the good relationship his child enjoys with the nonbiological father. A naturally evolving parent-child relationship is more desirable than one legally enforced. Children need space to develop maturity and the ark of security it affords. Both parents should work to ensure a secure space for this wholesome development.

Children of divorce need the ark of family peace.

Maturity helps adults successfully manage life's drama. Innocent and developing children do not possess this set of tools. Keeping the peace in an extended family becomes an ark for children who are living in the middle of a messy divorce. Lawyers of African-American clients observe that stepmothers present more problems than stepfathers do in cases of divorce and separation. Generally, the new man is ready to assume the fatherhood role. He is up to the task, especially if he is already taking good care of his own children. Usually, he will not cause extreme conflicts with the biological father. A stepmother, however, sometimes tends to feel hostility toward the biological mother of the children or may feel threatened by the other woman's presence. So, when trouble arises, the stepmother most likely gives impetus to conflict. According to divorce lawyers, seldom does the stepfather cause the same degree of trouble.

Consider another case where a woman who had been sleeping with two men gave birth to a child. One man had always been there for her. However, the faithful man was not the father of the child, though he thought he was. Eventually, the truth came out when the biological father wanted to establish a relationship with the child. Mama was angry because this man did not have the same kind of financial resources as the other longtime man in her life. So the father, her real "baby's daddy," was wrecking her life, while her child called the other man his "fake daddy." This situation created tension and drama at the child's basketball game where security officers had to keep the men separated. The grandmother defended her daughter, even though the daughter was running a game on both men. She was controlling access to the child while the grandmother was controlling the entire situation and getting paid.

This kind of family situation is a mess. Thankfully, some grandparents adamantly refuse to take part or to embroil themselves in this kind of manipulative drama. In fact, most adults cannot continuously deal with family drama. The lack of peace and dysfunction often becomes emotionally debilitating. If the drama wreaks havoc on the adults, imagine how family discord and disharmony adversely affect children in the midst of divorce. This is why children need an ark of peace in their extended family relationships.

Children of divorce need the ark of time-perspective understanding.

Parents must understand a young one's elongated time perspective. A child's perception of time—days, weeks, months, seasons, and years—differs from the perspective of an adult. To them, events and happenings should always occur sooner. "Are we there yet?" is a typical question of young children when they go on any trip. In a child's world, things take much longer to happen. Depending on a child's age and perception, a day may seem like a week; a month may seem like forever. Now if the divorce process seems to take an eternity for the parents, imagine what the divorce time span is like for a child.

When parents are going through a divorce and custody fight, they make accommodations for an extended battle. Most clients understand the process—the lawyer consultations, court appearances, negotiation sessions— the back-and-forth of it all. They settle in for the long-term—even if that "long-term" happens to be only a year or so. A young child perceives events of the same "divorce" as taking much, much longer to end. Every parent in a divorce process must empathize with the uncertainty and lack of control a divorce brings into the life of a child. How often will the child ask, "Is it over yet?" "Will daddy come back?" "Will we ever be a family again?" "How long is forever?" You must give your children a livable perspective on both the nature and timing of your divorce. Learn to fill their prolonged time spans with positive reinforcement and with comforting assurances.

Children of divorce need the ark of helpful therapy.

The way the drama of parental allegiance can divide the children's loyalties is difficult to stomach. Add identity confusion or weakened social development to the mix, and you have a real problem. Sometimes, trained therapists are the only ones who can help children sort through divorce matters and changing relationships. Although African-Americans generally are leery of submitting to emotional, mental, and psychological therapy, I nevertheless encourage using the services of certified professionals in these fields and cannot overemphasize the importance of parents following the therapist's advice. Otherwise, therapy is useless. Sometimes, a therapist will recommend that parents also receive therapy. Expect this recommendation since child behavior problems are often traceable to dysfunction in the family. When it comes to providing trained therapy in the African-American community, remember, "All resources are not created equal." In other words, family-type support services of the majority population are not as available in our communities.

The hands of caring parents can get very dirty as they make an ark for the emotional safety and well-being of their children, but their efforts can give children a fair chance to survive the storms and drama of their parents' breakup. Sometimes your good friends will question your sanity for relating to your ex with a measure of civility—"even after the way your spouse mistreated you!" Just tell the friends, "Excuse the mud on my hands. I am trying to create an ark for the benefit of my children. It's a dirty job, but it's all good."

Act Now 15 – The Children's Ark

The following action items will help ensure that you can find a way to make things work if you might—or indeed do—become the primary custodial parent. I suggest these tips to help you avoid some of the associated drama.

1) **Make a "Children's Ark Chart."** Use several columns headed: "Security," "Safety," "Sufficient Provisions," "Stability," and "Emotional Health." Under these headings, list several practical ways to help your children during and after your divorce proceedings.

2) **Understand your children's perspective on time.** Discover how they think about times and seasons. Practice using the terms they use to describe the sequence of things happening around them.

3) **Provide a safe space for your children before breaking any "bad news" pertaining to divorce or separation.** Even more than adults, children need a supportive atmosphere and time to process disturbing news. A comforting toy or favorite grandparent may help buffer them from

the storm. Especially be considerate of them when the information you share is about the other parent.

4) **Arrange professional therapy or counseling for your children.** Among other areas, ensure the counseling sessions focus on correcting any guilt feelings children have associated with their parents' divorce.

Up Next

Generally, a greater percentage of African-American parents exercise corporal discipline than any other group in society. Whether black families should continue this practice is culturally debatable. Increasingly problematic for divorced parties, both legally and socially, is the extent of corporal discipline used in child-rearing. The next section discusses issues related to discipline, affirmation, and behaving appropriately toward the children of divorce.

Chapter 16

Parenting Through the Pain

Discipline: "Spare the Rod?!"

The issue of how to discipline children generates its own set of complexities in the cross-cultural context of the African-American experience. Many black folks believe in a "whuppin" (as opposed to a "spanking"). They believe a fair and loving form of physical discipline can go a long way toward building character and preserving family and social order. Most of the older generations of African-Americans—especially those who came up under church influence prior to the 70's and 80's—were subject to some measure of "spankings." "Spare the rod; spoil the child" was the prevailing wisdom. Our parents, grandparents, uncles, aunts, neighbors, school teachers—our "village elders"—took care of wayward and rebellious children through "the art of corporal punishment." Based on the nature of the childhood offence, they gave us a "whuppin'," a "beatin'," or a "killin'"—depending on how much our childhood behavior deviated from expectations and good family upbringing. Did our elders love us? Certainly they did. Did they harm us for life? Probably not, and certainly not to the extent some persons would have us to believe. Did some parents and elders take the matter of corporal discipline too far or act out of anger and frustration? Unfortunately, some did.

The issues of divorce and separation interject a thorniness (or thorny-mess) into the subject of disciplining children. At the time the couple was living together, disciplining the children came naturally for either mother or father. However, when a breakup occurs, all bets are off, and drama often ensues.

Charges of child abuse carry a different kind of social impact in a single-parent environment versus a two-parent setting. In one context, both parents may encourage one another to use physical discipline. In the other context, the use of physical discipline by a newly-single parent is suspect. A divorced father can easily become the "heavy" and receive increased legal scrutiny and exposure when he administers discipline. A society increasingly against physical discipline adds fuel to the fire. Have you ever made note of the passerby who frowns and shows disgust or threatens to intervene when corporal discipline of children takes place in public? Beside the general pressure of societal norms, those who physically discipline children face possible legal repercussions. Depending on the locality, civil authorities can arrest, charge, and incarcerate parents who administer physical discipline. A charge of child abuse can legally engulf and emotionally destroy a good, very loving, and well-intentioned parent. There is no easy answer to this complex issue confronting parents, especially divorced parents, and divorce judges often provide little to no help. Many give the "company-line" when confronted with the issue of corporal punishment. Expect inconsistencies at best. However, I suggest the divorcee err on the side of alternatives to corporal punishment.

Rules and approaches to discipline in a remarriage bring their own set of surprises. These issues surface in divorce courts and with attorneys all the time. However, many parents are blindsided by this legal "intrusion" into what they otherwise consider their private business. For example, when a mother or father remarries, the biological father may not like the discipline his children receive from their stepfather. The tension mounts when the children are young or pre-teen girls. This apprehensive father may intervene to the point of starting a physical altercation with his ex's new husband or partner. On the other hand, he may exercise his legal muscle to protect his children from what he deems improper treatment by the new man in their lives. That is, he may aggressively interject discipline issues into the fray of the divorce or post-divorce proceedings and petition the court to remove his children from their mother's home.

It is a good idea for those who divorce and remarry to establish guidelines for disciplining their children. These guidelines should cover the role of a new spouse, stepparents, in-law grandparents, and anyone else in a position to administer discipline. Remember, "An ounce of prevention is worth a pound of cure." If you anticipate problems, you can determine in advance the course you should take to avoid embarrassing or drama-causing situations.

Showing Affirmation When the Script Flips

A parent should never discipline a child without giving affirmation since love and affirmation remove some of the sting. These attributes also ease some of the drama that occurs when a parent administers discipline in the context of divorce. In reality, discipline and affirmation are two sides of the same coin. Though changes occur for both parents in this area, mothers especially must review their patterns of affirming their sons. How a mother affirms her son may change during and after divorce. Whereas an irate ex may accuse a male parent of treating the children in a harsh way, the divorced mother may accuse her ex of treating the female children too fondly. She flips the script.

When it comes to the children, sometimes a father must walk a thin line between discipline and affirmation. A young girl needs a lot of affection from her father as well as warmth, care, fondness, stroking, and the like. In a natural way, she forms a strong and healthy bond with her daddy. A caring father should not take this bond with his young girl lightly, despite the potential misunderstandings others interject into the relationship. Divorce and separation can cause a fissure in the bond of affection between a father and his daughter. When a father becomes "absent" in his little girl's life, the separation creates a hole in her heart the size of a Mack truck. Whereas previously she had hope, expectation, and a measure of fulfillment, she now experiences a sudden and gnawing aloneness. The hole in her heart leaves her vulnerable and makes her susceptible to all kinds of emotional instability and predatory abuses. As a result, she may no longer feel loved or grasp for the straws of affection any male may use to lure her. A divorced father must stay connected to the life of his girl and fight for her emotional and psychological well-being. Even when your divorce or separation is creating untold grief in your life, you must still keep reaching out to your girl. You must do whatever it takes to assure her she is still, "Daddy's little girl."

A mother must likewise stay connected in a positive way to her sons. Some women have trouble emotionally adjusting to the sons of the ex who remind them of their former spouse. Many divorce attorneys or *Guardian Ad Litems* note these women perceive the image of their ex in the behavior of their sons and despise what they see. Though damaging for the sons, the perception and transference of negative feelings toward them is a sad fact. These irate mothers must remember their sons need affirmation, not just punishment or discipline. If you find yourself in this position, catch yourself before you inflict serious damage. You must learn to love, accept, and affirm your sons for being unique individuals. Don't baby your boys or thrust them into responsibility for which they are not prepared. Is a son really "the man of the house"?

A common saying is, "Black mothers prepare their daughters but protect their sons," while others say, "Mothers raise their daughters and pamper their sons." True as these statements appear, each primary custodial mother must realize her limits when dealing with an errant and rebellious son. Carefully draw the line before he reaches a "point of no return." That is, often a season comes when a black mother can no longer handle her son. Circumstances arise when it is too late to bend a tree. Some children do the wild thing and become completely uncontrollable. When a custodial mother reaches her "point of no return," she should call out for assistance from the child's father. Or, she must force the son to go live with his father, an uncle or another relative whom he respects and whose boundaries he is willing to accept. The ex may fault his former spouse for creating the problem by not letting him do his job long before the son became a problem. He may also complain that she now wants him to fix a problem for a son, who is now 15 years old, and going strong and wrong.

Appropriate and Inappropriate Behavior

Child abuse is a serious matter. Some parents become victims of false abuse allegations. Divorce opens the door for greater possibilities of accusations of child abuse. After a divorce, an accuser might classify the once innocent behavior of a parent toward a child as "suspect." Consider this scenario:

"I couldn't believe my ears," the distraught father said to his friend. "That 'b- - -h' hates me so much she accused me in court of trying to get it on with my own daughter. I'd never go there in my life! I just can't believe that woman would stoop so low."

The above scenario is real. During a divorce, some mothers accuse their ex of sexually molesting their daughters. They turn the normal affection of a father for his daughter into an illicit sexual encounter. The consequences of this accusation, and any legal repercussions, can be very destructive for both father and child. Divorced or separated fathers must view this drama against the backdrop of a disheartening social and moral reality: some men take sexual liberties with their own offspring. Incest is real. Child molestation is real, and sexual predators exist inside and outside of family relationships.

How does a divorced father relate properly to his children? Discipline and affection are allowable. Sexual encounters are totally out of order. When a man has an extreme emotional attraction to or excessive physical or sensual contact with his female children, it may signal inappropriate sexual activity. The kind of behavior toward a young daughter that may show fatherly affection when he is married, in the context of divorce, may appear alarming and result in charges of child molestation. Instances of such behavior may include kissing a daughter on the lips, permitting a daughter to sit on your lap, falling asleep in the same bed, and assisting with bathing or dressing. As a divorced or separated man, you need to protect yourself from accusations of sexual child abuse. A false accusation of inappropriate sexual contact with a minor child can destroy your good reputation, impede your future progress, and cause a slow burn in your life.

Adult Responsibility

Since your breakup, you probably no longer enjoy the sexual privileges and pleasure your ex provided. Yet, your sexual desires are still present. When you're hungry, all kinds of food look good to you. One day you may find yourself in a private space with the flirtatious daughter of your new girlfriend or one of your kid's female friends. The maturing teen girl searches for affirmation and begins looking to you to fill that need. She emotionally likes you as her "stepdad," and perhaps you now see your girlfriend's daughter in a way you never saw her before.

So one day, your girlfriend leaves you at her home while she steps out. In the meantime, her daughter emerges half-clad from the bathroom after taking a shower. The chance moment arouses you sexually. After all, you reason, she does not have any biological relationship to you; she is not your child. And while you would never sexually approach your own daughter, you begin thinking it is okay for you and your girlfriend's daughter to meet each other's sexual needs. Stop! You had better not go there. Make up your mind that under no circumstances will you cross that kind of sexual line. Leave the hot daughter of your new girlfriend alone. Keep her off limits.

Nor should you allow others in your household to step across forbidden sexual lines. For instance, sexual relationships may develop between foster children, or stepbrothers or stepsisters and biological children in the same household. Or, the same may occur between the children of different parents (e.g., a mother's son and a father's daughter). The repercussions resulting from these types of sexual relationships may also cause you some drama with legal authorities. Further, minor children who engage in these relationships can experience irreparable harm.

Occasions also exist for divorced mothers to engage in inappropriate behavior with under aged males. Mothers should guard themselves from touching or fondling sons and stepsons inappropriately. Any divorced mother who allows a male who is beyond a reasonable age to share her bed is opening a can of worms. She exposes herself to suspicions or charges of child sexual abuse.

Sometimes, a certain situation of abuse blindsides lawyers and others involved in a divorce case, such as when a biological or nonbiological mother perpetrates sexual abuse. I recall a divorce case where the court awarded custody of the children to the father while granting the mother supervised visitation rights. On weekends, the father would take his young daughter to stay with his mother, her paternal grandmother. During those times, the biological mother would stop by to see the girl, and on several visits, the mother sexually molested her young daughter. The little girl complained to her father, and the court launched an investigation that uncovered a habitual pattern of abuse by the mother. The father and just about everyone else was shocked and devastated by the discovery.

Act Now 16 – Parenting Through the Pain

Here are some ways a well-intentioned parent can avoid the pitfalls associated with giving physical discipline to a child. Without crossing any familial boundaries, there are many things you can do as divorced fathers and mothers to keep the bonds of your affection connected to your daughters and sons. Brother, Sister, safeguard your life and the future of your daughters and sons with a good fence.

1) **Make sure you clarify the distinction between discipline and abuse.** Where does discipline end and abuse begin? Pause and ask yourself whether your contemplated punishment is appropriate and corresponds to the offence, or if you are acting out of frustration and uncontrolled anger. Also, what is the difference between punishment and discipline? One helpful bit of advice suggests that punishment looks at the past and the wrong that was committed. However, discipline looks to the future and correcting the kinds of character flaws that will insure competency and success.

2) **Retool your understanding of the local laws regulating what a parent can or cannot do.** Discover which forms of discipline are permissible, and which forms you should consider borderline abuse. Treat the subject of discipline the same way you would renewing your driver's license. Ask yourself whether any changes have occurred in the "rules of the road" since you previously took the test. Yes, some rules and laws do change—and some of those rules and laws regulate physical discipline. Do not be denied your "license" to raise your children because you fail to learn the new changes that govern parent and child relationships.

3) **Learn other methods of discipline besides spanking.** Giving a *"whuppin'"* is not the sole method for altering a child's attitude and behavior. Learn new ways to mold a young life. Understand rewards and incentives. Remind yourself of how divorce and separation can turn the world of a child upside down.

4) **Curtail a child's manipulative behavior.** Some children expertly learn the art of manipulating a parent into not giving them discipline. A parent must guard against a child's devious attitude. Clearly communicate to the child the proper field of play. Say something like the following: "Mama is giving you discipline because you broke my rule for the third time. I've already given you enough warnings. Now I'm going to punish you. I understand the pain you feel from the family's breakup, but that is no excuse for you to disobey. So because of what you did, I am going to..." The errant child will soon get the point that manipulation does not work.

5) **Place your children's welfare above your own.** In some ways, a hurting father or mother must become transparent to their children. Often, a hurt person will shy away from opening himself. Do not let your own pain prevent you from meeting the deeper needs of your children. They also have pains and needs. Of course, you should never emotionally burden your young children; however, it may help your children to see your humanness and share their own disappointments with their parent. But beware: what you say to your children can get back to your ex who may later use the information against you!

6) **Make spending time with your children a priority.** Reallocate your time. Separated or divorced, you now have more free time—at least theoretically. Devote some of the time you once spent with your ex to your son or daughter. Make appointments with your child, and keep them. By your actions, let your child know she or he is a high priority in your life, even though you and her mother (or you and his father) do not get along anymore. A breakup can become a blessing in disguise if it translates into building a more meaningful fatherly or motherly relationship with your daughter, son, and any of your other children.

7) **Be open to seeking assistance from the other parent.** A child's mother or father, or another relative, can step in and give you assistance with an errant and rebellious son or daughter. Every parent should have limits when dealing with children. Know when to throw in the towel by turning your child over to someone else who can exercise firm control before the child implodes.

8) **Consider the possible sources of accusations.** Charges against you can originate from different sources. Most often, they may come from your ex. A family member or friend could plant seeds of suspicion in the mind of your ex. Charges could also come from your daughter's schoolteachers or any other mandated reporter. If they see something suspicious between a male parent and young girl, or between a female parent and young boy, the law may require them to report the matter to the proper authorities. Watch your public and private behavior.

9) **Be aware of the way you relate to biological versus nonbiological children.** Certain freedoms you take with your own girls are not permissible with your nonbiological female children. Hugs, kisses, lap-sitting, pats on the rear, bedroom visits, assisting in the bathroom, dancing, texting—all are up for re-interpretation during a divorce and afterward. Stipulate sexual boundaries in your home between nonbiological and biological children. Insure that everyone in the household understands and accepts appropriate space and guidelines for interactions between children who come from different parents.

Up Next

Extended family relationships are important. In-laws can play a major role in the lives of both divorced parties and their children. Divorce affects the way parents relate to fathers- and mothers-in-law, brothers- and sisters-in-law, etc. Marital separation also affects the relationship of children to grandparents, aunts, uncles, and cousins. All divorcees face the major question of how their divorce will affect the ongoing family relationships of themselves and their children. I provide some insight into these issues in the next section.

Chapter 17

Your Extended Family

Staying "In" With the In-Laws

When and how do you break the news about your divorce to your in-laws? If your divorce is impending, you know one thing for sure: you do not want your father- and mother-in-law to hear the bad news through the grapevine. Your major complaint is most likely not with them, but with their offspring you married. In most cases, it is the rule rather than the exception that your spouse be the first to know your plan to divorce. However, informing your spouse, children, in-laws, and extended family should run on parallel tracks. Sometimes, mitigating circumstances will require spouses to inform others first and their partners later as some marital relationships are dangerous or very complicated. Thus, breaking the news requires tactical expertise. You should make your move on several fronts simultaneously and expeditiously.

If you want to avoid some of the drama associated with divorce, show respect to your in-laws. Schedule a good time to talk with them; prepare what you will say and brace yourself for unexpected reactions. Let them hear the word from your own mouth. Better, let them hear the news from you and your spouse together—if you can agree to such an arrangement. Tell them you are divorcing, but realize that saying anything critical of their son or daughter will likely cause more drama. Be brief, and do not reveal all the gory details of the failed marriage. Be forthright and show as much graciousness as you can. Give your in-laws the general picture of the decision you made or that you and your spouse agreed to. Don't badmouth the spouse and try to show

how wrong they are and how right you are. Most know marriages are two-way relationships, and it takes both parties to succeed or fail.

The place and time you pick to share the news of your impending divorce (or your decision to start the process) are important. Pick the right setting and the right time. However, sometimes there is just no right place or time to tell your in-laws when you have decided to end your marriage. Once you tell them, prepare yourself for unexpected responses, which may range from depression and anger to exhilaration and joy. Many parents will be hurt and may encourage you to work out the matter. Some will express shock. After all, you are rejecting their son or daughter as a viable marriage partner. These parents might respond angrily, asserting their offspring deserved better in marriage than what you had to offer anyway! If mitigating drama is your aim, hopefully, you will not provoke a family feud. Your in-laws may not fully agree with your decision. However, you have won a great battle if, after hearing you, your in-laws still respect you. Assure them you will do everything within your power to preserve a sense of normalcy in their relationship with the children. However, your status with your in-laws will definitely change.

Once you have cleared the air with your spouse's parents, proceed to inform other family members in the order of your preference. Usually the order you choose will follow the order of those with whom you and your children had better relationships. Consider brothers- and sisters-in-law, aunts and uncles, nephews and nieces, etc. Ironically, sometimes your best relationship with your in-laws will exist, for example, with the wife of your husband's brother or with the husband of your wife's sister. Be assured, however, that word of your impending divorce will get around to the family soon enough. The family grapevine will take care of that. Just don't drop your bombshell at Thanksgiving or Christmas dinner, or at a birthday party, anniversary or other family event. There is no need for your news spoiling everyone's celebration.

What About the Others?

Whereas divorce can make a couple feel insecure, their divorce can also cause insecurity and uncertainty in the lives of their relatives. They, too, need a way to handle the breakup of your marriage. Even as you seek to lessen the drama in your own lives, you can alleviate some of the drama for your relatives if you share the story of your failed marriage. Your own siblings may be at the top of the list of those who need to know the status of your marriage. You may have kept a close brother or sister more up-to-date about your welfare than your parents. If so, break the news of your divorce to those siblings first. They may give you the initial love and affirmation you need to get over the shock when you hear yourself saying, "I am getting a divorce. I am through with my marriage." You can cry together.

Most likely, your siblings can strategize with you about the best way to tell your parents, many of whom are disappointed when their child's marriage fails to work out. Even if your parents went through a divorce, they still don't wish the same experience for you. Strangely, good parents will feel saddened, but encouraged at the same time. They want their child to be happy, not bound by an abusive, life-threatening, or dream-crushing marriage. Further, if your parents are emotionally sensitive, they will have detected your trouble before you disclosed your breakup. In some instances, it becomes necessary to brace yourself for a parent who says, "I told you so. You shouldn't have married him (or her) in the first place." You should anticipate such a response if you decided to get married despite your parents' objections. Prepare yourself emotionally to deal with parental payback or smack back. Parents are not perfect, and some are even mean-spirited.

The process of disclosing your intent to divorce is akin to notifying family members a relative has died. Many of us know very well how emotionally taxing the experience can become. Avoid inflaming a bad situation. Don't start or pour gasoline on a family feud. Sometimes emotions run high. A marriage brings extended families together. Don't allow your divorce to destroy good inter-family relationships and unity. Anticipate some relief once the word of your divorce is out. You will cross an important line by publicly revealing your personal plans. You will have done your part in clearing the air and setting a positive tone for going forward.

Getting "In" With "Big-Mama"

More drama occurs when a divorced party seeks to establish a new relationship with a different partner and a new set of in-laws, away from one relationship and into another. You have one time to make your first impression, so make it good. When meeting "Big Mama" or a new mother-in-law for the first time, you want to make a good first impression. Be prepared to invoke a recovery plan if your meeting heads south.

"Big Mama" can be a blessing or a curse disguised as a blessing. Whatever the case, when you first meet her, you should do your best to get on her good side as quickly as possible. This is to the children's advantage and especially to yours. Remember, "Big Mama" will naturally love her grandchildren because they belong to her son or daughter. However, she may choose to park her love with the grandchildren and leave it right there. If things between "Big Mama" and you become emotionally strained, she may only tolerate you.

Sometimes, the first meeting with "Big Mama" is awkward. She doesn't know what to expect; neither do you. She was (and still is) friendly with her former daughter-in-law with whom she still has a good relationship. The children from their union continue in her good graces. However, her son now has a new woman whom "Big Mama" must accommodate. She knows what her first daughter-in-law was like, but she has suspicions about you. Some of her suspicions are well founded. She knows or assumes you were flirting with and tempting her son while he was married. She heard through the grapevine that you just couldn't wait until his first marriage was over, and he finally got his papers. Therefore, "Big Mama" already has some preconceived ideas about you and your tactics. She knows, "It takes two to tango."

By meeting you, "Big Mama" knows her life has become a bit more complicated. Marriage becomes a family affair extending the relationship of a couple into the lives of their relatives. Divorce, too, becomes an extended family affair. It's like getting braids in your hair. Once two families become intertwined, it takes a long time to untwist the braids. Meanwhile, the tension pulls out some of your hair. "Big Mama" sees the complications of divorce and anticipates the mounting clouds of drama in her life. Moreover, she really doesn't need it. She has already lived long and worked hard. She has raised her own children, and now knows she will have to play a part in raising some of her grandchildren. She has already shared her kitchen with her first daughter-in-law, but now she will have to share it again with a second. Her living has moved from simplicity to complexity, from relative peace to potential family warfare by having one son connected by children to two women. Drama.

Where will they celebrate holidays? Should the grandchildren all show up at the house at the same time? Which grandchildren get preference at school and social events? When "Big Mama" has to play chauffeur and a scheduling conflict occurs, in which direction should she head first? On Mother's Day at church, what becomes the protocol between the older grandchildren and the children by the second wife? These issues and more will complicate "Big Mama's" life. So, when you meet her, sensitivity to her perspective is crucial, even though she may not initially say a thing to you about these matters.

Since you know you will eventually be meeting "Big Mama," try to orchestrate the meeting instead of allowing someone to force you into an impromptu encounter. Find out what she likes, and make plans accordingly. Keep it simple but significant. Reassure her you are not trying to take her son from her, but really desire to become part of the family. Remember, for the sake of her grandchildren, "Big Mama" must maintain a good relationship with her son's first wife. Don't ask too many questions during your first meeting. As time goes on, you will learn what you need to know.

What happens if your first meeting with "Big Mama" gets off on the wrong foot? Implement your recovery plan. You should have a good one prepared for quick activation. When all else fails, don't increase the drama by going off. Instead, acknowledge things aren't going well, and you would like to call or reschedule a personal meeting with her at a time when things are more relaxed. She'll appreciate the honesty, and the break will give her space to recompose herself for the next time.

Act Now 17 – Your Extended Family

Your in-laws are an important part of your family. Therefore, your breakup is bound to have a significant impact on extended family members, perhaps far more than you realize. The following tips can help you break the news and deal with the aftermath as well as welcome a new "Big Mama" into your life.

1) **Prepare a script with talking points.** These tidbits will help you share the news in a way that lessens drama. Perhaps you could email select individuals. Beware, however, any news you share electronically can get out of control in a hurry.

2) **Plan a "good" time to share your decision to divorce with your in-laws.** Share the divorce news with your other in-laws as soon as possible. You and your spouse should coordinate the time to share the news with your family, and then tactfully do it. Don't allow the grapevine to get the best of you. As many people as possible should hear the word from you. Choose the appropriate time to share the news with your children. If they are talkative, you might have to give them some ground rules.

3) **Share your news of divorce with trustworthy members of your own family.** Use their input to help you discern how other members of your family may react when they discover what is happening to you. Don't cause your parents unnecessary drama. Wisely break the news of your breakup, and let your parents down easy, especially if they are getting up in age.

4) **Nurture peace in your extended family.** If you can, convince your in-laws and relatives to keep the peace for the children's sake and for all others impacted by your divorce. Honesty and sensitivity go a long way.

Up Next

The next part of this conversation speaks to the **community dimension** of divorce and drama. The drama of divorce greatly impacts one's life and activities in the neighborhood, street, social gatherings, civic affairs, and other areas outside one's extended family. Thus, I will discuss such things as your friendships and your church relationships.

PART FOUR:

The Community Dimension

This section helps you recognize how divorce impacts you

and the community of which you are a part.

Chapter 18

Who Keeps the Friends?

Friends: Yours or Mine?

Outside the purview of the courts, divorce is a lot about friendships and relationships. Every couple has an investment of "friendship capital" in a marriage. When the marriage dissolves, each partner faces the challenge of maintaining the friendships the couple once enjoyed together. Thus, a divorcee will raise a crucial question between spouses about friends: "Which ones are yours, and which ones are mine?"

If by some farfetched chance a couple's friend(s) belonged exclusively to one partner or the other, the repercussions of their divorce would be minimal. Each party would claim his or her unique pool of friends and go their separate ways. However, we all know friendships just do not work that way. Certainly, a marriage partner has some friends more exclusive to him or her. However, most of a couple's friends relate to marriage partners as a unit. Couples usually enjoy common friendships as illustrated on the chart below.

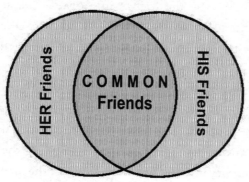

Imagine all the relationships and occasions where close friendships come into play. A married couple has work friends, leisure friends, church friends, club friends, sorority and fraternity friends, exercise friends, family friends, children's friends, school friends, professional friends, volunteer friends, neighborhood friends, long-term friends, girlfriends, boyfriends, married friends, single friends, young friends, older friends, ex-boyfriends, ex-girlfriends, and countless others. Some of these relationships are close; others are casual. Yet, in the African-American tradition, all of them are "friends." Some are even closer than family. When a divorce enters into the friendship equation, especially in a bitter divorce, sometimes a couple may force their friends to take sides with one spouse or the other, and the emotional toil can be both divisive and taxing. Even in tough divorce cases, the attorneys can find creative ways to settle the issues related to children and assets. However, such is not the case when dealing with "friendship capital." Divorce laws do not address this issue. For example, the judge cannot make a decision about which spouse gets to keep "Charlie," the neighbor friend who watches the house when the couple is gone. Nor will the judge make a ruling about "Shanna," the accountant friend who helps the couple complete their tax return every year.

Friendship Capital or Casualty?

The issue of "friendship capital" or "friendship casualty" often appears in divorce cases. For instance, in a contested custody proceeding, an attorney might subpoena a friend of the husband to testify on behalf of his client. Likewise, the wife's attorney may cross-examine the same friend! In some messy divorce situations, it is very difficult for a common friend to testify on behalf of one of the parties because, right there, someone will lose a "friend." This is friendship drama.

How do you negotiate the friends in a divorce relationship? A couple must settle their friendship matters outside the divorce court. On their own, they must personally negotiate a successful and informal agreement over their "friendship capital." If they fail in this area, some of their so-called "friends" may expose the separated spouses to recurring emotional upheaval, social isolation, and deceitful manipulation. For example, let's say their friends' holiday barbeque is approaching. How should the friends handle the matter? Should they still invite both divorced parties knowing they are still mad at each other? Should they invite just the female or just the male? By inviting only one, though, they risk creating other kinds of drama, as one of the spouses will end up getting hurt. Should there be any restriction on the invitations extended? Can you ask your friend not to bring his new partner? Attempting to play fair, the friends decide to issue an invitation to both exes, thinking it better for them to handle the matter as each sees fit. However, when the wife learns her ex has decided to attend the affair, her first inclination is to opt out. Then she has second thoughts. She remembers "Denise" usually comes to the gathering, and recalls how she used to flirt with her ex. The very thought of "Denise" fully exposing herself to him infuriates the wife. Therefore, she changes her mind and decides to attend the barbeque after all! "Denise" had better prepare herself. Chicken and ribs may not be the only thing on the grill! The holiday scene could turn nasty in a hurry!

Issues of "friendship capital" may revolve around gatherings at the workplace, in the community, at church, or in other social settings. Family gatherings also provide occasions for negotiating common friendships. Watch for those instances when you might face the drama surrounding friendship capital. Below are some scenarios to guard against:

- Sometimes, a "friend" catches a divorced male off guard. When he least expects it, a female "friend" abruptly speaks to him at the grocery store. She says, "At work the other day, I heard from your ex that you and she couldn't make it. You know, even though your ex and I have been working together for years, I really do not like her ways. I think you deserve something better. Tell me, what really happened between you all?"

- A divorced woman runs into the same types of situations when John, who plays ball with her ex, shows up unexpectedly at her house. "I just stopped by to see how you're doing and if you need help with anything," he says. "You know, John told the guys it's over between you two. To tell you the truth, I saw it coming. Really, John isn't all that he thinks he is. You can tell by the way that he handles himself on the court. Now, don't get me wrong. John is still my friend, but frankly, I'm glad you got him out of your life. If ever you want to know some other stuff about your ex, just say the word."

Obviously, in the scenes above, the so-called common "friends" lack integrity and other desirable characteristics. In both situations, they try to manipulate the ex of each divorced party. Remember, your "friendship capital" is a valuable asset. When divorcing, refuse to destroy this asset by acting unwisely. Most divorces leave some friends as casualties. However, they do themselves a favor when they determine not to let their pain, bitterness, and anger spill over and affect the lives of their friends. In some instances, the friendship relationships of divorced parties can grow through their division.

Act Now 18 – Who Keeps the Friends?

Here are some tips for negotiating your "friendship capital."

1) **Have a good talk with your ex about your mutual friends.** Reach a mutual understanding. Maybe you can agree not to badmouth each other to your friends. In addition, you can agree to keep each of your new homes open to your friends' children. In this way, you can decrease some of the drama and social isolation. Close the door on the manipulative and hypocritical tactics of so-called "friends."

2) **Spare your mutual friends from testifying in your divorce proceedings.** Whenever possible, don't cause them pain in the courtroom. Show deference, and you won't regret how you handled the situation.

3) **Think about you and your ex jointly issuing a cordial statement when the judge completes your divorce.** Your attorney can help you. Perhaps you can post your joint statement on Facebook or some other social media site. In the joint statement, define your relationship. Explain how you plan to conduct yourselves in the social realm. Speak words of encouragement to your friends. Some of them truly feel bad about your breakup. If you and your ex agree on how to define your relationship as divorcees, then you leave little room for others to define you or your ex negatively.

4) **Do not cut off your ex from his or her friendships.** That is, refuse to "demonize" your ex to others. Encourage your ex's friends to maintain a relationship with your ex and support him or her. Be gracious even if your ex is not. Prepare to lose friends you think are solid. Be ready for surprises. Eventually, you will preserve more of your pre-divorce

friendships by taking the high road. By refusing to badmouth your ex, you do a favor for your friends. They will appreciate and respect you for keeping them away from your drama.

5) **Set ground rules for yourselves when you and your ex must appear together in difficult and public social situations.** Those who fail to prepare are preparing themselves for failure. If your absence can make a better situation for your spouse, then properly excuse yourself.

6) **Help your children maintain their friendships.** Some divorces cause such a rupture in family relationships they cutoff the children from other family members and friends. Make certain your children maintain their friendships despite your divorce.

Up Next

The church is a large part of life for many African-Americans. The dimensions of church life are spiritual, cultural, and social. The impact of divorce for African-Americans on their church life, and vice-versa, is immense. Anyone who has been a regular attendee at a black church over the years has probably encountered a nasty situation of divorce at some point. When divorce occurs in the church fellowship, the drama can run rampant. The next section can help you curtail some of this church drama when divorce happens.

Chapter 19

You and
Your Church

The Word at the Church

Church is a very important part of the African-American cultural and religious experience. It is also a great social network for communication and relationship building. Any wise person will take heed to the "word at the church," whether the word is about social or political activities, community and cultural affairs, the neighborhood and schools, or national and personal concerns—it is always good to understand the pulse of the church when you are going through divorce. Your relationship with the church may change. You may be ostracized, judged, hurt, or even lose friends.

Many divorce clients also have a spiritual perspective and a sense of faith as Christian believers. They bring spiritual values to the legal table and wrestle with issues like, "What is the place of prayer in the breakup of my relationship?" "What does God really want me to do about my spouse?" "What is His will for my life in this situation?" "Would God approve of divorce?"

Sometimes the person contemplating a divorce has already spoken to the "elders" in their village and received the following words of encouragement: "I'm praying things work out for you." Some have received counsel from "Big Mama" or others who have challenged them to forgive and reconcile. They have counseled with their pastor or spiritual mentor. The ripples of divorce and separation can cause much drama in an African-American church. I recall the story of a church deacon who had been married for 30 years when he became romantically involved with a choir member, which led to his separating from his faithful wife. The deacon loved his children, so each morning, he would go back home to see his family, bring the newspaper, and have his regular cup of coffee. However, after his brief visit, he would go back to stay with his new woman. Had the deacon been a loner, perhaps his pastor could have successfully intervened in the situation. However, no less than 20 persons who were relatives of both the deacon and the choir member attended this church. Thus, their affair became an open scandal. The church began breaking apart. Members and family left the church, some even moved out of state. If this situation had occurred in a white congregation, generally speaking, the parties might have lost themselves in the social shuffle. However, in the African-American experience, church overlaps with how black people define community. Religious and social functions overlap and deeply influence one another.

When divorce takes place in an African-American context, we often find religious overtones in the mix. Many black people stay married for Christian reasons by understanding (albeit limited in many cases) what the Bible teaches about marriage and divorce. Marriage vows are spiritual and considered sacred. A couple feels the right thing for them to do is stay married "till death us do part," regardless of the circumstances. Divorce for them is wrong because their tradition teaches, "marriage is a forever commitment." Therefore, the right or "church" thing to do is stay together. Many call this, "the word of the Lord at the church."

Historically, marital relationships that did not receive validation in the larger society could receive affirmation in the church. The desire to have a "church wedding" was of high value. Moreover, it still is. Those who did not look favorably to the legal system could look favorably to the church. They respected the "preacher" and the church whose voice for many was "higher" than the legal system. African-Americans look to the church for support and as a forum. It is our safe-haven, especially during times of oppression. The church is the place where we express our voice and speak our peace.

A couple whose marriage is faltering faces both pros and cons when attending the same church. Of course, an obvious benefit is the mutual support a couple can give their children in a church setting. Perhaps, too, the practice of sitting together in church as a family can do a lot to keep church vultures away from their bleeding relationship. A drawback to cooperative church attendance is the emotional toll it can have on a couple who must learn to "wear the mask" before church members when their marriage is breaking apart.

Spiritual and Other Resources

The church has power: social power, spiritual power, power to make a difference, and power to influence change. People do a lot of talking at church, good and bad. When the right people discover your marriage is having problems, they may come to your aid. Many will pray and fast for your marriage. They may talk with you and express their understanding while others may send word through the grapevine to a spouse who is going astray. If your marriage fails, the Mothers Board or the Missionary Society at the church can surround your children with love and care. Many of them have "been there and done that." These righteous women of God will do all they can to help alleviate some of the pains of separation and divorce. They want you and the children to make it; they will put their spiritual, moral and other resources at your disposal.

Reconciliation and Mediation Services

Some churches offer reconciliation and mediation services to persons on the verge of divorce. These churches use the professional services of members and others associated with the congregation to help a couple whose marriage is rocky. Investigate the possibilities. Search online and call churches within your area to see what services are available. By using the reconciliation services of a church, you may save your marriage or at least smooth the way for an amicable parting during divorce. A prominent judge, who hears a great number of cases each year, firmly believes in "spiritual marriage counseling" to settle some marital and other disputes. In certain instances, it has been an effective resource in the black community for solving marital conflict, one that often "saves money, time, and stress" for everyone.

Peer Support and Mate-Finding

African-American churches can also give peer support to divorcees. Some churches have a ministry for single parents. Though mostly composed of women, single men often find marriage partners in this setting. In a particular church ministry for single parents, the women were most interested in remarriage (or marriage). It turned out every male who participated and received support from the single-parent group got married, several of them to women in the group. Single-parent groups focus on the children, while groups for single persons focus on marriage or remarriage. Sometimes, these groups of singles and single parents merge.

Safe-Haven from Abuse and Violence

Use the church as a safe-haven when the drama of violence erupts during marriage or divorce proceedings. Domestic violence and physical abuse occur too often in African-American households. Fleeing to the church is an expedient and quick option for a woman who finds herself in this type of crises. A church will usually help and protect you until help arrives from law enforcement and other agencies. The church can also provide a secure shelter for your young children and possibly safe temporary housing for you and them.

Divorced mothers should also consider steering their teens to the church as an alternative to the street violence running rampant in urban black communities. The number of shootings and homicides taking place in our communities is a disgusting scourge on black life. The weekend bloodbaths desensitize residents to the "matter of fact" manner in which violence mows down children, teens, and young adults of single mothers and divorced parents. Any wise African-American divorcee who loves her children will do everything possible to save them from the drama of the streets. An accessible option, though not foolproof, is getting the children involved in the youth program of a good church or a faith-based community group.

Some divorcees shy away from the church because they don't want everyone in the congregation to know their personal business, or the drama they face. The image they have of most church folks is one of people who think of themselves as better than everybody else. While some in the church fit that bill, most do not. Usually, no one who perceives all church folks as "sanctified and holy" hangs around the church long enough. Quiet as it is kept, a whole bunch of those church folks have a lot of drama going on. Many have learned the art of simply shielding the rough edges of their drama from others. But, spend a little time in the church house, and the truth will become evident: the lives (and lies) of these church folks are just like yours! Nobody's perfect.

Here are a few tips. When you go to church and get a chance to testify, tell your story just like it is. Don't make it pretty or gloss it over. By taking this approach, you will benefit yourself in a few ways. Foremost, if you tell on yourself, nobody else can tell on you. Your open testimony will blunt any gossip. In addition, "What comes from the heart reaches the heart." When you open up for real with your struggles and testimony about your divorce, you can expect others to open up, too. Consider something else. Don't just go to the church to get help, go also to give help. As a divorcee, you may have more time to volunteer in church activities. Take advantage of opportunities to serve others whose lives may be worse off than your living conditions. When your shoes are hurting, nothing is more therapeutic than helping someone who has no feet.

Act Now 19 – You and Your Church

The church is one of the most important institutions in the black community. As such, it can provide solace and help in times of emotional, spiritual and physical need. This is especially true for individuals who may be dealing with the drama of divorce. Below are some tips to help you get the most from your church experience.

1) **Assess the benefits of attending a church.** If your marriage is troubled or you face impending divorce, consider attending a church. Do your own fact-finding. Discover what the pastor and congregation have to offer those who are going through divorce or its aftermath.

2) **Discuss an impending divorce with your pastor or minister.** The church is there to help you. Refuse to suffer alone or in silence. Share your story and solicit prayer and support.

3) **Join a church group for divorced persons.** Some churches have special Sunday School classes for this purpose. Volunteer your services.

Up Next

Divorce brings closure. However, finalizing a divorce does not automatically end the drama it generates in your life. Life goes on. Social and personal development continues. Issues will surface. When you finally receive your divorce decree, you will probably ask yourself, "What's next?" Well, several things await you. Things like facing the reality that you really decided to break a bad relationship and need to plan for your future. You will especially have to wrestle with your new emerging identity. The next section, **Rebuilding Your Life After Divorce**, addresses all these issues to help you prepare for your future as a divorcee.

PART FIVE:

Now What? Rebuilding Your Life After Divorce

In this section, consider the positive and practical elements

you will need to rebuild a successful life post-divorce.

Chapter 20

So, Now That You're Legally Un-Coupled . . .

After-Court Wrap-Up Session

Relief has finally come.

Your divorce is final. You've got your papers and some of the things you wanted. You had to wrestle and wrangle about the terms, but at least you got something. You had to pay more money than you thought in attorney fees. Your life's been in an upheaval for quite some time. The many court appearances, attorney consultations, depositions, document collections, negotiation sessions, pre-trial conferences, and meetings have robbed you of your precious time. Now it's over. You have your divorce. The matter is settled, and you are free. So, "Court's over." Now what?

After the judge renders the final decision and brings your case to its destined end, you may want to open up emotionally. By experience, your lawyer knows you need to vent. You may begin talking in the courtroom, in the hallway, or on your way to the elevator. Your attorney may even invite you back to the office to tie up a few loose ends where, in the safe space of the conference room, you may find yourself having a therapy session. During the months of court appearances and the trial, you did not realize you still had all those feelings within you. You thought you had released them entirely. However—underneath the steady composure you managed to keep week after week—you were shielding your soft spot, your hopeful spot, and your denial spot. In fact, until the very end, you still held on to a slim thread of hope things would work out differently or at least work out a little better.

Now that your divorce is actually over, denial does not allow you to believe your life has turned out as it has. You ask yourself, "How could the person I loved have done such a terrible job on me and our children?" You tell the whole story one last time to your attorney. It doesn't matter that the attorney has already heard the painful story in court. Once more, you share; and once again, your attorney patiently empathizes, listening with understanding, but also with legal and functional reality. He knows the drama of life goes on, and wants to get you on the path of healing. One divorce attorney says the most satisfying thing about his practice is the fulfillment of seeing "persons who were once broken regain their self-esteem, love self again, and rekindle hope for tomorrow." Sometimes, if a client requires a deeper level of emotional and mental therapy, the attorney can refer them to a qualified counselor who can provide direction on how to continue as a viable member of society.

Experienced divorce attorneys have seen it all. They have a trained and practical GPS (Global Positioning System) for divorcees. When you open up, your attorney accurately knows your position in the post-divorce process. He can then orient your mental, emotional, and social position, as well as your potential for getting your life back on track. However, do not expect your attorney to raise you to maturity as a parent would a child. Instead, having done the legal work, your attorney could give you a good "wrap-up" session. You will be responsible for doing the rest. When you hear the judge's ruling and receive your decree, you may be a bit confused about your own whereabouts in the divorced world. The next steps you should take may be fuzzy to you, but your experienced attorney can set a course for you to follow as you transition from being married through separation, breakup and divorce to singleness. Compare the experience to the stages of grief: denial, anger, bargaining, depression, and acceptance.[32] Assume full responsibility of all your affairs as a divorcee. Begin or further your healing by taking charge of your life from the divorce forward. You will discover the more questions you ask, the more answers you will receive. When you ask the right questions, your attorney can direct you to the best resources for your unique situation. Just ask.

---

[32] DABDA-the Kübler-Ross model, commonly referred to as the **"five stages of grief,"** is a hypothesis introduced by Elisabeth Kübler-Ross, in *On Death and Dying*, New York, Rockefeller Center: Touchstone, 1969. March 1, 2013, http://dying. about.com/od/glossary/g/DABDA.htm. "Kübler-Ross model," *Wikipedia*, March 1, 2013, http://en.wikipedia.org/wiki/K%C3%BCbler-Ross_model.

A Divorcee's One-Stop Resource

A divorcee needs resources to assist him or her getting on with life, stability, security, and protection. Experienced attorneys can provide leads for their clients in any number of areas, such as financial advisors, therapists, realtors, insurance agents, social service agencies, tax preparers, law enforcement agencies, security firms, etc. Do not shy away from asking your attorney for guidance. In fact, imagine your divorce attorney as a "one-stop-shop" to help you stabilize the listing ship of your life as you sail through the rough seas of divorce. You should understand, however, there are limits. Expect to pay for additional services your attorney performs above the amount you contracted to pay for the handling of your divorce, although some resources may be free. From your personal viewpoint, your ex may have taken you to the cleaners on the asset side of your divorce. You can expect your attorney to empathize with your losses, but don't blame your attorney for the judge's decisions in favor of your ex. Nor should you emotionally put the lean on your attorney by hedging when it comes to paying your final bill. Pay your attorney what you owe, and pay timely. The attorney represented you, now do your job and pay. Don't ever think because you came out the "loser" in your divorce, your attorney should reduce or cancel the bill! That was not the legal deal.

If you take the course of a financial ingrate, you may find yourself back in court, this time facing your former attorney who will be suing you for legal fees. Be wise. Don't forget your divorce attorney knows about all of your business, including any assets you possess after divorce. If you financially stiff your attorney, be assured you will pay voluntarily or involuntarily.

Exploring Your New and Emerging Identity

Most life-changing situations have a downside as well as an upside. Divorce does not differ in this respect. It has its ups and downs, its good and bad aspects. Divorce breaks a special bond and separates the mates who once vowed or thought they would grow old together. At the same time, it can bring a measure of freedom into the life of either partner. A divorcee can use her new freedom to explore the personal aspects of life that a marital relationship could never offer. The "After-Divorce Action Plan" you prepare will do two things. First, it will help you handle your current realities. Second, it will help you successfully meet new changes and explore your potential.

Remember, freedom still has its consequences as stated in the old cliché, "Too much of something could be good for nothing." Usually, a person's freedom in one area of life translates into responsibility in some other area. This is especially true for a divorcee. Your freedom from a bad spousal relationship does not absolve you from handling your other responsibilities. A divorced person is still responsible for himself or herself and their dependents. Your divorce frees you in more ways than you realize. Legally, you are absolutely free from your partner. The law no longer considers you married or ties you to responsibilities related to your ex. Your status is now "divorced," "*single*," or "*available*"—however you choose to describe yourself.

The freedom you gain through your divorce also extends into other areas of your life. If the judge awarded your spouse custody of the children, then you are free from the daily responsibilities of childcare. I do not intend this statement to communicate insensitivity about the value of children. In no way would I consider a child some kind of "burden." The message is one about readjusting day-to-day priorities relating to child-rearing. Usually, a noncustodial parent has to pay child support, perhaps even some alimony. However, fulfilling those financial responsibilities is the legal extent of that parent's obligations as far as the court is concerned. If your divorce decree mandates that your ex pay off certain financial debts, then you are free from those bills as well. Your relief from servicing a mortgage or car note or from repaying an educational loan can take a tremendous load off your back and mind. I recognize, however, for some people, the emotional issues surrounding divorce linger and exploring their "new selves" is not as easy for them as it is for others.

When you obtain a divorce, your new circumstances place you in a position to explore the possibilities for your future—and some of these possibilities are fascinating. What are your likes and dislikes? What are the hobbies and activities you enjoy? What are the new interests you now have time to explore? Fill in the blank as you say to yourself, "*I always wanted to...but never got around to thinking about it until now.*" Dream during your divorce proceedings, and implement those dreams when your divorce is completed. An endless frontier presents opportunities for championing your freedom, unhindered by the restraints married life imposed upon you. Use the following questions to spur you in these opportune directions:

- How will I remodel or redecorate my home or apartment?
- What clothing styles do I really want to wear?
- What kind of foods can I now prepare for myself without having to think about feeding someone else?
- In which restaurants will I choose to treat myself?
- Which cultural places and events will I attend? Will I visit museums, amusement parks, concerts, and plays?
- What new intriguing places can I visit on my vacation?
- How can I improve my education?
- Under what circumstances am I too old to earn another degree or switch careers?
- Why may it be important for me to learn a second language?
- At what point should I start writing that book I've been putting off for too long?
- How can I wisely use my time to learn the history of some of my relatives?
- What is the benefit of volunteering at the local homeless shelter or a social service center in my community?
- I love growing things, so why shouldn't I plant a vegetable garden and participate in the farmer's market?
- Which exercise club should I join to lose a few pounds, even start roller-skating and steppin'?
- What capacity do I have to take steps toward becoming an entrepreneur?
- Which stocks should I use to invest the little nest egg I have?
- How important is it for me to devote myself to enhancing my spirituality?
- Since I have enough financial support from my divorce, for what reasons should I quit my job and consider home-schooling the children?
- In the next year, what is my plan for visiting social outlets for singles to meet new people and make new friends?

Breaking the Shackles

Many know the story of how animal handlers train a huge elephant. When the elephant is young, the trainers chain the gigantic creature by one of its legs. The large chain is too strong for the young elephant to break, so the animal submits. When the elephant gets full-grown, its tremendous size and strength would easily allow it to snap a chain as though it were a piece of thread. However, the elephant does not exercise its power to free itself. Why? Over the years, the physical chain has placed a psychological chain on the elephant's mind. The older animal still thinks it cannot break free from the same chain that confined it in its youth. So, the strong and mighty elephant continues submitting to this flimsy chain.

We can often liken a divorcee to a full-grown elephant. In many ways, the divorcee is still mentally bound to their ex-spouse and must break the shackles of the past marriage to gain the full freedom of his or her divorce. Are you a divorcee behaving like a full-grown elephant, shackled in spirit and mind by a past and binding relationship? If so, you are allowing unnecessary drama into your life.

Act Now 20 – So, Now That You're Legally Un-Coupled

By implementing the following you will empower yourself to tap the good resources of your attorney as well as adjust to your new un-coupled persona.

1) **Counsel with your attorney after your divorce.** Ask your attorney to schedule you for an appointment, as soon as possible, after the judge signs the decree. Prepare a good list of questions to ask your attorney. Nothing is too trivial a matter. Your attorney may not have all the answers. However, your lawyer can point you to resources in areas into which he or she cannot, or chooses not, to venture. Make sure your counsel reserves enough time for your debriefing.

2) **With your attorney's insight, make an "After-Divorce Action Plan" to guide your transition.** Perhaps you should make this plan before your divorce is final. Make timely dreams a part of the plan. Distinguish low-priority actions from high-priority areas you should address immediately.

3) **Make yourself a "Married versus Divorce Chart" with two columns.** Title the top of one column, "Married." Title the top of the other

column, "Divorced." In each column, list the differences in the areas of time, family living arrangements, money, friendships, vacationing, food and drink, and church. You may choose to do preliminary work on this chart before your divorce is final.

4) **Keep a journal of your feelings as your new life unfolds.** Make note when the light bulb comes on and enlightens your new legal status.

5) **Plan a vacation excursion for yourself, alone.** Bring no children, no friends, and no relatives. Go alone somewhere and get the best out of it. The future will present plenty of opportunities for you to enjoy your freedom with others.

6) **Rework your financial budget.** Plan for your immediate and long-term future. As a new divorcee, do not allow your finances to drift. Guide your financial future.

Up Next

As a divorced person, you must think ahead, sometimes far ahead. The time will come when you must resolve to forget the painful drama of your past. The next section will help you plan for your future.

Chapter 21

Taking Charge of Your Future

What Needs to Change?

The lawyer's wrap-up session can give you direction and prevent you from making hasty decisions that will negatively affect your future. Avoid knee-jerk reactions and the tendency to correct your marital failures overnight. Be reflective, not reflexive. Sometimes, your lawyer will offer radical advice: "You need a change." In one case, a certain divorce client contemplated moving out of state. She was 29 or 30 years old and confided she needed a fresh start. She wanted to change her surroundings, establish new social networks, and find a different employer. Her attorney's advice gave her the impetus she needed to take actions to better her future.

Your "After-Divorce Action Plan" can help you stay grounded while exploring your possible options. Keep your ship anchored while you explore new waters. Even if you choose not to explore, an anchorless boat can drift far away from shore. Keep your moorings. Stay tied to something trustworthy and fixed. Maintain some form of security.

Above All, Protect Your Future and Empower Your Children's

So what about your future? How should you plan to make things better for yourself down the road from divorce? Think about two main things. First, think about making those financial moves that most likely will insure your future financial security well into retirement. Based on available information and good advice, make the best decisions you can. The recent Great Recession reminds us no one enjoys the blessing of a crystal ball to predict the economic turns of financial markets. We now know all kinds of negative things can happen in the world and national economy that can potentially wipe out the financial stability of anyone on the local level. Second, a divorce is a good time to think about leaving a lasting financial legacy for your offspring. Give them a financial head start. African-Americans need to start thinking in these terms. If we are wise, we can financially empower future generations with a few strokes on a keyboard to complete a document and a pen affixing our signature. For instance, suppose the assets you gain from your divorce allow you to purchase a million dollar life insurance policy. Why shouldn't you think seriously about naming one of your children as your beneficiary? An effective life insurance policy is a simple way to accelerate and empower the progress of a family. (It works better than the odds of winning the Powerball lottery!)

Sometimes, the judge orders a father paying child support to get a life insurance policy, if he has none, and make his children the beneficiaries. In this case, the court takes the long-term view. If the father suddenly dies, the court seeks to insure that the children's financial support continues by virtue of the payout from his life insurance. The children need monthly income, educational and college expenses, and a degree of financial sustenance and stability in their lives. I recommend divorced parents follow the lead of the courts by taking the initiative to put these measures in place for their dependent children.

You must also think about your estate in times of divorce since estate planning and divorce issues often interrelate. Estate planning attorneys deal with trusts, estates, wills, personal and business powers of attorney, insurance, taxes, and the like. The legal advice an attorney provides in this area is generally useful for all people, whether married or single, either during a divorce, or once the divorce is completed.

Avoid "Playing Attorney" with Life's Critical Issues

You are probably thinking, "I don't have any more money to spend on a lawyer. The divorce cost me twice as much as I thought so the last thing I need is another lawyer in my pocket." However, you do not want to take any shortcuts with your future, an action that may later come back to haunt you, your children, or grandchildren. The first thing an attorney usually advises is for you not to "play lawyer" for your own affairs. Many people try to save a dollar by thinking they can bypass an attorney and do the legal work themselves.

Resist the temptation to use "internet" legal documents to prepare a Last Will and Testament, or for estate planning. In the overwhelming majority of cases, this practice creates a legal mess a lawyer must sort out later.

Attorneys know the finer points of the law that may escape the notice of those who desire to "play lawyer." This point was illustrated by a lawyer friend in the case of the pastor of a prominent church who created his will and trust via a popular internet website. He was an educated minister and felt he executed everything legally and properly according to the website. In his documents, the pastor took care to look out for the welfare of his wife, immediate family, the church, and some friends. Unfortunately, one day the pastor abruptly died. With great expectations, the family read his will and apprised the church of the same. However, when an attorney reviewed the documents, he discovered the pastor's will and trust were not legal. Contrary to what the pastor thought, he had not done everything correctly for a court to uphold the documents expressing his desires.

As one might expect, the documents created a nightmare for the pastor's family, the church, the friends, and everyone involved. The circumstances surrounding the pastor's homegoing turned what should have been a sad but joyous occasion into a drama of bitterness, hurt, anger, accusations, threats, physical altercations, and all the rest. At the very time proper preparations should have lessened the grieving process, the non-legal documents flipped the script. The lesson: secure the right kind of legal advice. I cannot emphasize this point enough. Few physicians can successfully perform surgery on themselves or choose to do so. Most people who drive cars are incapable of repairing them. At some time or another, each of us needs the help of a qualified professional in some area of our lives. Everybody's life and legal issues are different, and it's an honest fact that *simple wills do not exist.* Don't make cost the sole determining factor for whether you seek the help of a good lawyer or act as your own quasi-legal expert. Competent attorneys know the legalese and the fine points of the law that can escape the notice of lay people. The old adage says, "Either pay now, or pay later. But if you pay later, you will pay more." In this case, secure a lawyer experienced in estate planning.

A Prenuptial Agreement Before Remarriage

Second marriages dictate estate planning. In this regard, a prenuptial agreement may be of assistance. Its basic meaning is a contract a couple executes prior to their marriage, civil union, common-law marriage, or contract. Though no contract is absolutely foolproof, some persons use a "prenup" as a safeguard in case of divorce to cover such things as division of property, spousal support, or the forfeiture of assets on the grounds of adultery. Most divorced persons understand the importance of protecting their (remaining) assets in case a second marriage dissolves. However, a prenup is only workable if both parties agree. This agreement pre-supposes each party is not predicting the failure of the new relationship, but realizes the possibility of a breakup exists based at least on the experience of one party. The parties are realistic as, currently, more than half of all marriages end in divorce.

If you have children and see yourself headed toward a second marriage (or you are already in one), you may want to protect your own interests and your other assets with some form of a prenup. The future welfare of your children is too important to jeopardize. Allow your attorney to structure your prenup along with other legal documents.

Retirement Planning

Long-term planning for your future necessitates some sort of financial security in the form of a pension or other means of support when retirement time comes. Depending on the circumstances in a divorce, a judge can award a portion of a spouse's pension fund to the ex. Any divorced party will do well to review their retirement plans and any pension they hope to receive. Certainly, it is wise in this day of fiscal uncertainty to review the security of future retirement resources. You should submit your pension plans, IRA's, or Keoghs to the scrutinizing eye of an objective and shrewd financial advisor. Consider viable long-term options when nesting away your retirement egg. More likely than not, your divorce is a game-changer in your financial future.

Other Financial Instruments

Some married African-Americans possess huge amounts of money and immediate access to more. Sources and instruments of wealth may include annuities, lines of credit, money market accounts, insurance policies, stocks and bonds, etc. A divorce may have implications on these possessions or their use by either spouse. Meeting with a legal and expert financial advisor can help you sort out the losses, risks, and direction for proceeding when divorce occurs. Be prepared when you meet with your financial planner. Get up to speed on your financial situation beforehand. Think through the types of changes you may want to make in your financial affairs.

Federal and State Taxes

Brace yourself for a change in your tax filing status. The monies you have to pay for federal, state, and some local taxing jurisdictions are exposed. If you once filed your taxes under "Married Filing Jointly" or "Married Filing Separately," you are no longer able to do so as a divorcee. After a period, you will no longer enjoy the option or benefits of filing a return in the context of your marriage. You will now file as either "Single" or "Head of Household." Sometimes, those who file under a status outside of the two marriage categories may likely pay more taxes on their income.

Secure a sharp tax consultant to provide you with your anticipated tax liabilities. Give yourself sufficient time to spend some of your income on items that are legitimate deductible expenses. Acquire deductibles to soften the blow of the rise in income tax owed. Think ahead. Your financial future is worth the forethought.

Estate Planning

Divorce dictates estate planning during and after the process. A potential divorcee should apply the principle above to their will, trusts, life insurance policies, and other major assets. Many of us do not like to plan for death or even to think about it. Selfishly, instead of taking care of our business ahead of time, we leave the family to deal with it after our death. Rethink your will. Some attorneys recommend their clients review and update their will every two years. Some matters change more often than we realize. You want to place the management of your household and your money with the persons and in the places that satisfy you. The question is, "Whom do you 'trust' with your trust?" (Don't fail to consider any past divorce and the relationship implications on your estate.) Do not allow the monies from your insurance policies to fall under

NOW WHAT? LIFE AFTER DIVORCE 225

the control of your marital "adversary." Sickness and all kinds of things can happen during and after a divorce. Prepare for the worst-case scenario.

For instance, in a certain divorce case, the father was a drug dealer and the mother was terminally ill when their divorce was pending. At that time, the State of Illinois introduced the instrument of a "Standby Guardian" to allow someone to stand in for a parent over a 60-day period. The attorney quickly executed the instrument, and the mother died soon afterward. This course of action allowed the mother's friend to step in at the time of death and fight for the children. Because of the Standby Guardian instrument, the mother's friend received custody of the children, and the drug-dealing father received nothing. This case serves as an example of a mother who was willing to do some pre-planning. Some form of a Power of Attorney is also especially important when children are involved. Be explicit. Declare who should be guardian when your spouse is incapable. Provide detailed instructions on what your guardian should do on behalf of the children.

Life Insurance

When it comes to purchasing a substantial life insurance policy, many African-Americans think in terms of old-school men who used to carry life insurance amounting simply to burial policies. Some of our folks have paid tens of thousands over the years for a policy that was worth only a few thousand dollars upon their death! Frequently, I have heard a black man reflect this older generation's thinking, saying in essence, "I don't need all that insurance. If I get too big an insurance policy, my wife and children might start having some strange thoughts about my health and life. So I figure I don't really need that kind of money riding on my head. I only need enough money for them to give me a decent casket and grave." In other words, the brother is fearful his family might plot to take his life if his insurance policy pays too much above the minimum costs to bury him. Tragically, this thinking lingers in our community. Countless African-American men (and others) have no life insurance or do not have a policy that sufficiently covers the complete costs of their funeral. Consequently, too many men die leaving their survivors with nothing but a funeral bill!

Act Now 21 – Taking Charge of Your Future

You can't take the money with you, so leave your family as much cash as you can.

1) **Don't make an important decision about your future when you are under stress.** Give yourself some time to heal. Don't jeopardize what may be a good future by making a bad decision. Before making an important decision, run the matter by your attorney.

2) **Establish at least one significant routine that will change only in an emergency.** This will become your anchor and keep you grounded as you explore options for your future as a divorcee.

3) **Execute a Standby Guardian instrument.** Protect the interests of your children.

4) **Review the financial forms you filled out during your divorce.** The information you supplied provides an overall picture of your estate.

5) **Update your will or trust.** Make sure you remove the name of your ex to avoid them inheriting any money or property upon your death.

6) **Secure a prenuptial agreement.** It can protect the interests of your children and your assets when you anticipate remarriage.

7) **Make yourself a new long-term financial and retirement plan.** Use the help of a good financial advisor.

8) **Get advice from a certified tax preparer.** When possible, do it early in the year so you can implement certain strategies for money-shelters and thereby save some cash.

Up Next

Time brings about a change; so does divorce. A divorcee will face many challenging dynamics affecting (or arresting) their continuing identity development. Divorce provides an opportunity for you to explore being a new or renewed person. You can use the next section to help you maximize your divorce experience to redefine who you are. You can re-emerge into the world and declare, "Look out world, here I come."

Chapter 22

From Breakup to Breakthrough

Your Un-Married Identity

To one extent or another, most divorcees grapple with the dynamics of a changing identity. They face a struggle to adjust in a healthy and holistic manner and emerge successfully from the drama of their broken relationship. This journey begins with getting a grip on self, on your self-perception apart from your ex. Several kinds of experiences affect the life of a divorced individual:

- the emotional and psychological roller coaster of their anger, frustration, and lack of control;
- their anxieties about moving from the state of marriage to legal divorce, from living together to managing alone;
- the dashing of their spiritual hopes and dreams and their feelings of divine displeasure;
- the uncertainty of their future, especially the prospects for women of re-connecting in a new relationship;
- the "freedom" and grand opportunities of their breakup, exploring their new "single" status; and
- the financial independence of budget planning and freely allocating resources to meet their future desires.

Mediating Identity Issues

Personal, cultural, and social identity issues underlie all these experiences. They change and shift, sometimes quickly, at other times almost imperceptibly.

Many African-Americans face an identity crisis as members of a group living in a society often hostile to their racial and cultural experiences. Historically, since the days of slavery, white America has taught black people to hate themselves for being darker in color and different from whites in physical features. After centuries, the drama and aftermath of this self-hate remain and manifest in negative black cultural expressions, even into this 21st century. One dark-complexioned African-American attorney cites the case of a middle-aged African-American client who refuses to engage black people and avoids even gazing at them. The client's wife and children, the judge, the court administrators, and others who knew the man testified to his very deep antipathy toward African-descended people. This is but one example of the cultural self-hate at the root of many problems in the African-American community. When these problems intermingle in the relationship crises of breakups and divorce, a high level of drama ensues, and its repercussions are widespread.

Multi-Dimensional Connections

Wouldn't it be great if divorce only affected a person's living arrangements, and everything else remained the same? If this were the case, the divorced party could just move out of one house or apartment into a different one down the street and simply note their changed status by a new street address. But, alas, it just ain't so. Divorce affects not only marriage partners but also the interconnected cultural and social relationships of persons in a home, in a family, in a church, in a community, and in a society. As we have discussed in the previous chapters of this guide, divorce influences one's life along multi-dimensional lines.

- **The Personal Dimension –**
  - ✓ the foundation and roots of breakups, the different emotions of divorce and how a relationship deteriorates;
  - ✓ the realities of separating from a spouse and the continuing sexual and companion needs;
  - ✓ abuse and physical violence; the strains of interracial, homosexual breakups, and a husband's incarceration.
  - ✓ your shifting personal and social identity, and exploration of changes;

- **The Legal and Financial Dimension –**
  - ✓ how divorce moves you from counsel to court to conciliation to closure;
  - ✓ exposure of your assets and liabilities; the financial blues and the resetting of your standard of living;
  - ✓ the impact of child support orders on divorced fathers and some divorced noncustodial mothers;

- **The Family Dimension –**
  - ✓ the often devastating impact of divorce on both husband, wife, and their children;
  - ✓ the mother who sacrifices for her children, and the one who loses custody; the daddy who has custody and seeks to cope;
  - ✓ building an "ark" for the children's emotional security and preservation;
  - ✓ how divorced parents should discipline children, show affirmation, and avoid inappropriate sexual behavior;
  - ✓ how to maintain the bridges you build with extended family, in-laws, and others;

- **The Community Dimension –**
  - ✓ what to do about friends who are common to you and your ex;
  - ✓ how to keep friendship capital from turning into friendship casualties;
  - ✓ what to do about your divorce and church relations;

- **The "Now What?" –**
  - ✓ the fifth dimension of your divorce experience where you wrap up your legal matters;
  - ✓ how your lawyer can share additional resources as you look to the future;
  - ✓ what areas in your life need to change, and how you can best protect your future interests; and
  - ✓ coping with the new realities of your changing identity, as well as guiding and measuring your progress.

A theme weaves together how we handle these various dimensions of divorce. The goal is to seek peace and motivate growth in as many areas as possible. The result is the ability to withstand breaking down even though you are breaking up. A divorcee may successfully reach these goals by first honestly facing their identity crisis and mediating their immediate internal drama.

Where You Fit In

Have you ever gone through a bad experience, and felt at the time it happened only to you? "Why Me?" you asked yourself. "Why didn't this happen to someone else?"

Your divorce may have you feeling the isolation blues. The particular way your breakup and life are playing out may make you feel your situation is unique, a one-of-a-kind occurrence. Be assured, you are not "alone." Others share the kind of issues and drama you are experiencing. In this sense, your situation is not unique. Lawyers can work with you and help you make it through your nightmare. Trust me, there indeed is light at the end of the divorce tunnel. A good lawyer can help you to see where you and your divorce fit into the larger picture of social and marital breakups.

Other groups may use this book as a resource in their own professions. Perhaps you are a black psychologist, social worker, or mental health professional. Maybe you are a spiritual leader whose work repeatedly brings them face to face with the drama of individuals on the divorce spectrum. These insights into divorce drama can enhance your understanding about the kinds of legal or social issues faced by divorced persons. For example, consider the advice a counselor might give in the following situations:

A divorce happens in the lives of three different clients. All are African-American and approximately 40 years old. One client is male; the other two are female. In the first case, the female is a professional who married at 35 and has no children. In the case of the second female, we find she married at age 25, has four children, and works a common job. In the case of the male, he has three children, but is unemployed, having lost his license as a truck driver.

The counsel given to each of these divorcees will vary widely. In the "professional female's" divorce case, she is essentially back to being single. Her career gives her good earning power and potential, and she appears very available for the next prospect she meets. Whereas, the social trajectory of the "nonprofessional" divorced female is downward. She has four children in their early teens and younger. Any employment she finds will likely result in limited wages, or unreasonable or incompatible work hours. As far as a new marital relationship, she almost finds herself in "no-man's land." Many men who are available for marriage will not tie themselves down to a woman with kids or one who has little earning power, unless exceptional circumstances exist warranting such a relationship.

In the case of the "former trucker," his status is positive. Most likely, his wife has custody of their three children. With his background as a former trucker, any good work he finds is a blessing. In the meantime, he keeps himself afloat through the underground economy and gives something to the kids every now and then. With the scarcity of African-American males, his potential for remarriage is great. Likely, he will find a professional woman who will take him with any of his baggage. He probably will marry a woman who is willing to do far more than her share of supporting the household with him, despite the setback of him having lost his driving privileges—especially if he is good in bed.

Each divorce scenario presented has its own set of drama. My intention is to help lessen the drama of divorce for all clients and help them find themselves, identify options, and reach their fullest potential. I desire to situate each so they benefit from their future promise as restored divorcees—broken, but not bowed.

Victimized or Victorious

Most divorced persons consider themselves "victimized" by their partner in one way or another. That feeling can lead to depression. Pressures of church relationships and family members can add to your times of feeling down. Shame causes social embarrassment and can potentially lead you to isolation. In such a case, the Internet may become your friend.

If you are so inclined, you can use the social media on the Internet to re-establish your status following a divorce. Consider using a good professional networking site where you can exercise more control over the profile you present. Post a professional and attractive photo of yourself. In a straightforward and decent manner, share your profile, review your accomplishments, and state your goals. List your good qualities and assets. Discreetly present your story and a positive picture of who you are and what you do. Make certain your connections perceive your new single status. Additionally, you can share selective details of your story with a few of your connections. Underneath you are reserving the treasure of your life for someone who can truly respect you and appreciate the personal and professional value you bring to a relationship. You'll know the person when they discover you! In other words, make a good and upbeat impression as you reposition your status in the social realm. Check the tide of depression and isolation in your life. Emerge refreshed and proactive into the vast world of budding professional and personal relationships awaiting exploration. Be graceful and grateful. If your ex happens to read your profile, perhaps they may have second thoughts about your broken marriage.

Don't move too quickly, however, is the advice of one divorcee who recommends giving yourself at least 18 months of singleness following a breakup. You will need time to figure out who you are and recover from your "feelings of being lost" after the divorce and before you resume dating.

Crossing the Threshold from Pain to Change

Divorce is painful for most. By faith and wisdom, you can use the pain of divorce as a significant impetus in significantly changing yourself and your controllable realities. A friend of mine offers good insight when he writes, "Change is inevitable....Growth is optional....Choose to grow through your changes."[33] A person gains no merit if he or she strives to remain the "same" as before their divorce. What is the benefit? Even if he remarried his ex, he should still bring something new back into the old relationship. Otherwise, he probably will experience the drama of divorce the second time around. You should allow a divorce to usher your life into holistic transformation by becoming a new you. Intentionally shape your identity. Cultivate an image of the ideal person you wish to be. Like a phoenix, let a new you rise from the old ashes of your divorce.

Use your "After-Divorce Action Plan" as a starting point and criteria for measuring your outcomes. By doing so, you will change the way you think about yourself, and become proficient in renewing your identity along personal, social, and professional lines. Keep a holistic perspective. Deal with every imaginable aspect of your life. Embrace and empower yourself, your total self, in all dimensions of living. Your divorce has given you a great opportunity to do better for yourself.

[33] *Get Grown! And Keep Growing: The Self-Help Adult Maturity Handbook*, Walter A. McCray, YAMA 21st Publishers: Chicago. 1985. (Black Light Fellowship, Dist.)

Before the days of GPS, I heard the story of some urban travelers who got lost while traveling through the deep countryside. As the car meandered down the country road, they happened upon an old shack with a very old black man sitting in a rocking chair on the porch. They decided to stop and ask the man for directions.

"Do you know where Jones Road is?" they asked.

"No, I don't," the old man said.

"How about Sky Tree Street?"

"No, I don't know where that is, either."

"Then can you tell us how to find Rocky Lane?"

"Never heard of it," the old man said, calmly rocking his chair back and forth.

Finally, one of the travelers got so frustrated that the old man couldn't give them any directions, he blurted out, "Old man, you don't know nothing!"

To this the old man replied, "I know where *I* am."

The story speaks clearly. Some people cannot answer all the questions of others, but they know their personal whereabouts. Some of the people who may ask you a multitude of questions about the circumstances of your broken relationship and divorce may be wandering about themselves. As a party in an African-American divorce, you need to emerge from the broken experience by discovering anew where you are. Your identity as one formerly married may be undergoing a season of change, but you must reach a level of self-awareness, maturity, and wholeness where you can say with the utmost of confidence, "I know where I am."

Act Now 22 – From Breakup to Breakthrough

Once your divorce is final, you will truly be "on your own," facing a future that will have its share of uncertainties as well as opportunities. As a divorcee, you are now officially someone's ex-wife or husband, but this needn't be all that defines you going forward. Here are some tips to help you gain a clearer picture.

1) **Treat yourself.** Perhaps you have neglected yourself too long. If so, change your mindset. Every now and then, everyone has a right to pamper themselves, especially during and after the battles of divorce

proceedings. One suggestion is to set weekly or monthly lunch or dinner dates with trustworthy friends. Use the time to share private information with them so you won't feel alone or abandoned.

2) **Make a table comparing how your after-divorce identity has shifted.** On the left side, put "How I used to feel about myself." On the right side, put "How I feel about myself now." Answer these questions according to several different categories. For example, one divorcee cites her marital feelings of being "complete and sheltered." Post-divorce she feels "weathered, exposed, and vulnerable."

3) **Journal your prayers and hopes for your life.** Use a journal to gauge the progress you are making. List the three areas of your divorce that evoked the most pain. Determine to use the pain as an impetus for changes you desire to make. For example, the greatest source of pain for one divorcee was "single motherhood."

4) **Use your "After-Divorce Action Plan" as a basis for measuring your growth.** Be sure to thoroughly deal with each area of significance in your life. You should attach a timeline with deadlines for purposes of periodically checking your progress.

5) **Use the social network to introduce the new you.** Describe how you have successfully navigated and mediated the dynamics of your changing identity after divorce. Celebrate your emerging new self.

Lastly

Today is the first day of the rest of your life. Your caterpillar is turning into a butterfly. I have included several important documents as appendices. Some will help you understand some common terms related to the legal system and divorce in general. Other items will raise your consciousness about such things as financial reporting forms. Familiarizing yourself with these documents will help you to communicate more effectively with your attorney. They will also heighten your awareness of what to expect during your divorce proceedings. You can avoid some drama by staying prepared and forewarned. Good Luck.

Blessings and peace.

APPENDICES

Glossary of Common Terms

alimony – money for support of a spouse after separation or divorce

answer – pleading filed to respond to a divorce complaint

ark – a large, protective vessel

assets – items of value, property

baby's daddy – cultural slang for father

baby's mama – cultural slang for mother

Big Mama – cultural slang for grandmother

bornication – refers to many children being born outside of marriage

browbeat – to dominate, bully or intimate someone

child support – amount of money usually paid to the custodial parent for the maintenance and support of the children

cohabitation – two persons living together

common law marriage – a marriage existing by mutual agreement without the benefit of a civil or religious ceremony

complaint – the pleading used to commence a divorce action

confidentiality – the expectation that anything done or said will be kept private

contested – where one party does not consent to the divorce

cooling off period – required interval between the date of filing and entry of divorce

co-plaintiffs – two parties who sign a joint complaint or joint petition in a divorce action in states where this is allowed

Court Clerk – administrative person who handles the court papers, hearings and other matters

cover sheet – information sheet about the legal action and the parties involved that is filed with the complaint (also called an information sheet)

custodial parent – the parent who has physical custody of the children

deadlines – time within which action must be taken, such as filing an answer

decree – published command or judgment

defendant – the person whom the complaint is filed against (see also dumpee)

deposition – oral questions from one party to another

discovery – questions one party asks another by various means

dissolution – to dissolve or end, as in *dissolution of marriage*, terminology many states use instead of "divorce"

divorce – legal action that formally ends a marriage

divorcee – person who is newly divorced

domestic violence – emotional, mental, verbal and physical forms of abuse that occur in the relationship or marital home

"down low" – refers to heterosexual married men who engage in homosexual relationships

drama – emotionally tense and gripping events or actions

dumpee – spouse whom divorce action is filed against (see also defendant)

dumper – spouse who initiates the divorce action (see also plaintiff)

equitable distribution – division of marital property between husband and wife

ex – former husband or wife

fault grounds – basis for divorce, such as adultery

filing fee – fee that is paid at the time the complaint is filed

final judgment – the form which concludes the divorce after all the requirements of the case have been met

financial statement – statement of parties' assets, liabilities, and net worth

friendship capital – marital friendships retained after the divorce

ghetto divorce – married partners going their separate ways without first obtaining a legal divorce

Guardian Ad Litem – attorney appointed by the court to protect the children's interests

hearing – proceeding where testimony is presented before a judge

interrogatories – written discovery questions from one party to another

irreconcilable differences – a typical no-fault ground for divorce

joint complaint – complaint filed by both husband and wife

joint custody – agreement where both parents are entitled to care for and obtain information about the children

joint property – property owned by husband and wife equally

jurisdiction – the basis for the court to hear a particular case

liabilities – all debts and other financial obligations

litigant – someone engaged in a lawsuit

marital property – property acquired during the marriage

marriage – a legal union of two people established by a civil or religious ceremony

mediation – process used to achieve a solution, settlement or agreement in a dispute

military affidavit – document that states the divorce defendant is not on active military duty (Under the Federal Soldiers' and Sailors' Civil Relief Act, a divorce action may not be allowed to proceed if the defendant is on active military service)

no-fault – uncontested divorce

no-fault grounds – no need to prove actual fault grounds

noncustodial parent – parent who does not have physical custody

order of protection – a restrictive document issued by a judge or court of law in cases of domestic violence

petition – same as complaint

physical custody – one parent living with the children while the other parent has visitation rights

plaintiff – the person who files the complaint (see also dumper)

pleading – any complaint, answer, etc., is called this

Power of Attorney – document that gives someone the power to act for another person in legal and business matters

prenuptial agreement – a financial agreement made between a couple before marriage

Qualified Domestic Relations Order (QDRO) – an order that needs to be included in a divorce agreement when dealing with pension funds

remediation – legally improving a situation or correcting a problem

residency requirement – the length of time one or both parties may need to reside in a state before a divorce action may be filed

separate property – property not considered marital property

settlement agreement – agreement between husband and wife settling all property, child support, custody, and other issues

sexual shock – the reality that one's ex-spouse has a new sexual partner

shackin' – two people living together without marriage (see also cohabitation)

spouse – someone's husband or wife

summons – a document signed by the court clerk and served on the defendant that informs them a complaint has been filed

uncontested – divorce where defendant with action does not appear in court

Uniform Child Custody Jurisdiction Act (UCCJA) – act adopted by most states determining which state's courts have jurisdiction over custody matters

venue – the proper county in which to file the divorce

visitation – right of the noncustodial parent to visit with the children

waiting period – in some states, the amount of time between when the complaint is filed and the matter can be heard or a judgment entered

Client Intake Form

(To be completed by attorney)

Range Quoted:_____Retainer: _____
County for Filing:_____Terms: _____
                     Hourly:_____Office:_____Court:_____
                     Costs:_____

CLIENT INFORMATION

NAME:_____
                FIRST   Middle Initial   LAST
AGE and DATE of BIRTH: _____STATE/COUNTY or COUNTRY of birth: _____
Place where mail can be delivered to you confidentially:
STREET: _____ CITY: _____ ZIP CODE: _____
HOME phone number:_MOBILE phone number:_____
Email address: _____
SOCIAL SECURITY #: _____
State the total number of years of formal education your spouse has had: _____
If your spouse has a college degree, or degrees, state what those degrees are:
_____
_____

EMPLOYMENT INFORMATION:

Name of your employer: _____
Occupation (what you actually do): _____
Address of your employer:
STREET: _____ CITY: _____ ZIP CODE: _____
How long have you been employed by your current employer?_____
Work phone number: _____
How often are you paid? (check one):
                     ____Weekly ____Biweekly____Monthly
Your gross (before deductions) employment income per pay period:_____
Your net (after deductions) income per pay period: _____
If you have any income other than from your chief employment, state:
     From whom such income is received: _____
     Gross amount: _____ Net amount: _____

If you are not employed, state:

    Name of your last employer:_____

    Occupation (what you actually did): _____

    The amount of income you received from your last employment:_____

State the total number of years of formal education you have had:_____

If you have a college degree, or degrees, state what those degrees are: _____

YOUR SPOUSE

NAME: _____

          FIRST   Middle Initial   LAST

STREET: _____ CITY:_____ ZIP CODE: _____

HOME phone number:_____MOBILE phone number:_____

AGE and DATE of BIRTH: _____ STATE/COUNTY or COUNTRY of birth: _____

PHYSICAL DESCRIPTION: Ht:_____Wt_____Eye Color:_____Hair Color:_____

Identifying Marks/Scars:_____

BEST TIME TO SERVE SPOUSE: _____ LOCATION: _____

SOCIAL SECURITY #:_____

SPOUSE'S EMPLOYMENT

Name of spouse's employer:_____

Spouse's Occupation (what your spouse actually does): _____

Address of spouse's employer:

STREET: _____ CITY: _____ ZIP CODE: _____

How long has your spouse been employed by his/her current employer? _____

How often is your spouse paid? (check one):_____Weekly _____Biweekly ____Monthly

Your spouse's gross (before deductions) employment income per pay period:_____

Your spouse's net (after deductions) income per pay period: _____

If your spouse has any income other than from his/her chief employment, state:

From whom such income is received: _____

Gross amount: _____ Net amount: _____

If your spouse is not employed, state:

Name of your spouse's last employer:_____

Occupation (what your spouse did): _____

Amount of income your spouse received from his/her last employment: _____

YOUR MARRIAGE

Date of your marriage: _____

If separated from your spouse, the date of your separation:_____

City, county, and state in which you were married: _____

If applicable, wife's maiden name: _____

Does your spouse use any aliases? If so, list them: _____

If you were previously married, how many times? _____

As to each previous marriage of yours, state whether the marriage was ended by:

    (check one) _____Death_____Divorce

If your spouse was previously married, how many times?_____

As to each previous marriage of your spouse's, state whether the marriage was ended by:

    (check one) _____Death _____Divorce

If *you* have children by a previous marriage who are minors (under age eighteen), state:

    Whether in your custody _____or your spouse's_____

    What the support provisions are in the judgment of divorce:_____

If *your spouse* has children by a previous marriage who are minors (under age eighteen), state:

    Whether in your custody _____ or your spouse's _____

    What are the child support provisions in any judgment of divorce granted to your spouse? _____

If *you* or *your spouse* previously filed for divorce against the other, state:

    When (year): _____ What county:_____

    Who was your lawyer? _____

    Who was your spouse's lawyer?_____

If you have previously consulted with a lawyer about marital problems regarding this marriage, state the name of each lawyer and approximate date of each consultation: _____
_____

If you and/or your spouse received either psychological or marital counseling, state:

    Name and address of counselor:_____

    Who was involved in the counseling:

    (check one) _____ Husband _____ Wife _____ Both husband and wife

State the approximate time period (weeks or months) in which there was counseling, and approximately how many counseling sessions there were:

_____

_____

_____

Check all of the following that describe your marital problems:

___ Incompatibility ___ Lack of communication ___ Lack of interest in the marriage

___ Disagreements regarding your children ___ Infidelity ___ Drinking problems

___ Physical abuse ___ Mental abuse ___ Lack of common interests

___ Frequent and ongoing arguments ___ Late hours or absence from residence

(Place an asterisk (*) by the marital problem that you consider the most significant.)

Other (please describe): _____

CHILDREN

As to each child born to you and your spouse, state the following:

NAME   AGE   DATE OF BIRTH

_____

_____

_____

_____

The children are now in the custody of:

(check one) _____ Husband _____ Wife _____ Both

Describe any unusual health or psychological problems of any child: _____

_____

PROPERTY

MONEY ON DEPOSIT

As to any monies on deposit in any financial institution, state the following (if there is more than one such account, please describe on reverse side of page):

- *Joint accounts:*

Checking

Name of institution:_____Approximate current balance: _____

Savings

Name of institution: _____Approximate current balance: _____

- *Accounts in husband's name alone:*

Checking

Name of institution:_____Approximate current balance: _____

Savings

Name of institution: _____Approximate current balance: _____

● *Accounts in wife's name alone:*

Checking

Name of institution:_____Approximate current balance: _____

Savings

Name of institution:_____Approximate current balance: _____

As to any certificates of deposit or other money deposits:

● *Joint*

Name of institution: _____Name of fund:_____

Approximate current balance: _____

Husband's

Name of institution: _____Name of fund:_____

Approximate current balance: _____

Wife's

Name of institution: _____Name of fund:_____

Approximate current balance: _____

REAL ESTATE

Residence: _____

                    (Street Address   City, State   Zip Code)

As to all real estate, state:

Jointly held between you and your spouse: _____ If in one name only, state if it is you or

your spouse: _____

Purchase date: _____ Purchase price: _____

Your estimate of current value: _____ Balance of mortgage: _____

Interest rate: _____

Mortgagee (name of bank or savings and loan): _____

Amount of taxes and insurance, or state if included in the monthly payments: _____

Approximate balance of any second mortgage, and the name of mortgagee: _____

_____

Other Real Estate

If title to real estate is held in trust, state: _____

Name of bank or other institution holding title in trust: _____

Location of property (county and state): _____

As to all real estate, whether title is held in trust or not, state beneficial interest in the trust owned:

Jointly between you and your spouse: _____

If in one name only, state if it is you or your spouse: _____

Purchase date: _____   Purchase price: _____
Your estimate of current value: _____   Balance of mortgage: _____
Interest rate: _____
Mortgagee (name of bank or savings and loan):_____
Amount of taxes and insurance, or state if included in the monthly payments: _____
Approximate balance of any second mortgage: _____

AUTOMOBILES

Driven by wife:	*Driven by husband:*
Year:_____ Make:_____	Year:_____ Make: _____
Balance owed:_____	Balance owed: _____
Monthly payments: _____	Monthly payments:_____
To:_____	To:_____
Approximate date acquired:_____	Approximate date acquired_____
Other:_____	Other:_____
By whom usually used:_____	By whom usually used:_____
Year: Make: _____	Year: Make:_____
Balance owed:_____	Balance owed:_____
Monthly payments: _____	Monthly payments:_____
To:_____	To:_____
Approximate date acquired:_____	Approximate date acquired:_____

STOCKS AND BONDS

If you own any stocks or bonds, attach a separate sheet of paper on which you state the following:
Name of corporation: _____ Number of shares: _____
Approximate value of each share, or total value of all shares: _____

OTHER ASSETS OVER $500

If either you or your spouse has any assets that were acquired during the marriage, but not by gift or inheritance, and excluding household goods, which have a value of $500, describe each asset (*e.g.*, boat) and state the approximate value of each asset:

_____

_____

GIFTS, INHERITANCE, AND PROPERTY OWNED BY EITHER SPOUSE BEFORE THE MARRIAGE

Do you now own an asset with a value of more than $500 which you owned before the marriage and which has not been placed in joint ownership between you and your spouse? If so, describe that asset and state its approximate value:_____

_____

Does your spouse now own an asset with a value of more than $500 which your spouse owned before the marriage and which has not been placed in joint ownership between you and your spouse? _____

If so, describe that asset and state its approximate value:_____

Have you inherited any asset valued at more than $500 which asset has not been placed in ownership with your spouse? _____ If so, describe that asset and give its approximate value:_____

Has your spouse inherited any asset valued at more than $500 which asset has not been placed in ownership with you? _____ If so, describe that asset and give its approximate value:_____

Have you acquired any asset valued at more than $500 by gift from anyone? __If yes, has it been placed in ownership with your spouse? _____ Describe that asset, and give its approximate value: _____

Has your spouse acquired any asset valued at more than $500 by gift from anyone? _____ If yes, has it been placed in ownership with you? _____Describe that asset, and give its approximate value: _____

PENSION PLANS

If you have a pension plan or other deferred-income plan, such as employee stock option plan, profit-sharing plan, etc., whether vested or not, state the name of the employer providing the plan and how long you have been or were employed by that employer:

_____

_____

If your spouse has a pension plan or other deferred-income plan, such as employee stock option plan, profit-sharing plan, etc., whether vested or not, state the name of the employer providing the plan and how long your spouse has been or was employed by that employer:

_____

_____

HEALTH INSURANCE

• Do you have a policy of health insurance? _____ If so, indicate if:

Through employment: _____ Private plan: _____

• Does your spouse have a policy of health insurance? If so, indicate below:

Through employment: _____ Private plan: _____

LIFE INSURANCE

• Do you have a policy of life insurance? _____ If so, indicate:

Through employment: _____ Private plan: _____

Amount of death benefit: $_____

• Does your spouse have a policy of life insurance? If so, indicate below:

Through employment: _____ Private plan: _____

Amount of death benefit: $ _____

DEBTS

As to each debt owed by either you or your spouse, state:

• Name of creditor: _____

Approximate balance: _____ Monthly payments: _____

Describe item purchased, or the reason the debt was incurred: _____

• Name of creditor: _____

Approximate balance: _____ Monthly payments: _____

Describe item purchased, or the reason the debt was incurred: _____

• Name of creditor: _____

Approximate balance: _____ Monthly payments: _____

Describe item purchased, or the reason the debt was incurred: _____

• Name of creditor: _____

Approximate balance: _____ Monthly payments: _____

Describe item purchased, or the reason the debt was incurred: _____

As to other debts, describe in the same manner as above: (attach additional page if necessary)

_____

_____

AGREEMENTS OF YOU AND YOUR SPOUSE

If you and your spouse have made any agreements regarding custody of the children, visitation, financial matters, or disposition of property upon a divorce, state what those agreements are:

_____

_____

If there is other information related to your divorce that you believe your lawyer should know, please state: _____

_____

_____

_____

_____

_____

_____

REFERRAL

We wish to know how you came in contact with this firm:

Referral by another lawyer:

Name: _____

City: _____

General reputation of firm (several sources):

_____

_____

Referral by former client:

Name: _____

Yellow pages

Learning of firm, or member of firm, through newspaper, television, radio, or the Internet:
    (please specify):_____

_____

Other (please describe): _____

_____

_____

_____

_____

Financial Affidavit (Florida)

INSTRUCTIONS FOR FLORIDA FAMILY LAW RULE OF PROCEDURE FORM 12.902(c), FAMILY LAW FINANCIAL AFFIDAVIT

When should this form be used?

This form should be used when you are involved in a family law case which requires a financial affidavit and your individual gross income is $50,000 OR MORE per year.

This form should be typed or printed in black ink. After completing this form, you should sign the form before a notary public. You should then file the original with the clerk of the circuit court in the county where the petition was filed and keep a copy for your records.

What should I do next?

A copy of this form must be mailed or hand delivered to the other party in your case, if it is not served on him or her with your initial papers. This must be accomplished within 45 days of service of the petition.

Where can I look for more information?

Before proceeding, you should read "General Information for Self-Represented Litigants" found at the beginning of these forms. The words that are in "bold underline" in these instructions are defined there. For further information, see rule 12.285, Florida Family Law Rules of Procedure.

Special notes . . .

If this is a domestic violence case and you want to keep your address confidential for safety reasons, do not enter the address, telephone, and fax information at the bottom of this form. Instead, file Petitioner's Request for Confidential Filing of Address, ✏❑ Florida Supreme Court Approved Family Law Form 12.980(i).

The affidavit must be completed using monthly income and expense amounts. If you are paid or your bills are due on a schedule which is not monthly, you must convert those amounts. Hints are provided below for making these conversions.

Hourly - *If you are paid by the hour, you may convert your income to monthly as follows:*

Hourly amount × Hours worked per week = Weekly amount

Weekly amount × 52 Weeks per year = Yearly amount

Yearly amount ÷ 12 Months per year = Monthly Amount

Daily - *If you are paid by the day, you may convert your income to monthly as follows:*

Daily amount × Days worked per week = Weekly amount

Weekly amount × 52 Weeks per year = Yearly amount

Yearly amount ÷ 12 Months per year = Monthly Amount

Weekly - *If you are paid by the week, you may convert your income to monthly as follows:*

Weekly amount × 52 Weeks per year = Yearly amount

Yearly amount ÷ 12 Months per year = Monthly Amount

Bi-weekly - *If you are paid every two weeks, you may convert your income to monthly as follows:*

Bi-weekly amount × 26 = Yearly amount

Yearly amount ÷ 12 Months per year = Monthly Amount

Bi-monthly - *If you are paid twice per month, you may convert your income to monthly as follows:*

Bi-monthly amount × 2 = Monthly Amount

Expenses may be converted in the same manner.

Remember, a person who is NOT an attorney is called a nonlawyer. If a nonlawyer helps you fill out these forms, that person must give you a copy of a Disclosure from Nonlawyer, Florida Family Law Rules of Procedure Form 12.900(a), before he or she helps you. A nonlawyer helping you fill out these forms also must put his or her name, address, and telephone number on the bottom of the last page of every form he or she helps you complete.

IN THE CIRCUIT COURT OF THE _____JUDICIAL CIRCUIT, IN AND FOR _____
COUNTY, FLORIDA

Case No.:_____

Division:_____

_____,

Petitioner,

      and

_____,

Respondent.

FAMILY LAW FINANCIAL AFFIDAVIT

($50,000 or more Individual Gross Annual Income)

I, {full legal name} _____,
being sworn, certify that the following information is true:

SECTION I. INCOME

1. Date of Birth: _____

2. Social Security Number: _____

3. My occupation is: _____

4. I am currently
[✓ all that apply]

_____ a. Unemployed
Describe your efforts to find employment, how soon you expect to be employed, and the pay you expect to receive:

_____ b. Employed by:
Address:_____
City _____State_____ Zip code_____
Telephone Number_____
Pay rate: $_____( ) every week ( ) every other week
                ( ) twice a month ( ) monthly ( ) other:_____
If you are expecting to become unemployed or change jobs soon, describe the change you expect and why and how it will affect your income:

_____

_____

□ Check here if you currently have more than one job. List the information above for the second job(s) on a separate sheet and attach it to this affidavit.

_____ c. Retired. Date of retirement: _____
Employer from whom retired: _____
Address: _____
City_____State_____ Zip code_____
Telephone Number:_____

LAST YEAR'S GROSS INCOME: Your Income   Other Party's Income (if known)

     YEAR _____ $_____ $_____

PRESENT MONTHLY GROSS INCOME:

All amounts must be MONTHLY. See the instructions with this form to figure out money amounts for anything that is NOT paid monthly. Attach more paper, if needed. Items included under "other" should be listed separately with separate dollar amounts.

1. Monthly gross salary or wages   1.$_____

2. Monthly bonuses, commissions, allowances, overtime, tips, and similar payments   2._____

3. Monthly business income from sources such as self-   3._____
employment, partnerships, close corporations, and/or independent contracts (Gross receipts minus ordinary and necessary expenses required to produce income.)
(□ Attach sheet itemizing such income and expenses.)

4. Monthly disability benefits/SS   4._____

5. Monthly Workers' Compensation   5._____

6. Monthly Unemployment Compensation   6._____

7. Monthly pension, retirement, or annuity payments   7._____

8. Monthly Social Security benefits   8._____

9. Monthly alimony actually received
     9a. From this case: $_____
     9b. From other case(s): $_____
       Add 9a and 9b   9._____

10. Monthly interest and dividends   10._____

11. Monthly rental income (gross receipts minus ordinary and necessary expenses required to produce income) (Attach sheet itemizing such income and expense items.)   11._____

12. Monthly income from royalties, trusts, or estates   12._____

13. Monthly reimbursed expenses and in-kind payments to the extent that they reduce personal living expenses
(□ Attach sheet itemizing each item and amount.)   13._____

14. Monthly gains derived from dealing in property (not including nonrecurring gains) Any other income of a recurring nature (identify source)   14._____

15. _____   15._____

16. _____   16._____

17. PRESENT MONTHLY GROSS INCOME (Add lines 1–16) **TOTAL**:   17.$_____

PRESENT MONTHLY DEDUCTIONS:

All amounts must be MONTHLY. See the instructions with this form
to figure out money amounts for anything that is NOT paid monthly.

18. Monthly federal, state, and local income tax (corrected for filing
status and allowable dependents and income tax liabilities)
    a. Filing Status_____
    b. Number of dependents claimed _____   18.$_____
19. Monthly FICA or self-employment taxes   19._____
20. Monthly Medicare payments   20._____
21. Monthly mandatory union dues   21. _____
22. Monthly mandatory retirement payments   22._____
23. Monthly health insurance payments (including dental insurance),
excluding portion paid for any minor children of this relationship   23._____
24. Monthly court-ordered child support actually paid for children
from another relationship   24._____
25. Monthly court-ordered alimony actually paid
    25a. from this case: $_____
    25b. from other case(s): $_____Add 25a and 25b   25._____

26. TOTAL DEDUCTIONS ALLOWABLE UNDER SECTION 61.30,
FLORIDA STATUTES (Add lines 18 through 25)   **TOTAL:**   **26._____**
27. PRESENT NET MONTHLY INCOME (Subtract line 26 from line 17)   **27._____**

SECTION II. AVERAGE MONTHLY EXPENSES

Proposed/Estimated Expenses. If this is a dissolution of marriage case
and your expenses as listed below do not reflect what you actually pay
currently, you should write "estimate" next to each amount that is estimated.

HOUSEHOLD:

1. Monthly mortgage or rent payments   1.$ _____
2. Monthly property taxes (if not included in mortgage)   2._____
3. Monthly insurance on residence (if not included in mortgage)   3._____
4. Monthly condominium maintenance fees and homeowner's association fees   4._____
5. Monthly electricity   5._____
6. Monthly water, garbage, and sewer   6._____
7. Monthly telephone   7._____
8. Monthly fuel oil or natural gas   8._____
9. Monthly repairs and maintenance   9._____
10. Monthly lawn care   10._____
11. Monthly pool maintenance   11._____

12. Monthly pest control · 12._____

13. Monthly misc. household 13._____

14. Monthly food and home supplies 14._____

15. Monthly meals outside home 15._____

16. Monthly cable T.V. 16._____

17. Monthly alarm service contract 17._____

18. Monthly service contracts on appliances 18._____

19. Monthly maid service 19._____

Other:

20._____ 20._____

21._____ 21._____

22._____ 22._____

23._____ 23._____

24._____ 24._____

25. **SUBTOTAL (add lines 1 through 24)** 25. $_____

AUTOMOBILE:

26. Monthly gasoline and oil 26.$_____

27. Monthly repairs 27._____

28. Monthly auto tags and emission testing 28._____

29. Monthly insurance 29._____

30. Monthly payments (lease or financing) 30._____

31. Monthly rental/replacements 31._____

32. Monthly alternative transportation (bus, rail, car pool, etc.) 32._____

33. Monthly tolls and parking 33._____

34. Other: 34._____

35. **SUBTOTAL (add lines 26 through 34)** 35.$_____

MONTHLY EXPENSES FOR CHILDREN COMMON TO BOTH PARTIES:

36. Monthly nursery, babysitting, or day care 36.$_____

37. Monthly school tuition 37._____

38. Monthly school supplies, books, and fees 38._____

39. Monthly after school activities 39._____

40. Monthly lunch money 40._____

41. Monthly private lessons or tutoring 41._____

42. Monthly allowances 42._____

43. Monthly clothing and uniforms 43._____

44. Monthly entertainment (movies, parties, etc.) 44._____

45. Monthly health insurance   45._____

46. Monthly medical, dental, prescriptions (nonreimbursed only)   46._____

47. Monthly psychiatric/psychological/counselor   47._____

49. Monthly vitamins   49._____

50. Monthly beauty parlor/barber shop   50._____

51. Monthly nonprescription medication   51._____

52. Monthly cosmetics, toiletries, and sundries   52._____

53. Monthly gifts from child(ren) to others
    (other children, relatives, teachers, etc.)   53._____

54. Monthly camp or summer activities   54._____

55. Monthly clubs (Boy/Girl Scouts, etc.)   55._____

56. Monthly access expenses (for nonresidential parent)   56._____

57. Monthly miscellaneous   57._____

58.   **SUBTOTAL (add lines 36 through 57)**   58.$_____

MONTHLY EXPENSES FOR CHILD(REN) FROM ANOTHER RELATIONSHIP:
    (other than court-ordered child support)

59._____   59. $_____

60._____   60. _____

61._____   61. _____

62._____   62. _____

63.   **SUBTOTAL (add lines 59 through 62)**   63.$_____

MONTHLY INSURANCE:

64. Health insurance, excluding portion paid for any minor child(ren) of
    this relationship   64.$_____

65. Life insurance   65._____

66. Dental insurance   66._____

Other:

67._____   67._____

68._____   68._____

69.   **SUBTOTAL (add lines 64 through 68)**   69.$_____

OTHER MONTHLY EXPENSES NOT LISTED ABOVE:

70. Monthly dry cleaning and laundry   70._____

71. Monthly clothing   71._____

72. Monthly medical, dental, and prescription (unreimbursed only)   72._____

73. Monthly psychiatric, psychological, or counselor (unreimbursed only)   73._____

74. Monthly non-prescription medications, cosmetics, toiletries, and sundries 74._____
75. Monthly grooming 75._____
76. Monthly gifts 76._____
77. Monthly pet expenses 77._____
78. Monthly club dues and membership 78._____
79. Monthly sports and hobbies 79._____
80. Monthly entertainment 80._____
81. Monthly periodicals/books/tapes/CD's 81._____
82. Monthly vacations 82._____
83. Monthly religious organizations 83._____
84. Monthly bank charges/credit card fees 84._____
85. Monthly education expenses 85._____

Other: (include any usual and customary expenses not otherwise
mentioned in the items listed above)

86._____ 86._____
87._____ 87._____
88._____ 88._____
89._____ 89._____

90. **SUBTOTAL (add lines 70 through 89)** **90. $_____**

MONTHLY PAYMENTS TO CREDITORS: (only when payments are currently made by you on outstanding balances)

NAME OF CREDITOR(s):

91._____ 91.$_____
92._____ 92._____
93._____ 93._____
94._____ 94._____
95._____ 95._____
96._____ 96._____
97._____ 97._____
98._____ 98._____
99._____ 99._____
100._____ 100._____
101._____ 101._____
102._____ 102._____
103._____ 103._____

104. **SUBTOTAL (add lines 91 through 103)** **104.$_____**
105. TOTAL MONTHLY EXPENSES:
(add lines 25, 35, 58, 63, 69, 90, and 104 of Section II, Expenses) **105. $_____**

SUMMARY

106. TOTAL PRESENT MONTHLY NET INCOME
   (from line 27 of SECTION I. INCOME)   106. $_____

107. TOTAL MONTHLY EXPENSES (from line 105 above)   107. $_____

108. SURPLUS (If line 106 is more than line 107, subtract line 107 from
   line 106. This is the amount of your surplus. Enter that amount here.) **108. $_____**

109. (DEFICIT) (If line 107 is more than line 106, subtract line 106 from
   line 107. This is the amount of your deficit. Enter that amount here.) **109. ($_____)**

SECTION III. ASSETS AND LIABILITIES
   A. ASSETS (This is where you list what you OWN.)
   INSTRUCTIONS:

   STEP 1: In column A, list a description of each separate item owned by you (and/ or your spouse, if this is a petition for dissolution of marriage). Blank spaces are provided if you need to list more than one of an item.

   STEP 2: If this is a petition for dissolution of marriage, check the box in Column A next to any item that you are requesting the judge award to you.

   STEP 3: In column B, write what you believe to be the current fair market value of all items listed.

   STEP 4: Use column C only if this is a petition for dissolution of marriage and you believe an item is "nonmarital," meaning it belongs to only one of you and should not be divided. You should indicate to whom you believe the item belongs. (Typically, you will only use Column C if property was owned by one spouse before the marriage. See the "General Information for Self-Represented Litigants" found at the beginning of these forms and section 61.075(1), Florida Statutes, for definitions of "marital" and "nonmarital" assets and liabilities.

A ASSETS: DESCRIPTION OF ITEM(S) ✓ the box next to any asset(s) which you are requesting the judge award to you.	B Current Fair Market Value	C Nonmarital (✓ correct column)	
		husband	wife
☐ Cash on Hand	$		
☐ Cash (in banks or credit unions)			
☐			
☐ Stocks/Bonds			
☐			

☐			
☐ Notes (money owed to you in writing)			
☐			
☐			
☐ Money owed to you (not evidenced by a note)			
☐			
☐			
☐ Real estate: (Home)			
☐ (Other)			
☐			
☐			
☐			
☐ Business interests			
☐			
☐			
☐			
☐			
☐ Automobiles			
☐			
☐			
☐			
☐ Boats			
☐			
☐			
☐ Other vehicles			
☐			
☐			
☐ Retirement plans (Profit Sharing, Pension, IRA, 401(k)s, etc.)			
☐			
☐			

A ASSETS: DESCRIPTION OF ITEM(S) ✓ the box next to any asset(s) which you are requesting the judge award to you.	B Current Fair Market Value	C Nonmarital (✓ correct column)	
		husband	wife
☐			
☐ Furniture & furnishings in home			
☐			
☐			
☐			
☐ Collectibles			
☐			
☐			
☐			
☐			
☐			
☐			
☐ Sporting and entertainment (T.V., stereo, etc.) equipment			
☐			
☐			
☐			
☐			
☐ Other assets			
☐			
☐			
☐			
☐			
☐			
☐			
☐			
Total Assets (add column B)	$ _____		

B. LIABILITIES/DEBTS (This is where you list what you OWE.)

INSTRUCTIONS:

STEP 1: In column A, list a description of each separate debt owed by you (and/ or your spouse, if this is a petition for dissolution of marriage). Blank spaces are provided if you need to list more than one of an item.

STEP 2: If this is a petition for dissolution of marriage, check the box in Column A next to any debt(s) for which you believe you should be responsible.

STEP 3: In column B, write what you believe to be the current amount owed for all items listed.

STEP 4: Use column C only if this is a petition for dissolution of marriage and you believe an item is "nonmarital," meaning the debt belongs to only one of you and should not be divided. You should indicate to whom you believe the debt belongs. (Typically, you will only use Column C if the debt was owed by one spouse before the marriage. See the "General Information for Self-Represented Litigants" found at the beginning of these forms and section 61.075(1), Florida Statutes, for definitions of "marital" and "nonmarital" assets and liabilities.)

A LIABILITIES: DESCRIPTION OF ITEM(S) ✓ the box next to any debt(s) for which you believe you should be responsible.	B Current Amount Owed	C Nonmarital (✓ correct column)	
		husband	wife
☐ Mortgages on real estate: (Home)	$		
☐ (Other)			
☐			
☐			
☐ Charge/credit card accounts			
☐			
☐			
☐			
☐			
☐			
☐ Auto loan			
☐ Auto loan			
☐ Bank/Credit Union loans			
☐			

☐			
☐			
☐ Money you owe (not evidenced by a note)			
☐			
☐ Judgments			
☐			
☐ Other			
☐			
☐			
☐			
Total Debts (add column B)	$ _____		

C. NET WORTH (excluding contingent assets and liabilities)

Total Assets (enter total of Column B in Asset Table; Section A) $ _____

Total Liabilities (enter total of Column B in Liabilities Table; Section B) $ _____

TOTAL NET WORTH (Total Assets minus Total Liabilities)

(excluding contingent assets and liabilities) $_____

D. CONTINGENT ASSETS AND LIABILITIES

INSTRUCTIONS:

If you have any **POSSIBLE assets** (income potential, accrued vacation or sick leave, bonus, inheritance, etc.) or **POSSIBLE liabilities** (possible lawsuits, future unpaid taxes, contingent tax liabilities, assumed by another), you must list them here.

A Contingent Liabilities ✓ the box next to any contingent debt(s) for which you believe you should be responsible.	B Possible Amount Owed	C Nonmarital (✓ correct column)	
		husband	wife
	$		
Total Contingent Liabilities	$_____		

E. Has there been any agreement between you and the other party that one of you will take responsibility for a debt and will hold the other party harmless from that debt?

(   ) yes   (   ) no   If yes, explain: _____

_____

_____

_____

_____

_____

_____

_____

_____

F. CHILD SUPPORT GUIDELINES WORKSHEET. 🖊❏ Florida Family Law Rules of Procedure Form 12.902(e), Child Support Guidelines Worksheet, MUST be filed with the court at or prior to a hearing to establish or modify child support. This requirement cannot be waived by the parties.

[✓ one only]

_____ **A Child Support Guidelines Worksheet IS or WILL BE filed in this case.** This case involves the establishment or modification of child support.

_____ **A Child Support Guidelines Worksheet IS NOT being filed in this case.** The establishment or modification of child support is not an issue in this case.

I certify that a copy of this financial affidavit was: (   ) mailed, (   ) faxed and mailed, or (   ) hand delivered to the person(s) listed below on {date} _____.

Other party or his/her attorney:
Name: _____
Address:_____
City, State, Zip: _____
Fax Number: _____

I understand that I am swearing or affirming under oath to the truthfulness of the claims made in this affidavit and that the punishment for knowingly making a false statement includes fines and/or imprisonment.

Dated:

_____
Signature of Party
Printed Name: _____
Address:_____
City, State, Zip:_____
Telephone Number:_____ Fax Number: _____

STATE OF FLORIDA
COUNTY OF _____

Sworn to or affirmed and signed before me on _____by _____
.

NOTARY PUBLIC or DEPUTY CLERK
[Print, type, or stamp commissioned name of notary or deputy clerk.]

Type of identification produced _____
____Personally known
____Produced identification

IF A NONLAWYER HELPED YOU FILL OUT THIS FORM, HE/SHE MUST FILL IN THE BLANKS BELOW: [✎ fill in all blanks]
I, {full legal name and trade name of nonlawyer} _____,
a nonlawyer, located at {street} _____,
{city} _____ {state} _____ {zip}_____
{phone} _____ helped {name} _____,
who is the [✓ one only] _____petitioner or _____respondent, fill out this form.

Petition for
Domestic Violence Civil Protection Order (Ohio)

FORM 1O.O1-D: PETITION FOR DOMESTIC VIOLENCE CIVIL PROTECTION ORDER
Amended: July 1, 2010
Discard all previous versions of this form.

IN THE _____ COURT

_____ COUNTY, OHIO

_____ Petitioner	Case No. _____
_____ Address	Judge _____
_____ City, State, Zip Code	
Date of Birth: _____	PETITION FOR DOMESTIC VIOLENCE CIVIL PROTECTION ORDER (R.C. 3113.31)
V.	<u>Notice to Petitioner</u>: Throughout this form, check every ❏ that applies.
_____ Respondent	
_____ Address	**DO NOT WRITE YOUR ADDRESS ON THIS FORM IF YOU ARE REQUESTING CONFIDENTIALITY. PLEASE PROVIDE AN ADDRESS WHERE YOU CAN RECEIVE NOTICES FROM THE COURT.**
_____ City, State, Zip Code	
Date of Birth: _____	

❏ 1. Petitioner is a family or household member of Respondent and a victim of domestic violence and seeks relief on Petitioner's own behalf. The relationship of Petitioner to Respondent is that of:

❏ Spouse of Respondent ❏ Former spouse of Respondent ❏ The natural parent of Respondent's child ❏ Other relative (by blood or marriage) of Respondent? Petitioner who has lived with Respondent at any time	❏ Child of Respondent ❏ Parent of Respondent ❏ Foster Parent ❏ Person "living as a spouse of Respondent" defined as: • now cohabiting; • or cohabited within five years before the alleged act of domestic violence

❏ 2. Petitioner seeks relief on behalf of the following family or household members:

NAME	DATE OF BIRTH	HOW RELATED TO PETITIONER RESPONDENT		RESIDES WITH

3. Respondent has engaged in the following act(s) of domestic violence (describe the acts as fully as possible, add additional pages if necessary): _____

_____

_____

_____

4. Petitioner requests that the Court grant relief under R.C. 3113.31 to protect the Petitioner and or the family or household members named in this Petition from domestic violence by granting a civil protection order that:

❏ (a) Directs Respondent not to abuse Petitioner and the family or household members named in this Petition by harming, attempting to harm, threatening, following, stalking, harassing, forcing sexual relations upon them, or by committing sexually oriented offenses against them.

❏ (b) Requires Respondent to leave and not return to or interfere with the following residence and grants Petitioner exclusive possession of the residence:_____

_____

❏ (c) Divides household and family personal property and directs Respondent not to remove, damage, hide, or dispose of any property or funds that Petitioner owns or possesses.

❏ (d) Temporarily allocates parental rights and responsibilities for the care of the following minor children and suspends Respondent's visitation rights until a full hearing is held (include names and birth dates of the minor children):_____

_____

_____

_____

❏ (e) Establishes temporary visitation rights with the following minor children and requires visitation to be supervised or occur under such conditions that the Court determines will insure the safety of Petitioner and the minor children (include names and birth dates of the minor children):

_____

_____

_____

_____

☐ (f) Requires Respondent to provide financial support for Petitioner and the other family or household members named in this Petition.

☐ (g) Requires Respondent to complete batterer counseling, substance abuse counseling, or other counseling as determined necessary by the Court.

☐ (h) Requires Respondent to refrain from entering, approaching, or contacting (including contact by telephone, fax, e-mail, and voice mail) the residence, school, business, and place of employment of Petitioner and the family or household members named in this Petition.

☐ (i) Requires Respondent to permit Petitioner or other family or household member to have exclusive use of the following motor vehicle:

☐ (j) Includes the following additional provisions:_____

_____

_____

☐ 5. Petitioner further requests that the Court issue an *ex parte* (emergency) protection order under R.C. 3113.31(D) and (E) and this Petition.

6. Petitioner further requests that the Court issue no mutual protection orders or other orders against Petitioner unless all of the conditions of R.C. 3113.31(E)(4) are met.

7. Petitioner further requests that if Petitioner has a victim advocate, the Court permit the victim advocate to accompany Petitioner at all stages of these proceedings as required by R.C. 3113.31(M).

8. Petitioner further requests that the Court grant such other relief as the Court considers equitable and fair.

9. Petitioner lists here all present court cases and pertinent past court cases (including civil, criminal, divorce, juvenile, custody, visitation, and bankruptcy cases) that relate to the Respondent, you, your children, your family, or your household members:

CASE NAME	CASE NUMBER	COURT/COUNTY	TYPE OF CASE	RESULT OF CASE

I hereby swear or affirm that the answers above are true, complete, and accurate to the best of my knowledge. I understand that falsification of this document may result in a contempt of court finding against me which could result in a jail sentence and fine, and that falsification of this document may also subject me to criminal penalties for perjury under R.C. 2921.11.

Sworn to and subscribed before me on this _____ day _____

_____ of _____ , _____

SIGNATURE OF PETITIONER

DO NOT WRITE YOUR ADDRESS BELOW IF YOU ARE REQUESTING CONFIDENTIALITY. PLEASE PROVIDE AN ADDRESS WHERE YOU CAN RECEIVE NOTICES FROM THE COURT.

_____

NOTARY PUBLIC

_____

_____

Signature of Attorney for Petitioner (if applicable)

_____

Name

_____

Address

_____

_____

Attorney Registration Number

_____

Phone Number

Twelve Month Protective Order (Georgia)

ORI Number _____

THE SUPERIOR COURT FOR THE COUNTY OF_____
STATE OF GEORGIA

_____,

Petitioner,

Civil Action File

vs.

_____,   No._____

Respondent.

FAMILY VIOLENCE TWELVE MONTH PROTECTIVE ORDER

A hearing was held on this matter on _____, 20_____ for which the Respondent had notice as required by law and at which the Respondent appeared and/or had the opportunity to be heard and the Petitioner requested that the Protective Order entered in this case be continued. Having heard the evidence presented, reviewed the petition and the entire record concerning this case and for good cause shown, IT IS HEREBY ORDERED AND ADJUDGED:

1. That these proceedings be filed in the office of the Clerk of this Court.

2. That this Order applies in every county throughout the state and it shall be the duty of every court and every law enforcement official to enforce and carry out the provisions of this Order pursuant to O.C.G.A. § 19-13-4(d). Law Enforcement officers may use their arrest powers pursuant to O.C.G.A. § 19-13-6 and 17-4-20 to enforce the terms of this Order.

3. This Order shall be in effect for up to twelve (12) months from _____, 20_____ until _____, 20_____

4. That the Respondent has violated the Family Violence Act, at O.C.G.A. § 1913-1 [pcoOlJ et seq., by committing family violence, has placed the Petitioner in reasonable fear for Petitioner's safety, and represents a credible threat to the physical safety of Petitioner and/or Petitioner's child/ren. Respondent is hereby enjoined and restrained from doing, or attempting to do, or threatening to do, any act of injury, maltreating, molesting, following, harassing, harming, or abusing the Petitioner and/or the minor child/ren in any manner. Respondent is not to interfere with Petitioner's travel, transportation, or communication. Respondent shall not follow, place under surveillance, or contact the Petitioner at any place

of the Petitioner for the purpose of harassing and intimidating the Petitioner.

5.That the Respondent is enjoined and restrained from doing or attempting to do, or [pcoO2] threatening to do, any act of injury, maltreating, molesting, harassing, harming, or abusing the Petitioner's family or household.

6. That this Court determined that it had jurisdiction over the parties and the subject matter under the laws of the State of Georgia and Respondent received reasonable notice and had the opportunity to be heard before this Order was issued sufficient to protect the Respondent's due process rights and this Order shall be presumed valid and pursuant to 18 U.S.C. § 2265(a) shall be accorded full faith and credit by any other state or local jurisdiction and shall be enforced as if an Order of the enforcing state or jurisdiction.

ONLY THE FOLLOWING THAT ARE INITIALED BY THE JUDGE SHALL APPLY

_____ 7. Petitioner is awarded sole and exclusive possession of the residence at [pcoO3]

_____ 8. Respondent is ordered to leave the family residence immediately and law enforcement at _____ (sheriff or police department) is ordered to assist Petitioner in returning to the family residence and the removal of the Respondent. Respondent shall immediately surrender to law enforcement _____ (sheriff or police department) all and any keys, garage door openers and other security devices to the family residence and law enforcement shall insure that these are given to the Petitioner.

_____ 9. Respondent is ordered to stay away from Petitioner's and Petitioner's child/ren's [pcoO4] residence and workplace and/or school and any subsequent residence or workplace or school of Petitioner and/or Petitioner's minor child/ren.

_____ 10. Respondent is ordered to provide suitable alternate housing for Petitioner and/or Petitioner's children by _____

_____ 11. That Respondent is restrained and enjoined from approaching within _____ yards [i,coOl04] of Petitioner and/or Petitioner's minor children.

_____ 12. Respondent is ordered not to have any contact, direct, indirect or through another [pcoo5l person with Petitioner, by telephone, pager, fax, e-mail or any other means of communication except as specified in this Order.

_____ 13. That Petitioner is awarded temporary custody of the minor child/ren, namely: [pcooQ] _____ DOB _____ sex _____
_____ DOB _____ sex _____

_____ DOB _____ sex _____
_____ DOB _____ sex _____

Respondent is ordered not to interfere with the physical custody of the minor child/ren.

[pco06] Initial here *only if Respondent* is awarded temporary custody of the child/ren.

_____ 14. The _____ shall pay to the _____, for the support
of the minor child/ren, the sum of _____
Dollars ($_____) per _____, beginning
_____, 20_____

All payments are to be made by or to: income deduction order
                                           child support receiver
                                           by mail directly to the Petitioner
                                           or_____

_____ 15. Respondent is ordered to pay temporary support for the Petitioner in the amount of
$_____ every _____beginning _____
All payments are to be made by or to: income deduction order
                                       child support receiver
                                       by mail directly to the Petitioner
                                       or _____

_____16. Respondent shall have visitation with the minor child/ren according to the
following schedule, beginning_____
no visitation
no visitation until _____
supervised visitation, supervised by a third party as follows:
visitation every other weekend from Friday at 6 p.m. until Sunday at 6 p.m.
beginning_____
other visitation_____
circumstances concerning how Respondent shall pick up and return the minor
child/ren shall be_____
Strict compliance with this visitation provision shall not be a violation of the
restraining provisions of this Order.

_____17. Respondent, only when accompanied by local law enforcement, shall be able to
remove his/her clothing and personal items from the residence as follows:

_____

_____

On _____, 20_____ at _____ m.

_____18. (Respondent)(Petitioner)(both Respondent and Petitioner) [strike through appropriate] is/arc ordered not to sell, encumber, trade, damage, contract to sell, or otherwise dispose of or remove from the jurisdiction of this Court any of the property or pets of the Petitioner or joint property or pets of the parties except in the ordinary course of business.

_____19. (Respondent)(Petitioner)(both Respondent and Petitioner) [strike through appropriate] is/are ordered not to disconnect or have disconnected home utilities, change or have changed and/or cancel or have canceled auto, health or life insurance for Respondent, Petitioner, and/or Petitioner's child/ren or interfere with Respondent, Petitioner's and/or Petitioner's child/ren's mail.

_____20. Petitioner shall have sole, exclusive temporary possession of the vehicle: Make_____ Model _____Year_____ Color _____ Respondent shall immediately surrender all keys, proof of insurance, and registration to this vehicle to law enforcement and law enforcement shall immediately turnover said items to Petitioner.

_____21. Petitioner shall be allowed to remove the following property from the family residence for Petitioner and/or Petitioner's children's use _____ _____

On _____, 20____ at _____ and law enforcement_____ (sheriff or police department) is hereby ordered to assist the Petitioner during this removal.

_____22. Respondent is ordered to undergo alcohol/drug abuse evaluation and follow the recommended treatment.

_____23. That Respondent shall be required to return the following property for Petitioner and/or Petitioner's child/ren's use _____ _____

On _____, 20____ at _____ and law enforcement _____ (sheriff or police department) is hereby ordered to assist the Petitioner during this return.

_____24. Petitioner is awarded costs and attorney fees in the amount of _____
_____25. **FAMILY VIOLENCE INTERVENTION PROGRAM**
It is further Ordered that the Respondent shall make arrangements to begin a certified family violence intervention program (FVIP) within fourteen (14) days of the signing of this Order, or if appropriate within fourteen (14) days upon

release from incarceration. A list of local certified agencies will be given to the Respondent with this Order. Furthermore, Respondent shall appear before this court _____, 20____ at _____.m. for a hearing on the status of his/her application, attendance and/or completion of the FVIP. At that hearing, Respondent is ordered to present to this court a written status report from the agency providing the certified FVIP. The status report shall detail Respondent's application, attendance and/or completion of or failure to apply, attend and/or complete the FVIP and shall be signed by an officer of the agency.

OR

_____Respondent is ordered to undergo a certified family violence intervention program and comply with the attached compliance form.

OR

_____Respondent is ordered to undergo a certified family violence intervention program.

OR

_____Respondent is not ordered to undergo a certified family violence intervention program and the following reasons exist:

_____

_____

_____ 26. Petitioner/protected party is either a spouse, former spouse, parent of a common [pcoo7l child, Petitioner's child, child of Respondent, cohabitates or has cohabited with Respondent and qualifies for 18 U.S.C. 922(g). It is further ordered that the Respondent shall not possess or purchase a firearm or ammunition as restricted by federal law under 18 U.S.C. 922(g)(8).

_____ 27. It is further Ordered:

[pcoO8]

_____

_____

SO ORDERED this _____ day of _____, 20____

_____
JUDGE, SUPERIOR COURT
_____ County

_____
Print or stamp Judge's name

Violation of the above Order may be punishable by arrest.

NOTICE TO RESPONDENT

1. Violation of this Order may result in immediate arrest and criminal prosecution

    that may result in jail time and/or fines and/or may subject you to prosecution and

    penalties for contempt of court.

2. This Order shall remain in effect unless specifically superceded by a subsequent

    Order signed and filed, by operation of law, or by Order of dismissal, whichever

    occurs first. Only this Court can void, modify or dismiss this Order. Either party

    may ask this Court to change or dismiss this Order.

3. If after a hearing, of which the Respondent received notice and opportunity

    to participate, a protective order is issued which restrains Respondent from

    harassing, stalking or threatening an intimate partner, Respondent is prohibited

    from possessing, receiving, or transporting a firearm or ammunition which has

    been shipped or transported in interstate or foreign commerce for the duration of

    the Order. 18 U.S.C. § 922(g).

4. A person commits the offense of Aggravated Stalking when such person, in

    violation of a temporary or permanent protective Order prohibiting this behavior

    follows, places under surveillance, or contacts another person on public or

    private property for the purpose of harassing and intimidating the other person.

    This activity can subject the Respondent to arrest and prosecution for felony

    aggravated stalking, which carries penalties of imprisonment for not less than 1

    year nor more than 10 years and a fine of up to $10,000.00.

RESPONDENT'S IDENTIFYING FACT SHEET

(please complete as much as possible; one of these must be provided to
have the order placed in the National Crime Information Center registry:
Respondent's date of birth OR social security number)

Respondent's social security number is _____, date of birth is _____,
sex, color of hair _____, color of eyes _____height _____, weight
_____. Respondent's race is _____, ethnic background _____. Respondent
has distinguishing marks (tattoos, scars, etc.) _____.
Respondent drives a _____, license tag no: _____(Expires:_____)
and has a_____ (state) driver's license no.: _____ Expires:_____). Respondent's
home address _____ and is employed by _____ at
_____ and works from _____to _____on (days) _____.
Respondent has the following known aliases:_____.

PROTECTED PARTIES' IDENTIFYING INFORMATION

Petitioner: _____ DOB _____ sex ____ race _____
Other: _____ DOB _____ sex ____ race _____
Other: _____ DOB _____ sex ____ race _____
Other: _____ DOB _____ sex ____ race _____

❏ **Transmitted to Georgia Protective Order Registry** Date _____ Clerk _____

Rev'd 10/2008

Pursuant to O.C.G.A. § 19-13-3,
Petitioner assisted by
Name:_____
Address:_____
Phone:_____

Note to Judges: This form is promulgated as a Uniform Superior Court Rule under the
auspices of O.C.G.A. § 19-13-53. To order a specific provision, please initial in the space
provided. The court should delete or otherwise make inoperative any provision in the
standardized form which is not supported by the evidence in the case and in order to
comply with the court's application of the law and facts to an individual case.

About The Author

Lester L. Barclay is the managing partner of The Barclay Law Group, PC in Chicago, Illinois. A graduate of Oberlin College and Case Western Reserve University School of Law, he has practiced matrimonial law since 1985. In that time, he has earned a sterling reputation as a skilled litigator who seeks to maintain the family's integrity during and after divorce. His passionate calling is to help children who are so often collateral damage in custody and divorce matters. Frequently, the court appoints him *Guardian Ad Litem* to protect the interests of children in marital breakups. His influential and ethnically diverse law firm serves an equally diverse clientele. The firm's list of clients has included Alpha Kappa Alpha Sorority, Inc., the Estate of Emmett Till, the National Black Evangelical Association, and the handling of family law matters involving professional athletes Eddy Curry, Richard Dent, Antwaan Randle El, and Dwyane Wade.

In addition to his law practice, Barclay is a legal advocate for the disadvantaged and a helpful mentor to young attorneys. He also has been actively involved in civic affairs, serving as president of both the Chicago Office of Tourism and Culture, the Christian Community Health Center in Chicago, and as a member of the Illinois African-American Family Commission. Further, Barclay is a friend and advisor to many business owners, corporate executives, pastors, and civic leaders. Generous and compassionate, and in spite of his demanding schedule, Barclay has served as a teen Sunday School teacher for more than 20 years. He is a member of the National Bar Association, Cook County Bar Association, and the Chicago Bar Association.

Lester L. Barclay lives in Chicago with his wife, Dr. Sue Barclay, and their three children.